Date Due

OC15'88			

Winston Churchill's Toyshop

Major General Sir Millis Jefferis, K.B.E., M.C., Director M.D.I., 1941–1946.

Winston Churchill's
TOYSHOP

COLONEL
R. Stuart Macrae

F.I.Mech.E.

WALKER AND COMPANY
New York

First published in the United States of America
in 1972 by the Walker Publishing Company, Inc.

Published simultaneously in Canada by Fitzhenry &
Whiteside, Limited, Toronto.

ISBN: 0-8027-0398-4

Library of Congress Catalog Card Number: 72-83118

Printed in the United States of America

Contents

Illustrations

Introduction

THIS IS THE story of a rather unorthodox department known as M.D.1. (Ministry of Defence 1). Born at the War Office early in 1939 with a staff of one commissioned and one non-commissioned officer charged with the task of devising special weapons for irregular warfare, it rapidly grew up into an establishment equipped to design and develop new weapons for all three Services very quickly indeed. The orthodox design and development departments which were not given the same freedom from red tape found themselves quite unable to compete with M.D.1. Naturally enough, those in control of them took a great dislike to what they regarded as an upstart organisation and they had many sympathisers in high places.

M.D.1. was under the direct control of the War Cabinet, for there was no Ministry of Defence at this time although there was a Minister of Defence — the Prime Minister. It was not surprising, therefore, that those who wanted to disparage the establishment should choose to call it 'Winston Churchill's Toyshop.' The toys we produced were rather dangerous ones. In all, by the end of the war no fewer than twenty-six entirely new weapons designed by M.D.1. had been accepted by the Services and were in quantity production. They ranged from small booby traps to heavy artillery, aircraft bombs and naval mines.

I was privileged to be appointed second-in-command of the original War Office section almost at its inception and to remain in this position until the end of the war when my Director, Major-General Sir Millis Jefferis, KBE, MC, was appointed Engineer-in-Chief to the Pakistan army and I was put in charge of the establishment in his place. So I do know the whole story from beginning to end. In telling it, I shall try to be unfashionable and avoid running down my superiors and my colleagues. The characters in this book are none of them fictitious and I shall try to describe them all fairly whilst making no attempt to stress any failings they may have. If anything I say gives offence to anyone I should like to apologise to them in advance and assure them that this is unintentional.

I have an advantage over many writers of such books as this which are written a long time after the events described because I do not have to trust to memory. If I did the book could not be written at all, for my memory has never been my strong point. Not only am I able to refer to the very complete diary of events which I kept for myself from the summer of 1939 when operations started so far as I was concerned until the summer of 1947 when they finished. I also still have by me for reference a vast quanity of official files and records which I was able to rescue from M.D.1. Whitchurch when the premises were abandoned. I was nearly court martialled when as a witness at the Royal Commission of Awards to Inventors I disclosed that I had these documents in my possession. The Crown Counsel gruelled me about this and I became a temporary Press sensation under such headlines as 'Colonel kept top secrets at home.' But it all blew over. I was ordered to hand over all these documents to a Security Officer who would call to collect them from me. But he never did call, so I still have them.

To name everyone who helped Millis Jefferis and myself to build up M.D.1. would be quite impossible. Some names will come into the story; others will just miss doing so. But I should like to take this opportunity of thanking all those who served with me in M.D.1. — the Service personnel, the civilian staff, and the little Welsh factory girls — for their wonderful support and tolerance.

Books are supposed to be dedicated to somebody. I have given this matter considerable thought and there is but one answer. The only possible choice is Lady Jefferis for if it were not for her remarkably talented husband and the support she always gave him, M.D.1. would never have been created and this book would never have been written. Millis Jefferis worked himself to death during the war although he did live on until 1964. I like to think that if he were still alive he would approve of everything I say in this book and once again say: 'Good for you, Bobby.'

R.S.M.

I

How it all Started

'THERE'S A GEOFFREY somebody from the War Office on the telephone,' said my faithful secretary, poking her head round the door of my office. 'He wants to speak to you.'

'My dear Mrs Collings,' I said more or less patiently, 'you know as well as I do that we go to press to-day and that since we went pocket size I have to read and pass 96 of these flaming little pages which I hate anyhow. What is more, I have to finish the job by 3 o'clock. So please go away. If you can't deal with the chap yourself put him on to Worrall or Lord Southwood or somebody.'

Back came Mrs Collings two minutes later without apology. 'It's a Major somebody from the War Office,' she said firmly. 'and he insists on speaking to the editor. He says it's important.'

With a sigh, I emerged from my little pages and grabbed a telephone. 'Is that the editor of "Armchair Science"?' asked a slightly barking voice. I pleaded guilty. 'I have here,' said the voice, 'the current issue of your journal in which you have an article about a new and exceptionally powerful magnet. I want full information about this magnet right away please. This is most important.'

I explained to the Major that the article in question had been taken from an American publication, that the best I could do would be to write to the USA for further information, and that anyhow the actual performance figures for the particular magnet described might not be of much use to him. If he could tell me what he wanted magnets for I could advise him whether the Alnico one he had read about was the right answer or whether he would do better to use one of another material called Alcomax. In any case, if he wanted super efficiency from a magnet it should be specially designed for the job and here I could help him only if I knew what the job was.

A bit of throat clearing went on at the other end. Then the voice said rather hesitantly; 'Well, it's a bit awkward. I'm not at liberty at present to tell you what this is all about. Please see if you can let me have a little more information to go on with. Write to me at the War Office. The name if Jefferis — J-e-f-f-e-r-i-s — Major M. R. Jefferis, MIR, War Office, Whitehall. Thank you very much — good-bye.'

Now this was an easy one. I knew that M.I. stood for Military Intelligence and presumed that the 'R' stood for Research. So this magnet must be wanted for some new weapon that was on the secret list. Naturally this Major Jefferis could not talk about it to anyone until he was security cleared.

I happened to be just that, so after missing my lunch and scampering through my proof-reading in record time I settled down to write to Major Jefferis and tell him so. When World War 1 started I was at school; but a couple of years later I got tired of sitting for examinations whilst all this excitement was going on and persuaded my mother to let me become an engineering apprentice at the Westinghouse Brake & Saxby Signal Co. in York Road, King's Cross. Here I soon got tired of working a ten-hour day at 2d per hour setting up capstans for ladies who were earning over £20 per week just by turning the handles and pulling the levers so I decided I would like to join the Army, preferably as a sapper. My mother wangled an introduction to the King Sapper at the War Office — General Sir Binden Blood — and off I went to see him. Although frightening in appearance, he was very kind to me and assured me he would be delighted to get me a commission in the Royal Engineers. But not yet! I had admitted to being only just over 16 years old and I did not look even that. If I would look him up again, in say, eighteen months' time he would then be able to do something about it. In the meantime, he would put my application on record so that when I came back my name would be well up on the list.

Reluctant to return to my capstan setting, I eventually got myself a job as a trainee draughtsman with a small aircraft manufacturing company at the magnificent salary of £1 per week. I took to this job like a duck to water and was soon entrusted with the design of some of the metal fittings and parts of the control gear. So it was not surprising that when a Captain Lloyd-Lott of the Canadian army came along to the firm with a letter from Arm G, Air Ministry urging them to give him assistance over designing some special bomb dropping gear I was promptly attached to him and told to get on with it.

It was, of course, my first experience in weapons design. These were the days of trench warfare and it seemed that there was an urgent requirement for some device which would enable our airmen to winkle out the occupants of enemy trenches. Trying to strafe trenches with normal bombing was a most unrewarding business. Only a few bombs could be dropped on each run and it was unlikely they would land near enough to the trench to do damage. Lloyd-Lott's bright idea was to use a large number of very small bombs in place of the half dozen or so normal sized ones which could be carried and contrive some way of strewing them along the line of a trench so that many must find their way into it and do damage.

Where Lloyd-Lott had been clever was in deciding that if a special bomb had to be developed for this particular purpose and then put into production the war might be over before he got it. So he must find something that was already available and could be made to serve. Obviously the Mills hand grenade was the answer. One of its main uses was as a weapon for lobbing into trenches and it was now being turned out on such a scale that Ordnance could supply even large numbers for this special purpose without anyone having to go short. So far so good. But Lloyd-Lott's problem was how to contrive some very simple way of adapting this grenade for dropping from aircraft.

Normally, the operation of the grenade was as follows. It was completely safe until a pin was pulled out. Then it went on being safe provided it was clutched in the hand in such a way that a lever was kept in place. Only when the grenade was thrown would this lever fly off to release the firing mechanism. This consisted of a firing pin which hit a percussion cap to ignite a seven second delay fuse. When that had burnt through, detonation took place.

Obviously the pilot could not be expected to fly along pulling pins out of Mills grenades and dropping them down a chute or something. Even if he could be induced to try this he could not drop enough grenades to matter and they would probably go off at the wrong time. So we must think along different lines altogether. What was more, the solution must not involve having to make major alterations to the grenades such as scrapping the firing mechanisms and using in their place some sort of impact fuse yet to be designed. As usual, the answer was quite simple in the end although it took us some time to arrive at it. All we did was to devise a wooden egg cup into which the base of the grenade would sit in such a manner that the lever was secured just as well as it would be if held in the hand. The cup was of course fixed to the grenade. Its job in life was to shatter on impact with the ground —

3

any kind of ground — when the grenade was dropped from any height over 50 feet but to be sturdy enough not to crack in the normal way even if somebody was careless enough to drop the thing on the floor.

We had to use wood because plastic was hardly known in those days and quite a bit of experimenting was required to determine what wood to use, what thickness of wall was needed, and which way the grain should run. However, we ran into no trouble and soon had special woodworking machines turning out these cups like hot cakes. The next thing to do was to design the dropping gear and bomb crate, which for preference was to fit into the bomb bay of a DH 9. That was all right. We had a wooden frame of the required size and just stuffed it full of metal tubes of a diameter such that the grenades complete with cups could be dropped into them and be only a loose fit. I think we had 36 tubes each holding ten grenades or something of that order. Anyway it was quite a load.

I was responsible for designing release gear of which I should now be heartily ashamed. At the bottom of each tube was a grid hinged at one end and secured at the other end by a slotted eye which was penetrated by a slideable rod. This rod was necked down at intervals and it was simple enough to arrange that as it was moved along the grids would open in any order desired. Each line of tubes had its own release rod operated by a Bowden wire control so that the pilot could do a balanced dropping act if he wanted to. A pair of substantial safety grids had to be opened before any dropping could be done and another useful though accidental safety feature was that when the safety pin was removed from a grenade as it was being loaded into a tube it still remained as safe as houses as apart from being held by the wooden cup the firing lever could also be held by the tube.

Surprisingly enough, this awful contrivance worked quite well. I was whisked down to Orfordness, which was the hush-hush Air Ministry experimental station at that time, with the whole box of tricks in a large and impressive Cadillac which had been put at my disposal and after a week of trials there we seemed to be all in the clear. Instructions were given to my company to produce the first 100 of these bomb dropping equipments as quickly as possible and for my sins I was to accompany the first one to France to see if it worked there. I did not really mind because I now had a vested interest in this project. As my pay was still no more than £5 per week the company had very generously decided to pay me a royalty of £25 on each unit. The first one was completed in November 1918, just as the armistice was declared. All such orders were at once cancelled so I did not draw even my first £25 and avoided becoming a war profiteer.

Having made my number with Arm G, Air Ministry and proved that I could be useful as a weapons designer I now hoped to get a job of this sort. But I was only eighteen and obviously inexperienced, whilst there were soon plenty of experts queueing up for such vacancies. For a while I went back to helping to design aeroplanes; but this business folded up in due course and I had to resort to making my living as a technical journalist and trying to invent gadgets of one sort or another as a sideline. In time I became an editor of various technical publications and also took on consulting work. I was not doing at all badly and should have been quite satisfied with my lot. But for some unknown reason I still wanted to be a weapons designer.

Nobody could accuse me of not being an opportunist. This enquiry from the War Office was just what the doctor ordered. Having disposed of my proof-reading I settled down to write to this Major Jefferis urging him to check up on me at the Air Ministry and the War Office and then if he was satisfied over the security angle to tell me more about his magnet requirement and let me help him. I suggested we should meet for lunch at the Arts Theatre Club as soon as possible and we did. Jefferis was evidently a fast worker for it was only two days later that we were usurping a window seat at the Club and whispering away together.

Millis Jefferis was certainly no ordinary man. With a leathery looking face, a barrel-like torso, and arms that reached nearly to the floor he looked a bit like a gorilla. But it was at once obvious that he had a brain like lightning. I had always reckoned that I could keep a jump ahead of most people, but this certainly did not apply with this Sapper Major. He seldom had to stop to think, and when he did he would scowl horribly. Then he would give an infectious little chuckle so that one just could not help liking him.

This was in June 1939. Apparently the threat of war had been dispersed for a while, but anyone associated with the Press knew that war must come sooner or later — and probably sooner. What I did not know was that the much maligned big shots at the War Office, who were supposed to be doing nothing about anything, had not only been thinking along the same lines but had also been taking active steps on the quiet to get the situation organised. Jefferis confided to me that he had been pulled back from India to start a section at the War Office for devising weapons for irregular warfare. Why he was interested in magnets was because he was working on what he called a magnetic mine which would stick to the side of a ship when placed there by a diver and go bang in due course to sink said ship.

After lunch, brandy, and deep thought I offered to design such a mine for him free of charge. He gladly accepted this offer, and mentioned that he had a private bag of gold from which he could at least pay my expenses. That was good enough for me. I went back to my office and told my Managing Editor that as the current number had now gone to Press I proposed to take the three weeks holiday due to me.

My assistant, Geoffrey Worrall, was far more observant than I am. When I was preparing to write to the USA for more information about Alnico magnets, he informed me that they had some little ones in the window of an ironmonger's shop round the corner and offered to go and get some for me. After inspecting a sample I asked him to acquire their entire stock for me, which he did. Obviously these little magnets would not be ideal for the job, but they might give me a quick start. I paid the bill and hoped the bag of gold would work.

That is how it all started. On the face of it, it did not seem to be much of a start but I was quite content. It seemed to me that if I could devise this magnetic mine very smartly indeed I might well be established in the armaments design business before the war came along. And for once I was right.

2

Birth of a Limpet

THE NEXT STEP was to find somewhere where I could carry out a little experimental work. My own garage even though it had a bench and a bit of equipment was not good enough. I gave the matter deep thought and was inspired — as I often seemed to be throughout this exercise. A couple of years back when I had been editing a journal called the *Caravan & Trailer* I had come across a character called Captain C. V. Clarke, MC. I had met him because he had placed an advertisement in my journal for what appeared to be a most remarkable caravan, and I had decided I must go and have a look at this creation. So I visited him at his works in Bedford.

Clarke at once fascinated me. He was a very large man with rather hesitant speech who at first struck me as being amiable but not outstandingly bright. The second part of this impression did not last long. It seemed that after winning his MC in World War I and helping to wind up that affair, this Clarke was vaguely looking round for something to do when, having a brother who ran a large farm, he realised that there was an unfilled demand for trailers of one sort or another — particularly horse boxes. The existing trailers with two wheels seemed to him to waggle about too much so he thought it would be nice to have four wheels instead. Establishing himself as the Low Loading Trailer Company Ltd (Lolode for short) he then started to produce a range of trailers based on a very nice design of his having a low-slung chassis and close coupled wheels with a special suspension system.

This caravan was his latest brain child. It was an enormous double decker affair about the size of a London bus and streamlined into the bargain like something from the future. It had a built in lavatory which would now be called a toilet and a separate shower with hot and cold. In fact it could offer every mod. con. and I liked the look of it at once. But its performance on the road was the thing. Clarke assured me that because of his special chassis and suspension system one could sit in the main saloon when travelling at 40 mph not only pouring out drinks but also drinking them without spilling them and that he now proposed to demonstrate this to me. He did so to my entire satisfaction and as there were no breathalysers in those days, I was able to get back to London without any trouble and write a nice ‘piece about him.

Although I had not seen him since this initial visit, Clarke's unusual personality and his ability to view mechanical problems in an unorthodox way had always stuck in my mind. I decided that he was the man for me, jumped into my motorcar complete with rough drawings and my collection of magnets, and went off to Bedford. I had of course rung up Clarke to warn him that I was coming and given him a very guarded idea of what I wanted to talk about. He was operating from his private house which he had converted in some remarkable way into a works. Sweeping a number of children out of the living room which had also to serve as an office, he filled me up with bread and jam and some awful buns and then we got down to business. Nobby, as I soon came to call him, was enthusiastic as I knew he would be. 'Fine! How about starting to-morrow? Be here as early as you can. Stay here if you like; we can easily find you a bed.'

Next day we started in on making our first ship sinking device. Nobby created an experimental department by sweeping a load of rubbish and more children off a bench. We went shopping in Bedford and bought some large tin bowls from Woolworth's. Some local tinsmith was cajoled into dropping all his other work and fashioning for us rims with annular grooves to fit these bowls and plates which could be screwed on to close these rims. The rims were sweated to the bowls and as many of the little horseshoe magnets as possible were packed into the annular grooves so that the pole pieces were exposed, these pole pieces then being lined up by simply placing a keeper ring over the whole lot. To secure the magnets in place we at first poured bitumen into the groove, but later found that plaster of Paris was a better answer.

The idea was to stuff this bowl full of blasting gelatine or some similar high explosive and then screw the lid in place so that the device was sealed. It had to be carried by a swimmer. so we contrived a belt consisting of a 4″ wide steel plate, just long enough to span the magnet ring, to which were attached strips of webbing which could be tied round the swimmer's waist. Obviously the swimmer must not be unduly handicapped by having to travel under water with this contrivance so we wanted it to weigh next to nothing when submerged. Eventually after using up all the porridge in the house in place of high explosive for filling, juggling about with weights and dimensions, and flooding Nobby's bathroom on several occasions, we got this right.

Field trials were the next stage, and we carried them out in Bedford Public Baths which were closed to the public for these occasions. At the deep end we propped a large steel plate reasonably upright to represent the side of a ship and Nobby, who was an excellent swimmer, started his dummy runs. Nobby was exceedingly noble over this. Looking as if he were suffering from advanced pregnancy he would swim to and fro removing the device from his belt, turning it over, and plonking it on the target plate with great skill. We learnt a lot more than we had done in the bathroom. Our magnets were so powerful that when in the water it at first proved difficult to remove the mine from the keeper plate belt without the risk of rupturing oneself. So we had to experiment with various sizes of plate until we had one which gave the required hold and no more. The buoyancy too came in for adjustment as we found it advantageous to have slight positive buoyancy.

It took us only a few days to bring the development to this stage. We then had the basis of Jefferis' magnetic mine which could be planted on the side of a ship by a clever fellow without much difficulty and would stay there provided the ship were not a wooden one and that it was not unduly encrusted with barnacles. We could only hope that the enemy kept his craft in decent condition. At a solemn ceremony back at the works, I christened this thing 'The Limpet' — a name which stuck. It is just as well it did, because a quite different device produced by the Germans later on was called a magnetic mine and this could have caused much confusion.

So far so good. The next thing to do was to devise a delayed action initiator which would cause this gadget to go bang in anything between half an hour and two hours after its installation. There was nothing on the market that would serve the purpose but it was simple enough to think up something. All we needed was a spring loaded striker, maintained in the cocked position by a pellet soluble in water. When the pellet dissolved, the striker would be released to hit a cap to initiate a detonator which would explode a primer to explode the main charge.

All this was easy enough, but finding a suitable pellet was difficult.

There were too many variables. The powder itself was the first one, and the degree to which it was compressed the second one. The temperature of the water made all the difference, and of course so did whether it were fresh water or sea water. Expert chemists were called in to find us the answer, but they failed. One day a pellet would dissolve at a rate which alarmed us and would no doubt have alarmed a Limpeteer. The next day, a similar one might take several hours over the job and we did not want that. There was some hope of a Limpet staying put on a stationary target and every chance of its getting washed off if the target moved off at 20 knots or so as it might well do in time.

One of Nobby's children solved the problem for us. It was only a small one and, in sweeping it off the bench which it much preferred to its play pen, we upset it by knocking its bag of aniseed balls on to the floor. Whilst Nobby was doing a consoling act, I tried one of these sweets. It seemed to stay with me a long time, getting smaller and smaller with great regularity. After trying a couple himself Nobby agreed that this might well be the answer so we commandeered the remainder of the supply and started to experiment. I think I can safely claim to be the first man to drill holes in aniseed balls and devise a fitting to enable this to be done accurately and efficiently. We rigged up some of our igniters with these aniseed balls in place of soluble pellets and tried them out under various conditions. They behaved perfectly, and the next day the children of Bedford had to go without their aniseed balls. For not wishing to be held up for supplies we toured the town and bought the lot.

Eventually of course we acquired our supplies from the manufacturers, Messrs Barratt, who were most helpful when we went along to see them and were able to explain why their product performed in such a highly satisfactory manner. It is a precision job, made by dipping a core into vats containing sweetened liquid a specified number of times and for specified periods. The result is that nothing can be more alike than two aniseed balls. Drop two of them into a glass of water and they will both take exactly the same time to dissolve — which is what we wanted. I was a little disappointed that Messrs Barratt could think of no way of producing these aniseed balls with a hole through the middle but that did not matter a lot. My drilling fixture worked well enough.

For safety's or danger's sake, we equipped each limpet with two of these delayed action exploders. The aniseed ball part of the device had of course to be protected from damp whilst it was in store — and in fact until the Limpet was actually placed on its target. So what we needed was a closed rubber sleeve of some sort which could be pushed over the tube to seal it and be easily whipped off by the Limpeteer when the time came. Again the local shops were able to meet the requirement. We went round to the chemists buying up all their stocks of a certain commodity and earning ourselves an undeserved reputation for being sexual athletes.

That ends the story of the 'Birth of a Limpet.' We made the first few hundreds at Bedford and then had to rope in outside contractors when the war came along to meet the demand. In all, over half a million Limpets were made and issued for use. It is said that they accounted for hundreds of thousands of tons of enemy shipping and certainly this might well be true if the encouraging messages we received by courtesy of our Cloak and Dagger friends and their secret radio stations were anything to go by. Time and again we would learn that a number of enemy ships had been sunk in harbour by Limpeteers and take off our hats to these remarkably brave fellows. One such message was not so good though. It reported that some Italians had got hold of a supply of our Limpets and to date had sunk three of our ships with them.

This MkI Limpet did excellent work throughout the first three years of the war until I could get down to cleaning up the design and making the MkII then the Mk III. The container had of course not survived long in the form of a Woolworth's bowl and had become a proper metal spinning. But the little horseshoe magnets had survived. I now replaced them with four large Alcomax magnets designed for me by Neill's of Sheffield and flexibly mounted so that they could take up position on an uneven surface. But the biggest improvement was the replacement of the aniseed ball igniters by the department's 'L' Delay fuses which will be described later in this book. To be honest, this refined model worked no better than its primitive predecessor and oddly enough it never seemed to take on so well with the operators. Maybe this was because it was too refined. True, rubber sleeves were still used to afford initial protection to the 'L' Delays but they were now so small that they were useless for any other kind of protection.

3

Called up

WHILST THIS LIMPET work was going on, all was by no means quiet on the War Office front. Jefferis would want to see me every other day to know what progress I was making, and then to start talking to me about his other activities. It took me some time to learn the form. Apparently an enlightened sapper — Lt-Colonel J. F. C. Holland, DFC, — had been given the job of forming at the War Office a department to be known as Military Intelligence Research. He had been appointed the GSO 1 of this outfit and one of his first moves had been to rope in his old friend Millis Jefferis to run the weapons side of things.

At the start, the situation had been complicated by the fact that the so called Cloak and Dagger boys under the control of a mysterious Colonel Grand and the Foreign Office were involved in this adventure. But it had now been decided that they should break away from the War Office and go off on their own. This left Colonel Holland with a very much reduced bag of gold, Major Millis Jefferis, and an odd collection of Military Intelligence officers of which the most senior was Lt-Colonel Colin Gubbins — later to become Major-General Colin Gubbins in charge of the Cloak and Dagger department when it was reformed in the Special Operations Executive.

Joe Holland was a wonderful organiser. In no time at all, he had created Millis Jefferis a GSO 2 and the head of a brand new section designated MIR (c) which was charged with designing and producing special weapons for irregular warfare. In other words, Jefferis was to run a more or less legitimate outfit which was to produce unusual but respectable weapons, the gentlemen concerned all being in uniform and therefore not to be confused with saboteurs, whilst Grand & Co would get double the money for running a Cloak and Dagger outfit. That was reasonable enough.

I went through the list of assets with Millis. It added up to not very much. Apparently the apple of his eye was a thing he called a TV Switch which will be described later.

To go with the TV Switch there was a prototype of a Light Camouflet Set. Next there came a sample of a most elaborate booby trap mechanism made by some RE Field Unit goaded into it by Millis which neither he nor I ever understood, another RE booby trap mechanism he had inherited from somewhere or other, and a most impressive piece of mechanism weighing about half a hundredweight, which Millis had evolved to serve as a means for blowing up railway lines.

The final item was an idea for a Sticky Bomb on the design of which Millis had already got started. He had roped in the assistance of a Professor Schulman who was running the department of Colloid Science at Cambridge University and a Dr. Bauer who was apparently working with him. Dr. Bauer was already involved with the design of the TV Switch and was trying to improve its delay action mechanism. So was Millis. He had encouraged Venner's to make some very expensive clockwork delay mechanisms, but unfortunately he had specified that they should be 3" diameter whereas the TV switch was now reduced to 2" diameter. Obviously nothing could be done about this; but they were really excellent clocks and graced our various mantlepieces throughout the war.

For some invalid reason I always disliked this TV switch. It was a gadget for blowing up railway lines and had to be used in conjunction with boring equipment called a Camouflet Set. The official Camouflet Set, as issued to R.E. Field Units, consisted of an incredibly heavy piece of metal piping carrying an internal hammer in the form of a large slug of metal operated by outside handles. It required four sturdy Sappers to work this thing. Two had to hold the device upright whilst the other two applied themselves to the hammer head via the handles. In due course, if all went well, they would punch a 3" diameter hole about five feet deep in the ground.

The next trick was to drop down the hole a small charge of explosive and poop it off. This produced a pear shaped cavern at the bottom of the hole, which had then to be filled with some suitable medium velocity powder explosive such as ammonal. There was room for quite a lot of this stuff and, when it was detonated, bags of earth would be moved and a most impressive crater would be formed.

This is where Millis' TV switch came in. The Camouflet mine was made near or below a railway track. Designed as a tubular affair which would fit into the hole made for the mine, the TV Switch consisted of a delicate mechanism which once it was armed would close an electrical contact when subjected to the vibration caused by a train passing, and fire the mine — which would not be good for the train or the track. To ensure that the device was safe to install, at least in theory, there was a simple switch consisting of a fat pin of insulating material between two contact strips so that they could not close to complete the circuit to the vibrator mechanism until this pin was withdrawn. A spring was anxious to withdraw it but was prevented from doing so by a large chunk of salt. Above it was a container which could be filled with water, or any other liquid in an emergency. In theory, as I have said, one could install this device in complete comfort safe in the knowledge that it would be an hour or so before the salt dissolved and the thing became sensitive to vibration. Even then, it would take quite a shake to cause it to go off.

Unfortunately this salt delay was apparently too safe at times. If the ground were very cold the process of dissolving the salt would not only be slowed down but might perhaps be stopped, in which case the device would not arm at all. Bauer was busy trying to get over this little drawback by using in place of the salt delay a bellows filled with air, which was again under spring influence. Where he was clever was that, instead of trying to use an adjustable leak valve which could never be set accurately so that it might take five minutes or five hours for the air to leak away, he used specially moulded porous ceramic pellets. With these he obtained quite surprising accuracy and I must admit that when he said his delay was for an hour it was for that or thereabouts.

In spite of this, I developed a hatred for this TV Switch in any shape or form and especially with Bauer's delay. For my sins, I had later on to demonstrate this contrivance amongst many others to budding saboteurs and army Independent Units. Although reason assured me that it was a perfectly safe operation, whenever I had prepared my camouflet mine and had to push a TV Switch into the hole I always had visions of myself sailing into the air in a cloud of smoke, dust and small stones and then hearing a nasty bang.

I suppose Freud might have been able to explain this but I couldn't. Maybe the feeling was brought about by the fact that I was generally a bit unlucky with this camouflet mine demonstration. The idea, after showing how the TV Switch should be installed, was to remove it and then detonate the mine by dropping down the hole a detonator and primer at the end of a nice long length of safety fuse which could then be lighted at leisure. The result was always so impressive that I used to make this event the final item in my programme.

That was all right if it worked but if it failed to do so there was a most awful anti-climax and something simply had to be done about it. I was unlucky here and, whilst other demonstrators always seemed to get away with it, I ran into trouble more often than not. After waiting about five minutes for the big bang that did not happen I would get that sinking feeling. The Book of Rules clearly and emphatically stated that if such a mine proved to be a blind it must be left alone for a period of at least one hour and preferably two. So in theory one had merely to dismiss the audience, set a guard to keep anyone away from the spot, go away for a drink, and come back two hours later to deal with the situation in comfort.

I was always on the point of accepting this solution to the problem. But I never had the pluck to do it. On the last occasion when this dilemma arose I was demonstrating to an incredible number of Home Guards in Richmond Park on a Sunday. All had gone well up to a point, the faithful Sergeant Bidgood doing all the real work. Then an apoplectic Zone Commander who, in the last war must have been at least a General and probably a Field Marshal, arrived with his entourage and informed me that the entire demonstration was illegal because he had not authorised it. This was a difficult situation. I had been urged to lay on this show by Bob Porter of Boon & Porter Ltd, who is now I am very sorry to say with us no more, which firm was producing various booby traps for M.D.1., probably at a loss. He had joined the Home Guard and was anxious for his colleagues to learn about the contrivances he was making. So I had agreed to put on this show for him, although I was a little startled when he produced about 1,000 Home Guards to attend it.

Bob was only a Second Lieutenant in the Home Guard and was therefore rather shattered when this Zone Commander threatened to court martial him. I myself was only a Major at the time, but I could call on the War Cabinet for support. So I asked this Zone Commander to go away and got on with it. Readers will, I hope, appreciate the situation with which I was faced when on my final 'great spectacular' nothing whatever happened. Here was I the temporary hero of the Home Guard having seen off their Zone Commander for whom they seemed to have no real affection. To date, all the bangs had gone off in proper order. Now the last event looked like being a complete flop.

A man of courage would have told the spectators to push off and would then work according to the book. Looking round at the vast number of eager faces, I could not bring myself to do this. They all seemed to be convinced that I was the world's top explosive expert and that faced with a little hitch of this sort I would most certainly be able to deliver the goods. So after waiting five minutes or so with Sergeant Bidgood urging me to let him deal with this little matter, which no doubt he could have done better than I did, I had to crawl up to the hole with my knees knocking, drop down it another exploder at the end of a long length of slow burning fuse which I had already lighted, and walk away trying to look all casual. This time the mine did go off, and the result was entirely satisfactory. But this did not cure me of my dislike of the TV Switch.

In case any expert asks why I did not resort to electrical firing, I often tried this but with no better result. One could get a blind either way, which would involve dropping another detonating unit down the hole. Whether this unit was at the end of a length of fuse or at the end of a length of wire made no difference. It still had to be dropped down the hole and, if the mine decided it might as well go off after all and chose this particular time to do it, the operator might well suffer damage.

It was unreasonable for me to be frightened of the TV Switch. Eventually we made and issued thousands of these devices and no doubt many were used. Yet I never heard of any operator having an accident with a TV Switch through premature firing — which is more than I can say about some of the gadgets I designed myself.

The Light Camouflet Set was, oddly enough, very much like the standard Service one except that it did not weigh so much and drove a 2" diameter tube instead of a 3" one into the ground It could be operated by two men and carried by one if he were strong enough. Again, we eventually made and issued many thousands of these tools.

Next we come to the Pressure Switch, which was another device for blowing up railway lines. It seemed that, whilst serving on the North West frontier and building roads under fire for which he was very rightly awarded an M.C., Millis had taken a dislike to railways and was anxious to do them an injury. The TV Switch was his first means of achieving this end but it took a lot of installing and he wanted something simpler — some device that could be placed under a railway line and would trigger off a mine when the track was deflected by a train passing over it. That sounds easy enough but there is a catch in it.

16

Unless it is a very badly laid one, a railway line will not deflect much when a light engine runs over it. Therefore if any ordinary form of spring trigger device were used it would have to be an extremely touchy one and anyone like myself would certainly die of fright in even trying to use it. It was claimed that our museum piece booby trap device would serve in this capacity but to keep it on the safe side about an inch of travel was required from a plunger before anything happened. This made it very safe indeed, for seldom could a rail be deflected as much as that.

Millis had set out to solve this little problem, and had done so very cleverly indeed. He used a conventional spring-loaded striker in a barrel which when released would fire a cap to start things going. The striker was maintained in the cocked position by a steel rod hardened to the point of brittleness. This rod was secured to the closed end of the barrel by pinning. It then ran through a partitioned-off chamber, the compression spring and striker head coming after the partition. An orifice with a boss bearing was so placed in the top of the chamber section of the barrel that a plunger dropped into it straddled with its Vee end this hardened steel rod. The top end of the plunger had a head designed to sit comfortably under a railway line and a safety pin was provided. Running through the boss in the barrel and the plunger, it prevented the latter from being depressed. The device had to be packed up hard against the railway line and, if the operator packed it too hard so that the plunger was actually under load, he would find it difficult to pull out the safety pin. So he had no excuse for blowing himself up.

The clever part of the idea was that the device was completely safe to instal. Yet when a train came along the rail had to be deflected only a few thousandths of an inch to cause it to fire the mine. In other words, its operation depended on loading rather than movement. It was an excellent example of how Millis had a gift for tackling a problem from a new angle-and more will be given later. At this stage, however, Millis had not acquired the ability to design a neat device. It used to be said of any small component such as a switch designed by the Admiralty that it was all right if you could lift it. Apparently Millis had adopted this axiom. His first Pressure Switch was based on an enormous brass casting with everything else in proportion and, although one could lift it, it weighed just as much as the elaborate and unusable RE contrivance which he had discarded. Any saboteur equipped with a couple of these things and being pushed out of an aircraft would undoubtedly have dropped like a stone — parachute or no parachute.

17

To jump ahead with the story, the Pressure Switch was eventually redesigned so that it was a nice little job weighing only 6 ozs and costing only 3/6d each to produce in quantity. It became a most popular line and eventually no fewer than two and a quarter million were made and issued by M.D.1. It is a chastening thought that to-day an equally effective device could be made merely by mounting a micro switch on a plastic box containing a dry battery. But we did not have micro switches and small batteries in those days.

Mention has been made of the two extraordinary booby trap devices Millis had acquired which would qualify for a star position in any museum. One took the form of a substantial metal box equipped with a variety of knobs and little levers which made the outfit look like a nightmare attempt at making an early English wireless set. In theory, armed with this machine — if he were strong enough to carry it — the irregular soldier or saboteur was fully equipped to blow up absolutely anything in any way he chose. It was merely a matter of setting the levers in the proper positions and turning the knobs to the right places. Unfortunately there seemed to be no instruction book for this thing and nobody had the faintest idea of how it was supposed to work. I did volunteer to try to find out but we agreed it would be a waste of time.

The second booby trap was perhaps a little better, but not much. Only about the size of a miner's lamp and looking rather like one, it was said to be able to serve in any booby trap capacity and particularly for this blowing up of railway lines. As we had decided it was useless for this purpose, we perhaps rather unfairly ruled it out for other purposes as well and back it went into the cupboard. Later on when it was my cupboard I did decide to investigate this device a little further to see if anything could be done with it. I took it apart or at least started to do so. The action from then on was self-supporting and a series of bits and pieces impelled by powerful springs shot around the room. I never succeeded in re-assembling this contrivance but I kept some of the pieces to remind me how not to design a mechanism.

The Sticky Bomb effort was different. It was only in the idea stage. What was wanted, Millis explained to me, was a grenade which could be thrown at a tank and would stick to it for five seconds or so and then go bang, to blow a hole in said tank and disconcert the occupants. Apparently, there was a catch in it though. A high velocity or cutting charge must be used, and for this to be effective it must be literally plastered on to the target — a poultice charge the Sappers called it.

Having explained all this to me very patiently, Millis told me how far he had got with this job. It was not very far. This was another project over which he had enlisted the help of Dr. Bauer and Dr. Schulman, of the Colloid Science Department of Cambridge University. They had got as far as filling lengths of bicycle inner tubing with plasticine to represent high explosive, fitting them with wooden handles to enable them to be thrown, and dipping them in rubber solution to make them sticky. They then had to be carried in metal tubes if they were not to stick to the operator.

It appeared that all had not gone well at a recent demonstration of these sticky appliances in one of the quadrangles at Cambridge. Unfortunately this had been held before my time, and it seems that I had missed a most entertaining party. Like the performers in any Harlequinade, the demonstrators had hurled their sausages in all directions and found them to be quite uncontrollable in flight. Only by luck did anyone make contact with one of the metal bins used to represent tanks and if a missile did hit one of these affairs it would not stick. Neither would it poultice. In fact the experiment had been a complete and literal flop, and Millis had decided that he must find somebody who might have some new method of approach to the problem.

This was me, for as I had hoped, Millis was now rather pro me because of the quite good progress I had made over the development of the Limpet with the aid of Nobby Clarke. So at this meeting, which took place some time in July 1939, I was given quite a number of assignments. I was of course to go ahead with the Limpet and produce the first 250 directly the design had proved to be acceptable. The next order would be for 1,000. Next, would I take over the Pressure Switch and neaten it up a bit. I might also give thought to the design of a Pull Switch which could be included in a trip wire and would fire a charge when the wire was tugged and a Release Switch which could be concealed under a book or a lavatory seat or something of that sort and cause a bang when it was lifted. It was not until later on that I christened these devices with these names which I thought were quite good and descriptive ones. The Ordnance boys thought otherwise and changed them into numbers.

Of these items, the Sticky Bomb was by far the most important; so would I run up to Cambridge right away and see Schulman about it? So far as pay was concerned, as I was to be only unofficially attached to MIR (c) War Office as a kind of dogsbody, I could not be paid a salary but only expenses. However, I could not be expected to work for nothing and Millis had discussed this matter with Joe Holland. They had agreed that if I devised a weapon for MIR (c) and could arrange for its manufacture I should be entitled to make a profit on the contract, provided of course that the price quoted was a reasonable one. If I could not cope with the production and the War Office had to place orders elsewhere then I should be entitled to a commission.

This suited me fine. I had visions of great riches even if no war came along, and even greater ones if it did. Here I would be running my little magazines at quite a good salary, designing weapons in my spare time which is just what I had always wanted to do, and collecting fat cheques from manufacturers at frequent intervals. What is more, if there were a war I should be in a nice safe reserved occupation and nobody could pressgang me into being a soldier and going off to fight. Nothing could possibly suit me better. During the first world war when I was to receive vast royalties on my bomb-dropping gear I had visions of a large house at Hampstead, a Bentley, a yacht and a few other oddments. These now returned.

Nobby and I had done a little costing work on Limpets. His overheads were pretty low, so the asking price came to something like £8 a time out of which he could afford to pay me £2 commission. This was probably more than the profit Nobby was making himself, but he was like that. When I had disclosed this deal to Millis and he had discussed it with Joe Holland I found they were both happy about it. So was I. Visions of a first cheque for £500 on account of the order for 250 Limpets and then another one for £2,000 for the next order floated before me and I very nearly ordered the Bentley there and then.

It was as well I did not. I managed to get myself organised at Odhams somehow or other, but it was not easy. I was running two publications now — 'Armchair Science' and 'Gardening.' Where 'Armchair Science' was concerned I knew what I was doing and did not need to spend a lot of time on the job. But over 'Gardening' I was exceedingly vulnerable. Then or now, nobody could know less about gardening than me and I was a worried man from the day I inherited the editorship of this journal. To support me, I had been given a Consulting Editor called Richard Sudell who was exceedingly kind to me and supplied me with all the technical gen needed. But I still had to deal with contributors, and discuss with them the series of articles they were willing to write. Sitting in my editorial chair, I would solemnly give them my views on whether it were better to plant globe artichokes in

September or March and hope they would not see through me —
which they probably did

At first I had found this kind of discussion rather fun, like playing
ping pong. But now my mind would wander and I would find myself
thinking about Sticky Bombs instead of potatoes. What is more, I
would be away every few days going off to Cambridge to talk to
Schulman about various ploys or to Bedford to see how Limpet production was going on. Now I look back on it, I think Korda, who was
my Managing Editor at Odhams, was very good put up with me.
And I certainly could not have survived if Geoffrey Worrall and Mrs
Collings had not done most of my work for me.

This peculiar existence went on for about a month. Then, when I
was at Bedford on a Sunday afternoon messing about in the workshop with Nobby Clarke, Millis succeeded in running me to earth on
the telephone. 'Bobby,' he said, 'I just can't go on like this. I must have
your full time help. Be up here to-morrow at 10 o'clock. I'm going to
get you into uniform right away. No, there is no war yet but you can
call this an emergency. Tell Odhams Press that you have to turn in
your job there at once and that they must find somebody else to do it.
I'll get the Secretary of State to write to them if you like. Anyhow, be
seeing you to-morrow.'

My trouble has always been that I am weak-minded. Millis kind of
dominated me, and I really did want to design armaments rather than
edit articles about the growing of cucumbers. So a few days later I
found that I was a 2nd Lieutenant at the War Office in an Intelligence
Corps which had not yet been formed. This was put right later, but
in the meantime I at once rose to the rank of Captain in most spectacular fashion and was given the title of GSO 3 (General Staff Officer
Third Grade) and Second-in-Command to the boss of MIR (c) — to
wit, Millis Jefferis. All this I achieved without doing any square-
bashing at all. But that did not help me much because, when the war
was over and I left this job to join the Territorial Army, I had to do it
just the same.

My pay, I remember vividly, was £773 a year which was taxed, plus
allowances that were not taxed. This was put right later on when they
taxed the lot. I did not get stuffed into uniform right away because the
war had not started. But I did have to abandon all my get-rich-quick
ideas. Obviously if I was in the Army I could not collect commissions
on orders for weapons, so I had sorrowfully to tell Nobby Clarke that
as I was now the fellow who ordered these Limpets he must reduce his

21

quoted price by £2 per unit which he would now not have to pay to me.

Real nobility was shown by my ever loving wife Mary here, and I intend to leave out this page from any MSS she may read so that she has no opportunity of destroying it. For years we had lived reasonably comfortably but not in affluence. Here at last was a chance for us to be really well off and to send the children to the best schools in the world. Fortified by several large Scotches I went home to tell her that due to the force of circumstances this plan had gone wrong. that I was now in the Army, and that our income would now be even less than before. Not a moan did she utter. This may have been because I had taken the precaution of bringing home the remainder of the Scotch, with which I had fortified myself, and tipping it into her. All she said was: 'Of course, you could not possibly do anything else but join the Army.' Which drove me to the conclusion that women are far more patriotic than men.

Odhams Press treated me coldly in spite of the letter from the S of S which they had duly received. This was understandable, because the war had not yet started and nobody knew that it would. I did have to leave them at only a week's notice which must have put poor little Korda to great inconvenience and justify him for telling me that if I did this I could never get back to Odhams again after the war. I never did. Neither did he, poor fellow. He was unlucky enough to be killed by a flying bomb which fell bang outside Odhams premises in Long Acre whilst he too was outside.

4

Early Days at the War Box

LIFE AT THE WAR OFFICE was very strange at first. Millis had to share an office with Lieutenant-Colonel Gubbins, who also came under Joe Holland in some capacity or other. It was quite a pleasant office on about the fourth floor and as Gubbins was a half colonel it had a carpet. But it was not very large, and had to accommodate Gubbins plus his military clerk when he wanted to dictate letters and Jefferis with the same qualification — his henchman being a Staff Sergeant Bidgood. It was not many months before Gubbins sprang into fame through Joe Holland putting him in charge of running the Poles and the Czechoslovaks, a job which he did superbly well. He finished up as Major-General Sir Colin Gubbins, and quite right too.

It was all rather uncomfortable for me, as I had to squeeze myself into a corner of this office and wait in a queue if I wanted to telephone anybody. So I contrived to spend a lot of time outside it. Rapidly, I laid on a number of visits. Running off to Bedford to see how Limpet production was going along was a cinch. But I could not spend the whole week there. However, I soon found other avenues of escape. First, I was instructed to hie myself to Clerkenwell and find the workshop of one called Thomassin who had produced the first TV Switches for Millis and was now engaged in all kinds of experimental work for MIR (c) which he would not tell me about. There was also a Mr Tutt of Hulburd Patents Ltd at Acton whom I must see. He was making or about to make something or other for the section. Then, of course, I had the Cambridge Sticky Bomb alibi.

Thomassin turned out to be a remarkable old fellow. Of Swedish extraction, he had started this workshop in Clerkenwell some years back as the Kinematograph Engineering Co. How Millis had run into him I never knew; but there he was making TV Switches and various other bits and pieces for him. This workshop was a decrepit old place equipped with very ancient machinery. It looked as if it might fall down if a bomb exploded within a mile of it. But it never did. Old Thomassin always looked distraught but never was. He would plug away all night through the blitz producing stuff for us and never complain. One of the tasks that fell to my lot which I really liked was writing a citation for him for a B.E.M. I was almost ashamed about it, though, because he should have been awarded something much better. He will not mind now, for he died many years ago. He was a fine old man.

Finally I was instructed to go to Aldershot and dig out a Sergeant Tilsley there who was at one time a henchman of Millis Jefferis and in this capacity had been induced to give up most of his spare time to messing about with magnets for Limpets. This I did. Poor Tilsley had made up some kind of magnet pack weighing about a hundredweight which would have fallen off any target under its own power. However, we made it up to him later for he became a key man at M.D.1., Whitchurch.

Having worked all these outside contacts to the bone, I was forced to retire to the inconvenience of the War Office and squash myself uncomfortably into a corner of this small room, hoping to be able to secure the services of Staff Sergeant Bidgood so that I could deal with the vast amount of paperwork which I seemed to have encountered. This did not work out. One little flair I have is one for contriving to make myself comfortable. Stick me down in the centre of a vast Americanised office such as I encountered at Temple Press Ltd and later at Odhams Ltd and I would guarantee that within a month or so I would find some pretext for getting myself installed in my own office complete with every mod. con. including a secretary.

This I soon managed at the War Office. The key to the situation, I discovered, was a lady named Joan Bright, God bless her. In theory she was just Personal Assistant to our boss — Lieutenant-Colonel J. F. C. Holland, G.S.O.1 of MIR. Actually, she more or less ran the show. It was she who kept the Bag of Gold and an accounts book to show the hidden powers how the money had been spent. It was she, I found, who had told Millis he had better take me on and who had fiddled it so that I was taken into the Army so smartly. Obviously her influence was unlimited. I promptly made my number with Joan and explained my difficulties. The very next day, MIR (c) was allocated room 173 at the War Office, As a Major, Millis was not entitled to a carpet; but Joan wangled one for him. He and I could live in this room in comparative comfort, and we had a place for Bidgood when he was called in to take letters.

I may have mentioned that I am an opportunist. Obviously I must set about planning to take Joan out to lunch and get to know her better. There was no ulterior motive in this, except a business one. Joan was not that kind of a girl and everyone in the department knew it. What is more, my new colleagues informed me that I could forget about dating her up for lunch. It was well known that she would never go out with anybody under field rank and that Captains like me stood no chance at all.

This proved to be true. But I won in the end, although it took me a long time to do it. Joan had a flat in Curzon Street, to which I and the other Captains had never been invited. One morning to my great amazement she turned up at the War Office looking a little unsettled. The blitz was on, and it seemed that during the night a bomb had dropped in the area behind her flat and had not yet exploded. The recommendation was that all tenants should go away for a while and wait to see what happened. But Joan was a very strong-minded girl and was reluctant to do this. She seemed to regard me as an expert on unexploded bombs although in fact I knew nothing whatever about them and wanted me to go round to her flat with her to review the situation. At once I took advantage of this happening. I told Joan that if she would accompany me to a fortifying lunch at Taglioni's where I had some influence I would then accompany her to her flat and cast my professional eye over the site. This happened to be a day when all the Majors in the department were out and most of the Captains too, so I won.

The whole thing was extremely platonic. As a nervous type, the idea of tottering about in a flat on the third floor of a building menaced by an unexploded bomb did not appeal to me at all. But how could I get out of it? There was no escape at all. So I went to Curzon Street with Joan and spent a most unpleasant half hour inspecting the premises, trying to work out what would happen if the bomb went off and when it might do this, and how long it would take to remove Joan's furniture from this danger spot. I advised her to stay at the St Ermins Hotel for a couple of days where we had some influence and suggested that after this time lag we might have lunch together again followed by another look at the site. Whilst making this proposal I was shuffling out of the place at great speed, which Joan must have noticed. She gave me a look

25

of scorn and said she had decided to spend the night there anyway and hope that the bomb would not go off. She did, and it didn't.

That was the only time I succeeded in getting Joan to come out to lunch with me, although later on I did manage to achieve what she regarded as acceptable rank. She finished up by running some terrific Central Reference Library for the War Office, being lauded by a number of Generals and the Press, and finally by marrying one of them.

Life became quite pleasant at the War Office until the war started. Millis and I could park our cars in the quadrangle and make our way to our office through the visitors' entrance. Here an elderly but very charming Lieutenant-Colonel would greet us every morning and if one of us had a brown paper parcel tucked under our arm he would say: 'Ha! And what have you got there? Explosives, I suppose,' and he would laugh heartily at his little joke. 'One of us would reply: 'That's it, sir. Very high explosive this. We're trying to collect enough to blow up this place.' We would then proceed with dignity to our office and lock up in the filing cabinet the 6lbs or so of blasting gelatine we had been carrying. At times we had as much as 20lbs there, which was no doubt a court martial offence. It was wanted for filling experimental devices of one sort or another and we had nowhere else to keep it. To get hold of the stuff was easy enough. The Colonel Grand brigade which had broken away from us was now established at the St Ermins Hotel. They operated under the name of some business concern or other and although they did not as a rule wear false beards and dark glasses they got very near to it. They were always helpful and if we rang them up to say could we have some more of that cheddar cheese — say about 6lbs — they would have it packed up ready for collection by 10 o'clock the next morning. Of course one did not go to the St Ermins Hotel to collect this explosive. The drill was to be at St James's Park station at 10 o'clock the next morning and look out for a bowler hatted gentleman wearing a buttonhole and carrying a brown paper parcel in addition to a copy of 'The Times' . . . This gentleman had to be hailed and talked to for a couple of minutes during which the parcel would be transferred. Names were never used. Meeting these Cloak & Dagger boys in other places we would get to know their names, or think we did. But it was never any good. The Major Norman we had talked to last week would tell us that for this week he was Captain Walker or something of that sort.

This happy situation changed soon after the war started. Security was tightened up. No longer were we allowed to park our cars in the quadrangle or to use the visitors' entrance. We had to go in by the Staff entrance round the corner and be inspected by a Guard who would certainly not let us get by with a brown paper parcel of any sort. So we had to make other and more complicated arrangements. To make things worse, whereas we had seldom been called upon to produce our original passes we were now issued with new ones carrying our photographs which must be produced whenever we entered or left the building. This worried me more than most. Some photographer had been roped in in a hurry to take pictures of all the MIR staff. I was one of the first and was therefore an experimental job for him. The resulting print gave the impression that I was wearing a black shirt and uniform and made me look just like some senior member of the Gestapo. When I think of the thousands of times I had to see myself as this camera saw me it is a wonder that I managed it without committing suicide.

Of course with the outbreak of war the work of MIR (c) did not double. It was at once multiplied by about four. This did not suit me at all. Anyhow I had learnt that it was not the work you did yourself that brought success in life but the work you persuaded other people to do for you. Any of my colleagues at M.D.1. would confirm that I lived up to this principle. At the moment, MIR (c) consisted only of Millis Jefferis, myself and Staff Sergeant Bidgood. At the rate we were now going it was obvious that we would soon run down like clocks unless we found help. For a while we had secured the part time services of a Captain Jones RE, and Sergeant Tilsley but these had now been taken away from us and told to go to war. What I wanted personally was somebody who could take over from me at least part of the awful job of not only goading our contractors into stepping up the output of our products but also seeing that deliveries were made to the proper places, which was quite a complicated matter. After due thought I had the answer, for as I have said I seemed to be inspired over this M.D.1. operation. When I was at Odhams, I was assailed at all too frequent intervals by an over-enthusiastic but otherwise quite likeable red-headed fellow called Gordon Norwood. He dealt with the advertisement side of my two journals and I had soon learnt that however hard pressed I might be it was quite impossible to get rid of him until he had got whatever it was he wanted from me. He was persistance personified. Undoubtedly this was the man I wanted.

A telephone call to my ex-secretary got the thing started, and in a few days time there was Gordon Norwood sitting in Room 173 at the

War Office begging for work which was soon given to him. If Odhams had only known it, I did them a far worse turn in taking him away than I did in leaving myself. For the first few months with me, Gordon's job was practically nothing but sheer drudgery and he missed out on most of the fun and excitement. In fact, at one stage he was banished to a second office we had acquired in the basement where he could talk into a couple of telephones at once without distracting Millis and my-self. However, it all came right for him in the end. When eventually we moved out to Whitchurch he came into his own and became one of my senior executives. He stayed with me throughout the war except for a few weeks when he got called up and taken away by mistake.

Trying to look ahead a bit, it was obvious to me that I must quickly find some more contractors to enable me to meet the ever-increasing demand for MIR (c) stores. The existing ones which had been found by Millis were already working flat out for us. Thomassin was busy on TV switches and a variety of odd jobs. Tutt of Hulburd Patents was now on Pressure Switches. Bell's Asbestos were making the Light Camouflet Set. The one firm I had brought in, Nobby Clarke and his Low Loading Trailer Co, was so busy making Limpets that it was working to full capacity. I had orders to place and nowhere to place them.

Of course I knew plenty of large engineering concerns, but when I approached them and tried to place orders with them I soon found the catch. With the outbreak of war they had at once been tied to the Ministry of Supply and could accept orders only with its approval. The Ministry would certainly not agree to the War Office placing orders with such firms and would want to handle all our contracts for us. But I soon found that if we tried to do a deal with them on these lines we should get nowhere at all. As our products were not yet officially accepted ones their manufacture could be given no priority whatsoever and we should be lucky if we got any made in six months. In the meantime I had an impatient Joe Holland on my tail all the time urging me to produce more and more MIR (c) stores in less and less time. For he seemed to have made me responsible for this side of things and left Millis in peace.

The only answer was to find our own contractors — ones which were not tied to the Ministry of Supply — so that we could fix our own priorities. Fortunately we were free to do this because no problem arose over payments — thanks to our having our bag of gold. The thing to do was to look round for small firms which were not in the

35 Portland Place, London W.1., London Office of the International Broadcasting Corporation (Radio Normandie), requisitioned by MIR (c) in 1940.

Top: Deserted, forlorn, lifeless and awaiting a new owner, 'The Firs' Whitchurch, as it is today.
Below: The experimental workshops.

clutches of the Ministry and which were likely to be a bit short of work because of the war. Illuminated signs were obviously not going to be in much demand for a while. Franco Signs were well known to me, so I approached them right away. They welcomed me with open arms, put their main factory at Hendon at my disposal and rapidly reopened one at Bristol which had been closed down. Throughout the war they worked hard for the department.

By the same reasoning, it would seem that the makers of musical instruments would not be overworked for a while. So Boosey & Hawkes were roped in. They had an excellent factory at Edgware, and Geoffrey Hawkes spared no effort to help us. In fact we almost counted him as one of us, and Millis and I acquired a very good friend. Boon & Porter's garage was the next firm to be adopted and as time went on other garages and small engineering shops joined the party. It was not long before we had a very useful little manufacturing group.

Professor A. M. Low did me a good turn by introducing me to a firm called Midgley Harmer which specialised in the design and manu-facture of small mechanisms. I had first met Low a year or so back when I had got bored with editing 'The Caravan & Trailer' and he was looking for somebody to help him run 'Armchair Science.' I joined him, and the partnership was a very happy one. But unfortunately the publication did not pay and Jack Courtauld who had been subsidising it for years got rather tired of doing that. So when a Mr T. Korda who ran the 'World's Press News' made an offer for 'Armchair Science' and for me to go with it this was accepted. Korda then sold his com-plete outfit to Odhams Press and that is how I came to be there.

Low had remained Consulting Editor of 'Armchair Science' so I kept in close touch with him. When the war came along, he was bursting to get into the army and seemed to think I must have enough influence to fix this for him. But I had not and neither had Millis. For apart from being well over the age limit, Low was not very popular in the scientific world and the War Office people seemed to know it. Apparently where he had gone wrong was in styling himself 'Pro-fessor' on the grounds that he held a Chair of some sort at Farn-borough — the RAF research and development centre. He then followed this up by writing a number of scientific books for children and was looked down on for that as well. So far as I was concerned, none of this mattered at all. Apart from the fact that he had been and still was a very good friend of mine I knew that he had a first class brain and could be of help to MIR (c) over the design of special weapons. So when his application for a commission was turned down I got Millis to agree to let me enrol him as a kind of unofficial helper. It was in this capacity that he brought in Midgley Harmer Ltd., a firm which he had induced to make up the prototype of a device he was designing for us.

My manufacturing arrangements ran beautifully for about a month. Then Gordon Norwood who spent most of his time on the telephone in the office shook me awake and asked for help. It seemed that one of our little contractors anxious to get on with the job had ordered the necessary materials and had been told that they could not be supplied to him unless he quoted an official contract number. Could I please give him such a number? The great thing in this kind of operation is not to weaken and let on that you are in trouble, for in this way the other fellow loses confidence in you and your organisation. I spoke to him, apologised profusely for our oversight in not giving him a contract number, said I would consult my list right away and let him have one, and it would be – er – RIM 9401. This was not very difficult to think of in a hurry. 'RIM' was MIR backwards and 9400 was the war office telephone number.

I explained to him that all RIM numbers carried the highest priority and that he should mention this to his suppliers. He did, and it worked like a charm. What is more, it went on working throughout the war and nobody ever discovered that our contract numbers were completely phoney ones. In fact, late in the war when somebody formed a Munitions Priorities Committee or something of the sort of which I was made a member it gave me great pleasure when attending the first meeting to be presented with a schedule giving particulars of all contracts on hand. There was a long list of RIM numbers, and an encouraging footnote saying: 'These RIM numbers carry top priority.'

All this had happened before the end of November 1939. The report I was then able to send to Colonel Holland showed that the section was now actually in production with no fewer than eleven devices of one sort and another and was carrying out experimental work on five more. This was not a bad performance. In spite of it, though, I found later on that because of the ever changing situation at the War Office we should have been abolished or swallowed up by the Ministry of Supply in the near future if something had not happened on November 10 which transformed the entire outlook.

5

Operation Royal Marine

ON SEPTEMBER 1 Winston Churchill had been appointed First Lord of the Admiralty and had made himself exceedingly busy there. One of his first moves had been to enlist the help of his old friend, Professor Frederick Lindemann, who held the Chair of Natural Philosophy at Oxford, and install him in Admiralty House. Lindemann was to serve as Scientific Adviser to the First Lord and be concerned with any project which involved the use of scientific equipment or special armaments.

Millis, on the afternoon of November 10, 1939, received an urgent summons to present himself in Joe Holland's office to meet some Naval Officer. Two hours later, he arrived back at Room 173 in a highly excited state. It appeared that Winston Churchill, whom he had talked to for five minutes, had a scheme for immobilising the Rhine which called for the use of special mines and bombs. Neither the Admiralty nor the Royal Air Force had any armaments that could be made to serve this particular purpose, so Lindemann had been asked to see what he could do about it. From somewhere or other, he had learnt that the War Office had a department dealing in special weapons and had soon run Joe Holland to earth. After the brief session with Winston, Millis had been given a fair idea of what was wanted by Lindemann. Of course we had nothing to offer, but Millis was quite undeterred by this. He said he would start work on a design right away and be back in a week or so with a prototype weapon — which of course impressed Lindemann enormously. He kept his word too, for I have a note in my diary that we showed first rough models at the Admiralty on November 24.

The scheme was a grandiose one — typically Churchillian in its conception. Churchill was very annoyed with the Germans for

31

sinking some of his ships with magnetic bombs (not Limpets) and was anxious to get his own back. He considered he might do this with a bit to spare if he could contrive to sink half the barges taking supplies for the Germans down the Rhine and put that important waterway out of action for perhaps quite a time. This would be a very serious blow to the German war effort. It could be effected by feeding floating mines into the Rhine from the left bank above Strasbourg, which was French territory, and dropping others into it from aircraft.

Whilst it was known that the Admiralty and RAF had no armaments suitable for the job the exact requirement had not yet been formulated. Millis, of course, was full of ideas when nobody else seemed to have many and the next day had confirmed them to Lindemann in writing. So on November 19 the First Lord was able to send a Minute to the Controller, an extract of which reads as follows:-

'The type of mine required is therefore a small one, perhaps no bigger than a football. The current of the river is at most about seven miles an hour, and three or four at ordinary times, but it is quite easy to verify this. There must therefore be a clockwork apparatus in the mine which makes it dangerous only after it has gone a certain distance, so as to be clear of French territory and also so as to spread the terror farther down the Rhine to its confluence with the Moselle and beyond. The mine should automatically sink, or preferably explode, by this apparatus before reaching Dutch territory. After the mine has proceeded the required distance, which can be varied, it should explode on a light contact. It would be a convenience if, in addition to the above, the mine could go off if stranded after a certain amount of time, as it might easily spread alarm on either of the German banks.

'It would be necessary in addition that the mine should float a convenient distance beneath the surface so as to be invisible in the turgid waters. A hydrostatic valve actuated by a small cylinder of compressed air should be devised. I have not made the calculations, but I suppose 48 hours would be the maximum for which it would have to work.'

It would be around 6 o'clock when Millis got back to Room 173 and explained to me what was wanted, although not quite in the terms of this minute, which I did not see until some days later. I suggested to him we should rule out clockwork right away. His expensive Venner clockwork time switches, the purchase of which he now obviously hoped to justify, would not serve the purpose. First to design a new clockwork mechanism and then to get it produced in any quantity would take at least six months. How was he going to laugh that off with Lindemann when he had promised him something in a week or so. If we wanted delay mechanisms in a hurry what was wrong with using some version of my Limpet ones or his TV Switch affairs?

Millis saw the point, as he generally did, and ruled that after going round the corner for a little fortification to one of the Clubs which had kindly made us temporary members we should return to Room 173 and get on with the job. What is more, it must be given absolutely top priority and I must drop everything else in its favour. Couldn't Gordon Norwood take over my work? I explained that the unfortunate Gordon had already taken over the dullest part of it and that, as there was only one of him and he was already working harder than I was, this was no answer. Millis merely snorted and said he would ask Joe for more help — which he did the very next day.

If only Millis had lived in Roman times I am sure he would have become a Chief Flogger on one of those slave-powered galleons. This was, in fact, the first time he had kept me up all night, but there were many more times to follow. We had a drawing board but, as we were always going to places where we wanted to make sketches, it was seldom used. To cart it about with us was impracticable, and anyhow we could not both use it at the same time. So Millis had acquired some large drawing pads marked off in one sixteenth inch squares and they were just the job. To work with them, all one needed was a pencil, a ruler, and the ability to count squares. One could get the originals copied and I soon found that by using a suitable filter the background lines could be cut out so that nobody knew we had cheated. Millis's idea was that faced with a problem of this sort we should both have a go at it and let the best man win. Or maybe the two designs could be combined with advantage, which often happened.

As I have said, we had nothing in stock to meet this special requirement, but some of the ideas we were working on might fit in. One did — the one that Low was working on. Millis had a lust for destroying communications. Blowing up railways appealed to him most, but as a close second came the burning of pontoon bridges. He had vague ideas about a fire mine which could be floated down a river and would burst into flames on encountering a pontoon bridge. Low had started on this one and had got his Midgley Harmer firm to make up a little model to illustrate the firing gear he had in mind. It was quite good. He used a central tube in which floated a central rod, positioned by rubber diaphragms. Antennae sprouted out from it at the top end. When one of them hit anything the rod was displaced to make contact with the surrounding tube and off she went.

This struck us as being a good start, but no more. There were more difficult requirements to be met. The mine, dropped from an aircraft, must sink to the river bed and remain dormant for a predetermined period. It must then rise not to the surface but to a little below it and float down the river. One coming into contact with any shipping it must detonate with sufficient force to cause a wreck. Should it fail to be detonated after a certain time it must sink to the bottom and become harmless. Before the night was through, we completed designs for such a device and combined them. I must say that apart from Low's contribution for the firing mechanism which might be assessed at 10%, Millis was responsible for 60% and myself for only 30%.

The next day we got very busy. Low was asked to come along to Room 173 bringing his model device and the Midgleys with him. Father Midgley, as we came to call him, and his two sons had a very well equipped little engineering works at Park Royal. Given the idea and our rough sketches they retired there, and by the next evening Father Midgley had produced a most beautiful G.A. drawing of what we had in mind. Our main trouble in dealing with FM was that he would insist on preparing these beautiful drawings in ink for everything and making our sketches look exceedingly scruffy.

At this time the 'W' Bomb as we called it — 'W' being for water — was to carry 10lbs of high explosive and would be quite a sizeable affair. To try out the mechanism, we decided to produce some little scaled down models. They were attractive little things and operated in the following manner. When dropped into a tank of water, the bomb would sink to the bottom and stay there for perhaps five minutes. Through a chemical pellet dissolving away, a sinker weight would drop off and the bomb would then have sufficient buoyancy to rise to the surface. However, it did not quite do that because the freeing of the sinker also released a lid at the top of the bomb. When this came away, out popped a number of cork floats attached to the bomb by cords of such a length that when the floats reached the surface the bomb floated three feet below them. In this location, it was of course difficult to see.

The dissolving of another chemical pellet resulted in the central rod that released the lid continuing its movement until out sprung the antennae, contact with which would cause the firing. But further travel was needed before the rod was free to waggle about and the

34

device was fully armed. So it was really remarkably safe. Having risen to fame through my aniseed ball discovery, Millis now made me O/C of the dissolving pellet department and instructed me to find a quick answer. I did. Because of our wearing work and the need to keep ourselves going with alcohol I kept in room 173 a supply of Alka Seltzer tablets. I found these ideal for the job, and it was just as easy to drill holes in them as in aniseed balls. They were standardised for the 'W' Bomb and nothing better was ever found. What with the aniseed balls, the rubber appliances and now this Alka Seltzer, though, I was beginning to earn an unwanted reputation as a bit of a rake.

The heat was now being turned on. Winston had started a campaign to sell his 'Royal Marine' scheme to the Cabinet and had called his first meeting to this end on Monday November 27 at 12.30 am — sorry, Tuesday morning. Millis had been instructed to attend and to demonstrate this model, which he had already shown to Lindemann. We were both a little bothered about the device because we had not yet got it working well. In fact we had spent the week-end at Midgley Harmer's works making various modifications to it and now Millis was a little concerned because he was sure that even if it performed properly in the large glass tank I had had installed in the First Lord's room at the Admiralty for this demonstration somebody would be sure to ask him if he had tried it in deeper water and he would have to say he had not.

The answer seemed to be to go and try it in the Thames, so we did. This was a Sunday afternoon, and it was rapidly getting dark. Having motored as far as Chiswick Bridge we decided that this was about as far as we could get. By great good fortune, we found there a Sea Scouts depot in operation. It was agreed that Millis would go up on to the bridge and drop the bomb from it whilst I would mobilise a few Sea Scouts with a boat and chase the bomb down river to see how it behaved. There was a slight time lag, because the bridge was guarded. With commendable promptitude, Millis in his Major's uniform demanded that the guard should be turned out and stated that he had come to inspect it. It was and he did — after which he dropped the bomb. It was never seen again. In the Sea Scouts' boat, I followed its probable route — but nothing happened. Being an extremely honest man Millis owned up, which I think is more than I should have done. In the excitement of the moment he had forgotten to withdraw the safety pin, with which we of course equipped all our wares. So the bomb had just dropped to the bottom of the river and stayed there.

Back I had to go to Park Royal and rout out the Midgleys to get another sample made by the following night.

There was a sequel to this episode. Months later, I was summoned to Joe Holland's office. He had in front of him a massive file originating from Southern Command and proceeding in orderly fashion through Eastern Command, C-in-C Home Forces and almost the King. The gist of it was that on the evening of November 26, some officer of field rank who claimed to be a General Staff Officer had contrived to make his way on to Chiswick Bridge and throw from it a bomb, which fortunately had apparently not exploded. This was a most shocking occurrence, and every effort was to be made to trace the officer concerned and take immediate disciplinary action. It had been suggested that this officer was with MIR at the War Office and that was why the file was now directed to the GSO1 of MIR.

I explained this little matter to Joe Holland, who was not in the best of tempers through having a bit of tummy trouble. He was drinking a glass of milk, which he appeared to view with distaste, and eating some ham sandwiches. Suddenly he made up his mind, rang the bell for a messenger, consulted a list, and jotted down a number, 'Bring me this file, please,' he said, 'and quickly!' It did turn up in about five minutes — a most massive affair. Joe showed me the title. It was some sort of history of the design of the bayonet, starting from just after the Boer war. Joe untied the red ribbon on this massive parcel, opened it at somewhere about the middle, slapped into it this complaint file complete with all the minutes written by VIPs, added a half eaten sandwich for luck, retied the red ribbon, and rang for the messenger again. 'That's the end of that one, Bobby,' he said with a sigh. 'It will never be found now.' It never was. I always admired Joe, even if he did throw files at me on occasion.

I was not invited to this first meeting at the Admiralty. Millis assured me that it went all right and that Winston was so keen on the 'W' Bomb that he had instructed him to get it into production right away. So we retired at once to the Midgley depot and worked through the night on production drawings. The very next day we started to get our manufacturing circus lined up for this job and Joe Holland authorised us to spend £500 out of the bag of gold to help the good work. We did get three firms started on tooling up, but had to stop them very smartly when the Admiralty advised us that after consideration they thought the bomb or mine should carry a 20lb charge instead of a 10lb one.

36

This sounded easy enough. All we had to do was to scale up our drawings by increasing the container dimensions by 25%. But as we were working for the Admiralty, we now found ourselves caught up in their red tape. What was worse, as the RAF had been brought into this operation, we had to contend with their red tape as well. This rapidly brought us to a complete halt. Our designs must first be submitted to the Ordnance Board for consideration. Then, if they approved, the Design Department at Woolwich would have to prepare proper production drawings of our 'W' Bomb before it could be made.

Extracts from my diary make the position all too clear. Here they are.

November 10 Work on the 'W' Bomb put in hand.

November 24 Admiralty shown rough model. Very interested.

November 27 Instructed by Admiralty to get 10lb bomb into production.

November 29 Production drawings completed and supply arrangements made.

November 30 Initial finance obtained and arrangements made to start tooling up.

December 4 Tooling stopped as result of Admiralty report. Woolwich asked to prepare drawings of larger models and make samples.

December 9 Jefferis attended Air Ministry conference 10.30 am re 'W' Bomb. Discussion afterwards with Wing Commander Bennett. Green of ESS (Franco Group) informed of suggestion that his company should co-operate with Midgley Harmer so that the 'W' Bomb could be manufactured by the combined concerns almost under one roof. Macrae visited Midgley Harmer to put in hand experiments with soluble ball disarmer for 'W' Bomb. Bennett phoned to say 'W' Bombs would be five in a box with two or more boxes per plane.

December 11 Jefferis down with 'flu. Called to see Midgley who stated that Fisher, of Air Ministry, Harrogate, had spent the morning there discussing production details for 'W' Bomb.

December 12 Jefferis still down with 'flu. Macrae visited Midgley Harmer to adjust model of 'W' Bomb. Phoned Woolwich in hope of getting drawings of new models put in hand there on December 4. Nothing finished yet. In absence of Jefferis, Macrae attended Admiralty conference at 10 pm and demonstrated model of 'W' Bomb to Sir Kingsley Wood. Transpired during conference that First Lord was under the impression that 'W' bomb was actually at the production stage, which is not the case. First Lord referred to Tedder as being in charge of production and reaffirms that he wants 10,000 W Bombs by February 1.

My diary goes on like this for pages and pages. We had an awful time. On December 17, Millis had to go into Millbank Hospital for an operation through having developed a boil on his bottom, and that left me holding the baby. This was just at the time that Winston Churchill was really getting cracking with his campaign for selling his Royal Marine project to the Cabinet. He kept on laying on meetings at half an hour after midnight which came to be known as his 'Midnight Follies.' In Millis' enforced absence, I had to attend all these and demonstrate our model to everyone from the Prime Minister dowwards. The trouble was that Winston was a born showman and that the 'W' Bomb was his greatest act—for the simple reason that although he could talk about the other weapons he wanted to use for this project the 'W' Bomb afforded the only practical demonstration.

Everything did not always go well. We were invariably short of demonstration models, because we were always modifying them or losing them in trials. Given even shorter notice than usual about one of these meetings I had to dash out to Midgley Harmer's place, put some bits together in a great hurry, and dash back to Admiralty House for a Midnight Follies meeting at 12.30 am. I should explain that Mr Churchill was exceedingly cunning over these arrangements. Instead of trying to sell his Royal Marine plan to the Cabinet as a whole he worked on the members individually, asking one and only one at a time to sit in on one of his conferences on the subject.

I was getting pretty good at this act myself. Feeling rather like a professional conjurer, on the cue 'Captain Macrae will now describe the "W" Bomb,' given by the First Lord I would get to my feet, say my little piece about the little model I was holding, and before dropping it in the glass tank so that its functioning could be clearly seen by all I would demonstrate how the lid would come off and the antennae pop out through the chemical pellet dissolving by slowly undoing a nut at the base until this happened. I had, I thought, pretty well perfected my performance. At the previous meeting a few days or nights back the guest of honour had been Sir Samuel Hoare and everything had gone so well that he had congratulated me. This, however, was an even more important occasion. The visiting VIP was the Prime Minister himself, Mr Chamberlain.

All eyes upon me, especially Winston's, I went smoothly into my routine. Holding up the model, I slowly undid the nut to demonstrate the arming process. As I have mentioned, this device was assembled in a great hurry and somehow or other an early type central rod had crept into it, this rod having only a few turns of thread on it instead of the prescribed half inch of it which was required for this demonstration. The result was that just as I was in full spate the assembly came to pieces. Antennae, rods, springs, and a tin lid shot up into the air and descended in various parts of the room making tinkling noises. I was left holding the body of the bomb and that was all.

It was always said of Mr Winston Churchill that when put out he could produce the most horrible and intimidating scowl. This is true. He did so now, and roared out something in which I think the words 'bloody incompetence' occurred. With all the dignity I could assume, which wasn't much, I said: 'I apologise for this slight hitch, sir, and if you will proceed with the next item on the agenda for the moment I shall be happy to demonstrate the 'W' Bomb in five minutes time if you will permit that.' All I got was a growl. Thoroughly unnerved, I went round the room collecting my scattered components and was preparing to return to my seat when I realised I had not the pluck to do that. The table was a large one, covered by a blue cloth which descended almost to the floor on all sides. There was a gap by my chair because of two empty seats. On the pretext of retrieving a final and imaginary component I ducked under this tablecloth, sat down well under the table with my bits and pieces spread around me, mopped my brow, sighed with relief, and set about trying to put the flaming thing together again.

About five minutes later I wriggled up into my chair, rather flushed but otherwise in working order, caught the First Lord's eye by waggling my model about, and in due course received his order to continue my demonstration where I had left off. In the tank, the device I am glad to say functioned perfectly and the entire audience made encouraging noises afterwards — which was very kind of them because I was the utmost junior officer present. I should add that a day or two later when I had to report to the First Lord on 'W' Bomb progress in spite of his preoccupations he remembered the incident, told me he was sorry he had lost his temper for the moment, and actually commended me for my resourcefulness although I had not shown all that much.

These Midnight Follies had been rather fun when Millis and I had attended them together. We always found plenty of time for a few snifters beforehand. Then, when we got back to room 173 and, at around midnight were getting ready to go to our meeting, Millis would more often than not find he had not got his Sam Browne, without which he would have been improperly dressed. He would promptly requisition mine, and I would be left to scuttle round the War Office until I found some kind officer willing to lend me his. I was always lucky.

Without Millis' moral or immoral support I did not seem to do so well. Single-handed I had to argue with Admirals, Air Marshals and all kinds of big shots and try to goad them into action. Here again the diary tells its story:–

Friday December 22. Tests of 'W' Bomb at Walton postponed until midday on account of fog. Went straight to W.O. and arranged for various goods to be rushed to Thomassin's for crating and despatched by night train to Scotland en route for Finland. Left Bidgood to find lorries and loading parties for collecting material from Aldershot. Explained to Young routine inspection of T.Vs and made him responsible for seeing they were in order before being crated. Bidgood to superintend crating at Thomassin's. Young to arrange matters at station and accompany consignment to Leith.
Question of percussion caps for Pressure Switches arose. Tried to hustle up the 1,000 from ICI, Birminham but no hope of getting them in time. Rather than dismantle igniters, without which Woolwich would not supply caps, decided to send as many complete igniters as possible with consignment.

Phoned Tutt to see if any Pull Switches were completed. No luck. He's held up for springs.

Left W.O. at 11.25 am. and arrived Walton 12.15 pm, just in time for test. Three bombs dropped, two attached to wooden dummies to act as buoys. The other had small parachute. Buoy idea no good, as cables again broke during drop.

Drop was from 800 feet at 250 mph. Two instalments. Pilot succeeded in grouping most effectively, placing the bombs exactly where asked. This shows that given the requisite skill the bombs could be dropped successfully into a canal.

All bombs hit the water with a crack and everyone was convinced that the detonators had fired prematurely. On the way out in the boat, Currie (Commander Currie of the Design Department at Woolwich) was already redesigning centre tube assembly.

Inspection then showed that bombs had behaved perfectly on this occasion. Evidently we were very unlucky on previous day and it looks as if the main fault was in not having the lids securely attached by their cables. The slightly lightened model, dropped exactly as before, had armed properly by the time we reached it and fired perfectly when touched with an oar. Battery blown out by detonator. Came down in due course, unfortunately missing Currie and smashing a glass affair in the boat.

Second bomb with parachute had also armed itself and not being artificially buoyant was floating in correct position 3 ft. below surface. Fired immediately it was touched.

Third bomb had lid sealed on to ensure it rising to the surface. It was the only one to be dented in at the side, but was not badly damaged.

Conclusion was that the suggested remedy of adding a drogue would certainly get over all troubles, but that it was also advisable to strengthen lid attachment and adopt cork floats. Everything else in order.

Agreed that eight or more trial bombs fitted with drogues and slightly stronger lid attachments must be dropped soon as possible to settle the matter. Currie & Co decided next Thursday would be earliest time. Unable to cajole them into making it Wednesday. Agreed to give them all assistance. Tried out my three-minute pellet and found it took six minutes in the ice cold water. Agreed to make more pellet experiments although do not consider a six-minute delay disadvantageous.

Retired to Mitre by myself for lunch, Currie having planned to stop elsewhere on his road. Received message for Currie from Huskinson, who had been unable to attend trial. Wanted to be rung at 2.30. Had fixed appointment with First Lord at 4.30. Waiter giving message visibly impressed. Is this publicity necessary?

Cut lunch, went to Acton, and got Midgley started on pellets. Phoned Huskinson 2.30 and told him results, and agreed to accompany him to see First Lord. Went to office en route to see how big push for Finland was going. Phoned Low and tried to get him to abandon his early 'W' Bomb patent application and join Midgley and this department in new claim. Want to avoid risk of action after war.

Met Huskinson ten minutes before appointment and showed him drawing of modified lid attachment. First Lord again asked for news of Jefferis and particulars of his operation before getting down to business. Evidently he is determined to get to the bottom of this matter.

Huskinson reported progress and I put forward his suggestion for a conference of production experts and manufacturers. First Lord jumped at this idea and left Huskinson to arrange details. Said everything must be done to get going. Said DAP (Director of Armaments Production) must attend. I mentioned that Midgley & Co were going ahead with tooling for pressing base on the chance of getting order, that they were willing to work over Christmas, and that we had a line on fifty tons of sheet steel for the bomb bodies if wanted.

Afterwards, was treated by Huskinson as long lost brother. He confided the fact, already known to us, that Tedder had done nothing whatever to get production going. Said he was seeing Tedder that evening to warn him of impending Winstonian kick in the pants. We agreed that Midgley should contact Wright of Woolwich with Ordnance Board authority so that ideas could be co-ordinated. Silly to have him drawing bits at Acton with Currie drawing the same bits a different way at Woolwich. Huskinson will advise me directly meeting is called.

Visited Clerkenwell to find Bidgood just loading up the last crates. Done a good job of work. Went to Millbank to report to Jefferis. Schulman and Bauer had been to see him and tried to raise his temperature by describing their hitherto deadly secret experiments. They are working on a hydraulic gun. Jefferis very intrigued and thinks it may be a good thing.

Explained to Jefferis that the stock cupboard was now bare and arranged to order the following, subject to Col Holland's approval. 1,000 TV Switches, 500 Pressure Switches, 500 Pull Switches, 50 Light Camouflet Sets, 200 Striker Pattern Delays. The TV order to be split so that a second firm can get into the run of making them. Must not be dependent on one supplier.

That is a report of just one day's work on the part of MIR (c) and I have given it in full just to show that we had other work on hand apart from the 'W' Bomb. However, that project continued to be given top priority. There were more trials at Walton Reservoir, more meetings, more arguments and more frustrations. A most awkward stage was reached when the First Lord and Professor Lindemann had both entered a fool's paradise and were convinced that 10,000 'W' Bombs were actually being made ready for the Royal Marine operation whereas we knew that this was not the case. But we could not explain that to the First Lord and his Scientific Adviser because we were dealing with too many big shots and were completely outranked. The First Lord had entrusted Air Vice Marshal Tedder with making the production arrangements. He was supported by Group Captain Huskinson of the Ordnance Board, Commander Currie (RN) of the Design Department, and Uncle Tom Cobley and all. Any complaints we made could almost be classed as mutiny. So we just had to plug along and do the best we could.

Suddenly there was terrific action. Having done the rounds and sold his Royal Marine operation idea to the entire cabinet, Winston Churchill decided that his next move must be to sell it to the French. The next thing I knew was that I was left a message by a Captain Fitzgerald at the Admiralty, whom I had met at all the Midnight Follies meetings, to say that as Major Jefferis was hors de combat the First Lord would like me to accompany him to France to demonstrate the 'W' Bomb to General Gamelin and other French VIPs. I dearly wanted to go on this expedition, but at this time I was really up against it in all directions so I left Joe Holland to decide the issue. Joe was a pretty good sort. He could easily have instructed me to stay put and get on with my job. But divining that I rather wanted to go on this party he instructed me to do just that.

I had a frantic time off-loading my work on to Gordon Norwood and anyone else I could find to do it, trying to get the production arrangements for the 'W' Bomb unstuck so that the First Lord would not be lying when he assured the French that 10,000 were actually being made, acquiring the full sized models and the minature versions for demonstration to the French whilst assuring myself that the latter would not fly apart as they had done at my unfortunate Midnight Follies demonstration, and trying to placate Millis who was now liable to burst his boil and a blood vessel as well at the thought of being left out of this party.

In the event, I reported for duty at Charing Cross station at 1.15 pm on Thursday January 4 and was directed to the 'First Lord's Special Train.' There I met Millis, in an extremely bad temper, boil and all. He had discharged himself from Millbank and arrived on the hop, Mrs Churchill, or "Clemmie" to the First Lord, came to see him off and contrived to have a word with all of us in turn. There could be no more charming lady.

I had a worrying journey down to Dover, in spite of the lunch and the drinks. Millis informed me that after due consideration during his many sleepless nights he had decided that the 'W' Bomb was of poor design, mainly because it depended on electrical fiiring to which he strongly objected. He therefore intended to devise a mechanical version fired by the displacement of elements and seeing that I was here I might as well help him in this good work. This put me right on the spot. Here was I, briefed to demonstrate to the French the Mk I 'W' Bomb which was supposed to be in production and here was Millis saying that this device was no good and that we were now replacing it with a Mk II, as yet not designed. It was most awkward. I played for time.

Something had gone wrong when we arrived at Dover. In theory, we were supposed to board the destroyer *Cardington* there. But for security reasons or something of the sort the *Cardington* had been sent round to Folkestone and so road transport had been laid on to take us there. It had been laid on in a hurry and not well enough. As the most junior officer of the party I found myself allocated to a Utilicon carrying the luggage and arrived at the *Cardington* about quarter of an hour after the rest of the party was aboard. It was most impressive — to me anyway. As I trotted up the gangway all by myself I found myself faced with a whole row of Admirals and the entire ship's crew lined up on deck. Dressed in a very old trench coat which I had kept from the First World War I felt I could not be representing the War Office to its best advantage. What is more, I was not at all sure about the drill, for I was unaccustomed to boarding destroyers with the First Lord waiting to receive me. However, a faint bell rang somewhere in my head and told me the thing to do was to salute the quarterdeck. This I did so smartly that I almost fell backwards into the sea. But all was well. Pipers piped, sailors dashed about, and we were off in no time at all.

It was a most interesting voyage. The party was really a very small one, for unlike some of our modern Ministers Winston Churchill did not believe in taking a crowd about with him. It consisted in the main of the First Lord, Professor Lindemann his Scientific Adviser, Lt-Commander Thompson, his faithful bodyguard, a Mr Hopkins, who was a naval construction expert from Bath, a detective and a secretary, Millis Jefferis and myself. I am sure I was the lowest of the low, and perhaps that was why all the NOs were so kind to me. They at once rushed me down to the Wardroom where, after filling me up with pink gins, they made me an honorary member of their mess so that I was

The author, Colonel R. S. Macrae.

The 'Prof.' who was first Professor Lindemann,
and later became Lord Cherwell.

entitled to buy them drinks at around 8d per shot. It made me realise what I had missed through being turned down for the Navy!

We were allowed up on the bridge, provided we kept out of the way. Winston, attired in some enormous naval overcoat and a kind of yachting cap, spent most of the voyage there. He was particularly fascinated by the Azdic and would breathe down the operator's neck until the poor fellow got the jitters. And so did we! The wretched instrument started letting off beeps at intervals so that we felt sure there must be a U-Boat only a few yards away waiting to torpedo the First Lord and ourselves into the bargain. But this did not happen. We landed quite safely at Calais.

The French were evidently on their mettle. The train provided to take us to Paris was even more lush than its British counterpart. Bemedalled French officers joined the party and welcomed us. The bar, they explained, would remain open throughout the night and there were sleeping compartments for all of us. Dinner would now be served. It was.

At about 10 pm, I had ideas about retiring to bed. Millis had other ideas altogther. On the pretext that he would be unable to get to sleep because his boil was hurting him he dragged me into an empty compartment, presented me with a new drawing pad he had thoughtfully brought along for me, and suggested we should both get busy on the design of his Mk II mechanically fired 'W' Bomb. My plea that we should forget about this Mk II business for the time being and concentrate on selling the Mk I to the French, which was what we were there for, fell on deaf ears. It appeared that why Millis was so anxious to get these drawings done was so that he could show them to Lindemann before we met the French, explain how much better his new design would be than the original one, and suggest we should be permitted to cancel our demonstration of the latter.

As both Winston Churchill and Lindemann now regarded Millis as a kind of wizard who could produce new armaments out of a hat in a hurry and as they believed that 10,000 of these Mk I 'W' Bombs were actually in the course of manufacture, I could think of no better way of his ending a beautiful friendship than this one, and told him so. Millis could not see it this way at all, but I did succeed in sowing a seed of doubt. I was able to make a bargain with him. I would sit up all night working on his new design if he would promise me not to mention it until after we were back in London — if then.

About 2 am, Millis decided his boil might let him get a little sleep

45

after all, so we packed up. On my way back to my own compartment I had to pass through the magnificent saloon bar and was delighted to find that it was still functioning although I seemed to be the only customer. Soon after I had settled down with my whisky and soda, though, an impressive figure in a kind of siren suit came in. Seeing the place was empty but for me, Winston took the seat opposite. He could hardly go anywhere else without appearing to be very rude, and anyway he had now forgiven me for messing up the 'W' Bomb demonstration at the last meeting. When he got his brandy we chatted away quite merrily and I was able to remind him that some years back I had written an article about him and his hats of which he had approved.

This really got us on friendly terms. Winston pulled out his cigar case and was just about to poke it under my nose when his eye fell on my three pips. He then hastily changed his mind; it would be wrong to waste a good cigar on a mere Captain. He ordered me another drink instead, which was on the house. I got my own back next morning, though, when I saw Tommy (Commander Thompson) with whom I had become quite friendly. When I told him what had happened he dug out one of the big boxes of Winston's cigars which he had to carry round everywhere they went and presented me with half a dozen.

The First Lord seemed to be in no hurry to get to bed, which was not surprising. For this was his favourite working time, as I well knew from my attendances at Midnight Follies. I was having a most interesting talk with him which I was hoping would go on for a long time when up loomed the Prof. who settled down beside us. He was fully and faultlessly dressed as usual although I am quite sure he had been to bed. No doubt he had arranged to be informed if the First Lord moved out of his compartment and that was why he was here — for he hated Winston to be out of his sight with somebody else perhaps working on him.

'Ha,' said Winston with commendable but unusual tact, 'Prof. you are just the man I wanted to see. Now please explain to me in simple language exactly how an Azdic works.' Prof. promptly did so, and then went on to deal with further queries on technical subjects. There is no question that he had a wonderful gift for being able to give a concise yet easily understandable explanation of this kind right off the cuff. What is more, I found later that he was about the only fellow associated with Winston with the ability to meet his constant demand: 'Pray let me have an immediate explanation on one sheet of paper

46

only.' The rest of us could seldom manage it in two, especially as Winston insisted on our using typewriters equipped with the largest and most space-consuming type available.

Prof's appearance rather spoilt my party. I now felt a bit of an intruder, as it seemed likely that important matters of State were to be discussed. So without waiting to be asked to take myself off I did that and went to bed. On our arrival in Paris, we were whisked off to the Crillon, a vast hotel which had apparently been commandeered by the government. There was plenty of room for us. Even I was given an enormous suite having a bathroom with big bidets and one of the largest baths I have ever seen in my life. In it, I could easily have demonstrated the full size 'W' Bomb and I thought of doing so. But instead I snatched a couple of hours sleep before we all went off to demonstrate our wares to General Gamelin complete with staff and Admiral Darlan complete with his also.

I must say that Versailles was pretty impressive. There were beautifully dressed soldiers all over the place and our party was received with the fullest military honours. Winston Churchill gave an exposition of his Royal Marine scheme to the assembly, speaking mainly in schoolboy French which everyone seemed to understand quite well. In rolling tones, he would say something like: 'Le bombe descende à bas de mer — er — a bas du fleuve. Il reste la pour peutêtre cinque minutes. Enfin, il ascende jusqu'à il est une metre au dessous le surface. Il s'arme. Il voyage le long du fleuve jusqu'a il rencontrer un bateau. Bang. C'est fini.'

The French are an exceedingly courteous people. Not a smile could be seen on any of their faces during this remarkable performance. I hope our party behaved as well, but I am not too sure about it. I am glad to say that our 'W' bomb demonstration then went off without a hitch in spite of my shaking hands and there were even a few muttered 'Bravos' at the end of it. Some of the limelight was stolen from me by this Mr Hopkins, who was included in the party. He was a naval constructor from Bath who had devised a tank which was at the same time an entrenching machine. Instead of travelling along the surface of the ground, it excavated a trench for itself as it went along and could therefore in theory advance with great safety. The little model worked quite well, and the French with their Maginot line ideas just loved it.

There is a sequel to this one. Our Captain Clarke of Bedford had had a similar idea, but his machine was a more ambitious one. Instead of excavating its way along at a snail's pace, it laid and fired explosive charges in front of itself so that progress should be very much quicker than with the Hopkins model and also less liable to be seriously obstructed. Nobby had submitted his idea to the Royal Engineers Board from whence it had come along to MIR (c) — which served him right. After our return from Paris, we handed over Nobby's scheme to Lindemann and left it to him to sort things out. He did that rather well. Nobby was created an Assistant Director of Naval Construction in due course, a post which he hated, and made Hopkins' assistant for designing and producing this frightful machine. So far as I know, no prototype was ever completed. Nobby managed to escape from this post a few months later and get back into the army.

The second Military Mission gave us lunch after our morning's work — and a very good one too. It was headed by the Duke of Windsor, who was of course delighted to get the opportunity of entertaining his old friend and supporter Winston Churchill. I retired hurt afterwards, and swore never to drink plum brandy again. Millis was being a bit stand-offish with me, perhaps having regretted giving me his undertaking to keep quiet about his Mk II design. He went off to dinner with Captain Fitzgerald to whom he had taken a great fancy and did not ask me to join them. On his return, he informed me that he was going off to Strasbourg the next day with Fitzgerald to find a place from which 'W' mines and any others could be pushed into the Rhine, that I would not be wanted on this voyage, and that my orders were to get back to the War Office as smartly as possible and get on with some work. I put this down to the boil,

There was thick fog the next day, and no aeroplanes were flying. Eventually the Military Attache managed to get someone else thrown off a cross channel boat sailing in the evening so that I could get on it complete with all my bombs and a note to the Customs people instructing them to leave me alone. It was a miserable journey, with everyone lined up on deck wearing lifebelts in case we were torpedoed — this apparently being a favourite pastime of U-boats in foggy weather. But nothing happened.

Millis turned up a few days later, and we soon got back into the old routine. We had gathered that Winston's sales campaign had not gone too well, and the Prof. confirmed this. The French were intrigued with his idea and thought it would work. They would like to join in putting it into practice, but were frightened to do that. These were the days of the phoney war. Paris was still a gay city — not even blacked out. The French view, and it was an understandable one, was that life in their country was quite pleasant at the moment in spite of the war. Everybody was happy and nobody was getting hurt. They were the nearest to the Germans. If they joined us in this scheme to blow up German barges in the Rhine this might well make the Germans cross and it was they who would then have to suffer, not us. The Germans might at once retaliate by bombing Paris to pieces, an operation for which it was well known that they had the capacity. Therefore, let this excellent scheme be postponed for a while.

It was, which was just as well because in spite of all our efforts the machine had got clogged up with red tape and there was no hope of producing either the 'W' Bombs or any of the other weapons required for Operation Royal Marine in time for carrying out the good work in February as originally planned by the First Lord. Let me again quote from his book 'The Gathering Storm.' Incidentally my copy bears the following dedication. 'To Colonel Macrae. Whose co-operation at M.D.1. I valued so highly during the war. Cherwell.' Co-operation? This from the Prof. is about the highest compliment he could pay. It infers that I might be his equal, which of course he did not mean. Still, he might have limited it to 'help' or 'assistance.'

The Minute I want to quote from this book is one written on January 12 1940 by the First Lord to First Sea Lord, Controller, DTM, Rear-Admiral A. H. Walker and Professor Lindemann. Headed Operation 'Royal Marine' it reads as follows.

1. This matter was fully discussed in France with high Military authorities, and various arrangements have been made. Captain Fitzgerald and Major Jefferis have seen the necessary people and should now furnish me with reports of their work. The French Military men point out that they control the head waters of the Saar and the Moselle, in addition to the Rhine, and that many possibilities are open there. All are convinced that we should not act until a really large supply of the needful is in hand. Not only must the first go-off be on the largest scale at all points, but the daily and weekly supply thereafter must be such as to keep the tension at the highest pitch indefinitely.

2. It is, of course, understood that while all action is to be prepared the final decision rests with the governments.

3. In all circumstances, I am prepared to postpone the date from the

February moon to the March moon. Meanwhile, every exertion is to be made to perfect the plan and accumulate the greatest store.

4. A meeting of all concerned will be held in my room on Monday night at 9.30 pm. By this time, everyone should be able to report progress and everything should be concerted. I am asking the Secretary of State for Air to be present to hear the reports. These may be individually presented, but those concerned are to consult together in the interval. Above all, any obstacle or cause of undue delay is to be reported, so that the operations can be brought to full readiness as soon as possible. We may be forced to act before the March moon.

Somehow or other, we did manage to perfect the 'W' Bomb and build up an adequate stock of it by the end of March. It was, of course, the Mk I that had been adopted. Millis had tried hard to sell his Mk II design to Lindemann; but as Lindemann now regarded me as the fellow responsible for production of all MIR (c) weapons he summoned me to the Admiralty to have a talk about this matter before making a decision. I had to tell him that if we tried to swap bombs in mid-stream in the manner suggested there could be no hope whatever of turning out the required quantity by the end of March. Perhaps a little unfairly, I mentioned that Millis had now fallen out of love with his Mk II version and had started to design a Mk III one. That settled it, and I was instructed to concentrate on the Mk I.

In the meantime, the First Lord had been hotting up his sales campaign for operation 'Royal Marine.' The War Cabinet was now enthusiastic about the scheme and wanted to put it into practice right away. But the French could still not be induced to agree to a date. The French Ministers were coming to London on March 28 for a meeting of the Supreme War Council, so the First Lord persuaded the Prime Minister to make 'Royal Marine' the top priority item on the agenda. In Winston Churchill's own words: 'Mr Chamberlain opened with a full and clear description of the scene as he saw it. To my great satisfaction he said his first proposal was that 'a certain operation, generally known as "The Royal Marine" should be put into operation immediately.' He described how this project would be carried out and stated that stocks had been accumulated for effective and continuous execution.'

The French remained obstinate and refused to say 'Yes' to this proposal. It was left to the First Lord to try to talk them round.

Quoting again from his account of the matter he says: 'The War Cabinet were very ready to let me begin this carefully prepared offensive plan and left it to me, with Foreign Office support, to do what I could with the French. In all their wars and troubles in my life-time I have been bound up with the French, and I believed that they would do as much for me as for any other foreigner alive. But in this phase of Twilight War I could not move them. When I pressed very hard, they used a method of refusal which I never met before or since. M. Daladier told me with an air of exceptional formality that ''The President of the Republic himself had intervened and that no aggressive action must be taken which might only draw reprisals upon France.'' This idea of not irritating the enemy did not commend itself to me.'

Winston Churchill never won this particular battle. But operation 'Royal Marine' did take place after all — in May when France was invaded by the Germans. Quoting this time from Vol II of Mr Churchill's 'The Second World War' he says: 'From the moment of the invasion we began operation ''Royal Marine'', the launching of the fluvial mines into the Rhine. In the first week of the battle nearly 1,700 were streamed. They produced immediate results. Practically all river traffic between Karlsruhe and Mainz was suspended, and extensive damage was done to the Karlsruhe barrage and a number of pontoon bridges. The success of this device was, however, lost in the deluge of disaster.'

In all, some 20,000 'W' Bombs were made and issued under the arrangements made by MIR (c) and a great number of them was used. Then the Ministry of Aircraft Production took over from us as the weapon had been officially accepted by the RAF as a service store. Of course this bomb or mine was just the job for causing a bit of trouble for canal or river traffic in any theatre of war and we were soon told that it was in extensive use. So we felt entitled to clock this up as our first big success. It proved to be even more than that in time, for this adventure had brought MIR (c) to the notice of the man who was to become the most powerful in the land. In due course he was to save us from being abolished or swallowed up by some Ministry of Supply research department.

6

Booby Traps

IT MIGHT APPEAR from the previous chapter that the 'W' Bomb and operation Royal Marine were taking up most of our time. This was not so. All our other experimental projects had to be kept going, and new ones were added to the list almost every day. For because of the 'W' Bomb business our fame had spread and we were being asked to design armaments for the Royal Navy and Royal Air Force as well as for the Army. What is more, our standard lines were soon in such great demand that we just could not get them turned our fast enough. Looking back, it is hard to see how we managed. Fortunately Joe Holland realised we were up against it and would lend us officers when they could be spared from other work. I am still grateful to the first two, Captain Young and Lieutenant Walters, for the noble way in which they helped us out — working a 16 hour day as we all had to do.

At the end of 1939, apart from the 'W' bomb we were in production with the Limpet, TV Switch, Light Camouflet Set, the Pressure Switch and the Pull Switch. The last named was a newcomer — one I happened to be able to pull out of the bag. Booby traps set off by a trip wire were a popular idea, but the only device for firing them was the standard service igniter. This took the form of a spring-loaded striker in a barrel and a cap holder with percussion cap secured to the business end of the tube with a screwed collar. The cap holder had an extension tube on to which a No 8 detonator could be slipped or into which the end of a length of fuse could be inserted. A split pin running across the tube kept the striker in the cocked position and to fire the device one had merely to pull out the pin.

Actually, this igniter had been designed to replace matches for lighting a length of safety fuse and it was perfectly all right for that purpose. But as a booby trap initiator it was a dead loss. First it had to be very securely anchored somehow or other in such a way that it would stay put whilst the pin was pulled out. This could be done if there were a tree handy and a large staple. Even then, the prospects for success were not good. For the pull required to remove the pin was an unknown quantity. For safety's sake, the ends of the split pin would have been parted in the first place. When closed up again, it would be anybody's guess how strong a pull would be needed on a line to tug out this pin. Maybe a man could trip over the wire without doing that, which would be most unsatisfactory.

Millis, who was busy with higher thoughts, asked me to have a go at this one. With my nice new uniform, I was wearing a khaki shirt with a detachable collar. The front stud I was using I had always considered to be a clever little gadget. It had a detachable head which was as firm as a rock when in place. But pull out a little centre pin and the head would be pulled out. This was done by having a thin split tube attached to the head, the end of which was bulged out a little. The body of the stud consisted of a kind of hollow button from which projected a stem in the form of another little tube. To assemble the stud, one had to pull out the centre pin in the head as far as it would go, push the split tube right home, and then return the centre pin to its home position. The end of the split tube would have passed through the other tube, and pushing in the centre pin would expand it and make quite sure that it could not pass back again.

In reverse, this was just the action that was wanted. So sitting in Room 173 improperly dressed with my collar stud in front of me I got busy on my drawing pad and an hour later the Pull Switch was born. It was the quickest and most successful job I have ever done. The official description of the device reads as follows:–

'The Pull Switch is a device to be used in conjunction with a trip wire for firing a mine. It is particularly useful for booby trap work. Designed to operate when a direct pull of about 4 lbs is applied to to the release pin it fires a percussion cap in a holder exactly the same as that supplied with the Mk III Service Igniter. With the cap holder in position the switch measures approximately 4″ overall by $\frac{5}{8}$″ in diameter and weighs $2\frac{1}{2}$ ozs. It consists of a head into which is screwed a housing tube containing a plug with a restricted opening. At the other end of the tube is a screwed collar for attachment of the cap holder. Inside the housing tube is a striker head attached to a hollow spindle, which runs inside a compression spring. The end of this hollow spindle carries a small head which is split, so that when it is compressed the diameter is reduced. When this split head is forced through the small hole in the housing tube plug, a spring loaded release pin at once enters and expands the head so that it cannot return, although it is now under the influence of the compression spring.

'A safety pin can be inserted through the head and release pin so that the latter cannot be disengaged from the split head and it is impossible for the striker to fire the cap. Without a loading spring on the release pin, a pull of 1 lb will free the striker. The pull required can therefore be varied by having a stronger or weaker loading spring. The standard spring used calls for a 4 lb pull.'

The great feature of this device was that it could be so easily anchored; in fact if desired it could be included in the trip wire line and not attached to anything else. The exact pull to set it off being known, it was a simple matter to tension the trip wire enough but not too much. And setting the trap was so safe. When the work was completed, one merely had to pull out the safety pin from the Pull Switch. If it nearly fell out or came out very easily all was well. If it were at all tight it meant that there must be an initial load on the release pin so that it would be highly dangerous to remove the safety pin and readjustment was called for.

Prototypes of this Pull Switch were made the next day by the faithful Thomassin. A fortnight later we were in full production with it. The extraordinary thing about it was that unlike most mechanisms it behaved perfectly right from the start and gave no trouble at all. It never had to be redesigned and throughout the war almost three million were made and issued at a cost of 2/6d each. This was good value for money.

We now had the Pressure Switch which fired when a load was applied to it and the Pull Switch which fired when a pull was applied to it. To complete the series and catch up with the Germans who rather specialised in such mechanisms we needed a Release Switch — something that could be hidden under a book or perhaps a lavatory seat if one were feeling unkind and would explode a charge when the object was lifted. Bobby got the job again. But I did not mind because by now I rather fancied myself for this kind of work. This time I did if anything a little better. Although press tools had to be made in this case, my Release Switch was in full production in a fortnight and almost two million were made and issued eventually, the cost being

2/3d each. Again, the design was right from the word 'go' and was never changed.

In appearance, this device resembled a flat oblong hinged box with open ends. It measured 3″ x 2″ x ¾″ and weighed only 5 ozs. To the front of the body of the box on the inside was anchored one end of a strong leaf spring. The other end of this spring carried a hammer head which when the spring was released smacked a little striker resting on the percussion cap in one of our standard cap holders. This cap holder was pushed through a hole in the front of the box and kept in place by the striker itself which was rivetted to a pivoted spring clip. When the leaf spring was bent back through an arc almost as far as it would go, a hole in the hammer head registered with two other holes — one in the back of the box and another in a small anchor ear turned up from the base of the box. A safety pin could then be slipped through these holes to maintain the device in the cocked position.

On the lid of the box being closed and pressed right down, one edge of a retaining ear punched out of the lid and given a 45 degree angle engaged the leaf spring and pushed it just a little further so that the load was taken off the safety pin and it became quite loose. This was rather clever stuff. It meant that the trap could be set with perfect safety. The minimum load needed to keep down the lid was 1½ lbs. A book like this one would do that. But if it were a borderline case nothing could go wrong. After setting the trap, the operator merely had to give the string attached to the safety pin a gentle tug. It should almost fall out, in which case he could then walk off and congratulate himself. If it were at all tight, however, this would be a sign for him to turn pale, hastily disconnect the charge, and try again. You will see that we did everything we possibly could to safeguard the lives of our saboteurs and ensure that they blew up the enemy rather than themselves. This was fair enough, for they were exceedingly brave fellows. It is one thing to design a device of this sort and perhaps demonstrate it with a live charge with everything in one's favour. It is quite another thing to have to creep about enemy occupied territory and set up such a trap and risk being shot at any moment. This thought always shook me, and still does.

As I have said, the surprising thing about these three booby traps is that they all worked right from the start and could not be improved upon. What we did manage to do later on, though, was to improve on the caps. Sad to state, they at times failed to fire although our

55

strikers were calculated to hit them twice as hard as necessary. Nothing can be more discouraging to the saboteur than to take a lot of trouble to lay a trap of this sort and then find that it has failed to function. So even though the percentage of failures was quite small we felt we must do something about it. This service percussion cap assembly was all right in its way but we wanted something much more sensitive. At this time we were working very closely with Imperial Chemical Industries and they soon found for us the answer in the form of a little 1.7 grain detonator which was only about the size of a percussion cap but instead of needing a blow of 3 in/lbs to set it off only had to be prodded lightly with a needle point. Eventually we adopted this detonator for all our booby trap and like mechanisms and thereafter never received any reports of blinds.

There is a sad sequel to this story of our three famous switches. Towards the end of the war when fellows had to be dropped in jungles and trot around carrying a lot of equipment the question of weight became all important. Light as our switches were nobody wanted to have to cart about a dozen of each because they did not know what was wanted. So I sat down to design a Universal Switch which would do any of these three jobs. Why on earth I had not done this before I just do not know. The complete device weighed only 3 ozs and measured $2\frac{3}{16}''$ long by $\frac{1}{2}''$ square. The body was a neat little casting with a couple of lugs having holes in them so that it could be screwed in place if desired. It had the Pressure Switch cocked striker and hardened steel spindle. A load of 35lbs was needed to crack this spindle and fire the switch. To make it easier to instal under a railway line there was an extension piece which could be fitted to the head of the pin which did the fracturing and then unscrewed until the unit was nicely wedged under the line.

Where the device differed from the Pressure Switch was that instead of the hardened steel spindle being pinned to the barrel so that the striker could be released only if it were fractured this spindle was held by a flange on it which came up against the release or shearing pin. The release pin was mounted in a rotatable turret rivetted to the body. It was kept there by a cross pin which consisted of a tube through which passed a wire, looped at both ends. The turret was slotted so that when the fat part of the pin had been drawn clear the release pin would be released, the thin wire passing through the slots.

Used as a Pull Switch, this device had merely to be included in a trip line, which was easily done because the turret head would swing round to any suitable position. As the cross pin could be pulled out either way, one had only to fit a tension spring in the line to ensure that the mine would be detonated if the trip wire were either tripped over and pulled or cut. Used as a Release Switch, a load of 2lbs would suffice to keep the release pin in place. And of course the usual safety device was included — a super one this time. It consisted of a spring clip with a two foot length of cord on it. This went through a vertical slot in the body and interfered with the striker. If for one reason or another the striker were released this clip would trap it and that would be that. The safety clip would be irremovable and nobody could get hurt.

I really thought I had done a marvellous job of work here and might get knighted for it. This little gadget would do absolutely everything. A man could carry a dozen in his pocket and be able to cope with any booby trap situation. Pop the thing under a crate, for example, the necessary mine having been laid, and the mine would go bang if the crate were lifted. It would go bang just the same if a fat man sat on it. Likewise it would go bang if a trip wire were pulled or cut. Surely nobody could ask for more than that. These things cost only 3/4d each and were packed in neat little cardboard cartons each holding the switch itself, a loaded cap holder, an adjuster so that the device could be set under a railway line, and two No 6 woodscrews to anchor it if necessary. It was the perfect 'Do it yourself' kit for the saboteur. A tin box holding ten of these miraculous mechanisms plus a few spare strikers and loaded cap holders weighed only 1 lb 9 ozs and measured only $6\frac{1}{2}'' \times 2\frac{3}{4}'' \times 3\frac{3}{8}''$. You would think that no professional saboteur could afford to be without one. But no, they were all married to the standard Pull, Pressure and Release switches and nothing else would interest them. Only 30,000 of my wonderful Universal Switches at 3/4d a time were made and issued. I doubt if many were used, or that the device is now included in the Ordnance Vocabulary in which the other switches most certainly still appear. The life of the inventor is hard.

It was not until the Spring of 1940 that we produced our most unfriendly booby trap device which we called the AP or Anti-Personnel Switch. The existing anti-personnel mines were clumsy and expensive and could not be installed quickly. What was wanted was some little gadget which could be included in the equipment of the ordinary soldier and with which he could quickly make a track unusable for anyone following after him. Millis had vague ideas about fixing up

.303 cartridges in some way so that they would fire when trodden on. At this time, Imperial Chemical Industries at Ardeer, Ayrshire, were working on several projects for us and I had to visit them almost every week. I talked to them about this new requirement and found that two of their experts had started to develop something on the lines Millis had in mind.

We got down to it together and soon evolved a satisfactory design. We had a gun barrel in the form of a tube about 8″ long closed by a spiked plug at one end and having a flange at the other end. This had to be driven into the ground, and we had a drift which enabled it to be hammered into hard ground without suffering damage. Into the tube was then dropped a little assembly consisting of a headed rod carrying a powerful compression spring surmounted by a metal sleeve. An umbrella spring — the kind that enables one to put a gamp up and down — was let into the spindle and so placed that when the sleeve was pushed down and the spring beneath it was fully compressed the umbrella spring would pop out to lock it there. Next on the spindle came a striker head with extension tube. Finally, on top of this cocked assembly was lowered the .303 cartridge, the tip of which would project about ½″ above ground level. We used a pointed steel bullet in place of the normal one.

The action of the device was as follows: when the bullet was trodden on the cartridge would be pushed down the tube. The striker head in contact with it would also be pushed down, and the extension tube as it moved down the spindle would collapse the umbrella spring. When this was flush with the spindle, the sleeve would be released and under the influence of the compression spring would give the striker head a hearty kick in the pants so that the cartridge was fired. The unfortunate fellow who was doing the treading would then get shot through the foot and any other part of his anatomy which happened to be in the line of fire. The troops soon christened this device 'The Castrator.'

Like all our booby traps, this one was very safe to install. If by any chance the assembly had not been properly cocked and was inclined to function on a hair trigger basis so that when dropped into the tube it flew apart this did not matter at all provided the operator was not peering down the tube at the time. With the same qualification, even if by some odd mischance the cartridge were fired it would not matter, for the bullet would sail harmlessly into the air and it would be indeed unlucky if it hit somebody on landing. Anyhow, although 1,439,450 of these A.P. switches were made and issued I never heard of anyone having an accident in the field with them. They were certainly a cheap and effective way of keeping down the birth rate of the Germans as they cost only 2/- each plus another shilling for the cartridge.

Although I heard of no accidents in the field with the A.P. Switch I heard of one that took place in the Admiralty and very nearly got me court martialled. This was later on in the war when an enthusiastic Naval Officer who had got involved in some Combined Operations planning came out to see me to learn something about our 'irregular warfare' appliances. I explained everything very carefully to him and also gave him instruction pamphlets telling him exactly how to handle the sample devices he wanted to take away. When it came to the A.P. switch, I would at first give him only the blank cartridges equipped with wooden bullets which we used for training purposes. But I had been unwise enough to demonstrate this contrivance to him by installing one with a live cartridge and then giving it a smack with a 2″ wooden plank — which of course the bullet pierced. He was very anxious to be able to repeat this performance for the benefit of some of his Combined Operations pals; so in the end I weakened and let him have a few live cartridges.

About the middle of next morning, a blast of noise came from my telephone. When the sounds became intelligible, I found I was talking to a very irate Admiral. It seemed that he had been sitting in his office at the Admiralty hard at work when suddenly there was a bang and some missile came through the floor narrowly missing his chair and what was sitting on it. On investigation, he had found that some officer on the floor below had been fooling about with some lethal weapon with which I had provided him. Had I no sense of responsibility, sir? Did I not realise that this was a most serious offence? I would be hearing a lot more about this. Click. In fact I did not hear any more from this Admiral, whose name I never discovered. Maybe on enquiry he had been advised to pipe down because it was well known that his ex First Lord strongly objected to any interference with our establishment.

Much as I always liked and admired officers of the Senior Service — and I worked with many of them as the war went on — I did find many of them a little carefree when dealing with explosives. There was a Lieutenant Golding who was attached to our establishment for some time to help in some experimental work being carried out for the Admiralty. This involved using explosives, and I was horrified one day when one of our Sergeant Majors reported to me that this officer was walking about the place carrying not only a supply of electric detonators but also a dry battery in his pocket. I had him hauled in right away and asked him if this were true. With a disarming smile, he admitted that there was some truth in the statement but that everything was quite all right and I had nothing to worry about. For he kept the detonators in one trousers pocket and the battery in the other — and he demonstrated this fact to me. 'What,' he asked, 'could be safer than that?'

I explained patiently that if he went on like this sooner or later he would in a moment of mental aberration contrive to get both detonators and battery in the same pocket. As I did not want to have any eunuchs about the place he would cease this practice at once. He retired hurt; but he was more hurt a few weeks later. For he slipped back into his old ways, and the inevitable happened. He was extremely lucky, because, although he was quite badly burnt, his love life was not affected — not for long anyway.

That concludes the chapter on booby traps — intentional and unintentional ones. We will now return to the War Office to see what is happening there to MIR (c).

Norman Angier, O.B.E., Assistant Director M.D.1.

Lt.-Col. L. V. S. Blacker in full dress uniform.

The monocle is missing.

Major C. V. Clarke, M.C.
("Nobby")

7

The Widening Field

DURING THE FIRST HALF of 1940 we got busier and busier. All the top brass in the War Office had now learnt of our existence and wanted to know more about the peculiar weapons on which we were working. First, the Deputy Chief of the Imperial General Staff ordered me to lay on a demonstration for himself, the ACIGS, and the Director of Military Operations. After several postponements, this was done on February 15 with highly satisfactory results. The DCIGS was so impressed that I had to repeat the performance a few days later for the CIGS himself, General Ironside. After that, hardly a day passed without some General or other popping into Room 173 to inspect our bag of tricks and I soon came to be regarded as a professional conjurer.

Millis hated this kind of show and usually managed to dodge them on the grounds that he had an important meeting at the Admiralty or Air Ministry. He liked to get away from the turmoil of Room 173 and had every excuse for doing so. Lindemann was now constantly demanding his presence at the Admiralty to discuss some ploy or other whilst the Air Ministry having seen how smartly he acted over the 'W' Bomb were now asking if he could do some other design jobs in a hurry. In particular, they wanted an improved delay action fuse and also an untouchable device for the General Purpose bomb.

There was a move at this time to attach Millis to the Director of Scientific Research on the pretext that this would give him the right to have all his design work carried out by the Design Department, Woolwich. As a Sapper, 'The Shop' at Woolwich was Millis' natural home so this plan had some attraction for him. But it had not for me. Already it was becoming clear that the Ministry of Supply strongly disapproved of this pirate design section which had sprung up from nowhere without its co-operation and was rapidly making a name for itself. They decided that the sooner it was embodied in their machine the better, and this was the first move in that direction. I was quite sure that if Millis were attached to the DSR, MIR (c) would very soon be abolished and we should find ourselves appointed to the Design Department where we should be new boys without any pull whatsoever and Millis would be quite unable to exercise his special talents. I explained all this to Joe Holland who at once saw the point and with a little help from Lindemann squashed this proposal.

The long-suffering Gordon Norwood, who was my only assistant at this time with the exception of Staff Sergeant Bidgood, was in great demand. Millis could never seem to understand that I was working him flat out as well as myself and that if either of us dropped out the work of MIR (c) would soon grind to a halt. Time and again I would return from some expedition or other to find that Gordon had been instructed by Millis to drop all his ordinary work and tackle some special job. A little plan from the DCIGS for flooding the Rhine was a good example. Because of operation 'Royal Marine' Millis was now regarded as an expert on this river. He was delighted when the DCIGS asked for his help. A little research work must be done, he said, to ascertain water levels and that sort of thing but fortunately he had on his staff just the fellow for that and would put him on to it right away. The man, of course, was Gordon Norwood and this time it took me several days and the threat of mutiny to get him back to his proper work again. After that, I got better at it. A note in my diary for June 15, 1940 is short and to the point. 'Norwood lent by Jefferis to Wing Commander Bennett for special job. Found it would last at least a fortnight, so cancelled the arrangement.'

Patriotic citizens were by now bombarding the War Office with ideas for new weapons. Oddly enough, at first these found their way not to us but to another MIR section where they were dealt with by a Captain Adams who in peace time was a barrister. He did pretty well seeing that it was not his line of country but on learning of our existence used to visit us regularly to cross examine us for technical information. He then cunningly arranged for these things to start coming direct to us with requests that we should report on them. The worst kind came through the Secretary of State himself and were brought to us by his frock-coated messenger with a red sticker on them saying that a reply must be given within so many hours. When we were desperately trying to do about six things at once it was a little trying to have to stop and write a report on why it was impracticable to design a small airship which could take to the water and become a submarine or something of that sort.

There were lots of perpetual motion experts offering us free power, the old favourite of having a battery to drive a motor to drive a dynamo which would in turn charge the battery being an idea which we could bank on receiving almost every day. The death ray merchants were also numerous and gave us a bit of trouble. Most of them proved to be students of H. G. Wells and we often wished he had never thought of arming his Martians in 'The War of the Worlds' with heat rays which shrivelled up everything. Here I had better not mention names, although I have them on record. One gentleman with an Italian name, and accompanied by his solicitor, was shepherded into Room 173 by the S of S's messenger and therefore had to be attended to. He would produce no designs or descriptions. His idea was too deadly secret for that — literally. He turned pale and shuddered as he thought of its awful implications. All he would tell me was that it involved a split heat ray, not just an ordinary one like the Martians had. He would demonstrate its efficiency to me at his Notting Hill laboratory by killing rats at a range of 30 yards or so. But I must understand that range was merely a matter of power. To bring down an aeroplane flying at 30,000 feet would be no trouble at all if enough kilowatts were available.

Reluctantly I agreed to attend a demonstration and left him to fix the date. It did not surprise me at all when he postponed it on three occasions but what did surprise me was when he did not cancel the fourth appointment. But it all came right in the end. I went along and in due course was admitted to a very bare shed equipped only with a number of portable lighting units of the kind found on any film set or in any photographer's studio complete with cables trailing over the floor. I saw no rats, although I am sure there must have been some around for it was that kind of place. The inventor was most indignant when I asked him why he needed all this portable lighting. He implied that if I did not know the difference between portable lighting units and his split ray heat generators I was unworthy of my job and that he would feel it his duty to inform the S of S of this. I made my peace with him and suggested that we should now get on with the demonstration. Again I was in the wrong. Apparently when I had enquired about the range of his ray I had not seemed very impressed when he talked about 30 yards, so especially for my benefit he had been trying to step up the power and the range before I arrived. As a result, he had burnt out all his heat generators. It would take him at least a fortnight to make replacement ones and cost him a lot of money. He felt that in the circumstances the War Office should contribute to this and would I please see the S of S about it? I would not, so we parted on not very good terms. I heard no more from him.

The next death ray merchant who reached me by courtesy of the S of S was even more troublesome. Or rather it was not he himself who was so troublesome as his sponsor who claimed to be an ex-army Captain and a very influential fellow. Again no particulars of the device could be disclosed but I would be horrified if I attended a demonstration. The S of S, I was told, had said he would be prepared to attend one if I would advise him to do so after we had had this talk and I had learnt all about the idea. So would I now please report to him right away and tell him I was satisfied he should make this move? Another thing — could I please arrange Police protection for them before they left the building. The enemy had got wind of this war-winning invention and they were being followed.

Being a bit frightened of the S of S, I did ring up Scotland Yard about this matter and gave them a laugh. My customers did not hear it, though, and went off quite happily. Two days later I received a panic telephone call from the gallant Captain from Brighton. The situation was now desperate, he told me. They were after him, and unless I could get the Police round quickly to the address he would give me he would be finished and this great invention would be lost to the enemy. For my own protection, I at once rang the Brighton police and that was the last I heard of the matter. No doubt the enemy abducted this fellow, although I was not advised of the fact. I only wish they had also abducted the other dozen or so death ray merchants that followed in his footsteps as well.

A great deal of our time was now taken up in trying to equip the various Military Missions which were springing up left, right, and centre. The first one was for Finland. A Major Coombe and a Captain Whittington-Moe seemed to be involved in this one, together with Lieutenants Munte and Croft whom I labelled the Finnish Commercial Travellers. They were all frightfully enthusiastic and even induced me to train them in demolition work on Sundays. Four Independent Companies were also rapidly formed and I received a stern memo. from Joe Holland saying that we must give priority to supplying them with our devices and instructing them in how to use them. This memo. was dated April 25 which was a Thursday and it closed with a sentence saying that these four Independent Companies must all be equipped and trained by the following Tuesday. Joe always was an optimist!

We managed it, near enough. Bidgood went to Dymchurch (No 2 Company) and then on to Suffolk (No 3 Company). I went ot Newcastle and then on to Edinburgh to look after the other two companies. We took some of the gear with us whilst the rest followed by road or passenger train. Surprisingly, it all turned up in time thanks to the almost superhuman efforts of Gordon Norwood and Sergeant Tilsley who had now been posted to us in view of this emergency. I flattered myself that I was working myself to death and was chastened when I realised that these others were working even harder.

Millis missed all this excitement, but found some with more danger in it for himself. He contrived to talk Joe Holland into letting him go to Norway to get some practical experience in blowing up railway lines. The idea was that Sergeant Tilsley was to follow him, but not yet thank goodness. Filling his haversack with Pressure Switches and blasting gelatine, off he went early on the morning of April 18. The RAF had arranged to pick him up at Hendon and fly him to Scotland, where he was to board a Sunderland flying boat which would take him on to Norway. Millis arrived at the War Office that morning in a bit of a flap to make his final arrangements. I wanted to drive him to Hendon, but it was one of those mornings when everything had gone mad and even Millis agreed that I could not possibly get away. The Transport Pool could not help us. as they were fully booked up with Generals and mere Majors just had to wait in the queue. So it was agreed that Millis would drive his own car to Hendon — fortunately he had it in the courtyard — and that I would have it collected from there at leisure.

Off he went and two days later I received a signal to say that all arrangements had worked well and that he had landed up in Norway. Fine! The next day a policeman arrived at the War Office and as deputy for Major Jefferis I had to accept a summons. It appeared that in dashing to Hendon to catch his aircraft he had exceeded the 30 mph limit along the Finchley road and been well and truly pinched. He must appear in court in due course.

Busy as I was, I took time off to write what I thought was a crushing letter to the Hampstead Police. I reminded them that there was a war on. I explained that my superior officer had to get to Hendon in a hurry to go off to Norway. Speed limits, I pointed out, were admittedly very necessary in peace time but in wartime it must be understood that army officers in the course of their duty were entitled to disregard them. Writing this masterpiece on War Office notepaper and signing it as a General Staff Officer I thought that would be that. But not a bit of it. A month later, I was advised that the case had been heard and that as Major Jefferis had not appeared and put in a defence he had been fined £6, which sum must be paid immediately. I gave up, for I reckoned that if I had to fight this one I would have no time left to fight the war. But it gave me some satisfaction to send the money out of my bag of gold anyway so that the country had to pay whichever way one looked at it. The sad sequel was that Millis was back again by this time and tried to insist on returning this £6 to the fund on the grounds that it was a personal debt. It cost me at least four large Scotches to talk him out of this one. I have never known a man who was so awkwardly upright.

Poor Millis did not have much of a party in Norway. He arrived just at the wrong time when our forces were on the run and from the time he landed he could do nothing but scuttle around trying to avoid being picked up by the Germans. He had no time even to look at a railway line, apart from blowing it up. However, when he got back to Room 173 on April 30 he was able to write a most valuable report on the situation in Norway which went to the CIGS and then to the P.M.

MIR (c) had become involved in chemistry amongst other things. As a New Year's present, Joe Holland had given me two little bottles containing liquids. He had made it clear that they were not drinkable. One he had christened 'Motorists Delight' and the other 'Superscent.' Joe was always one for titles and should have been an advertising king. The title of the former portion was not truly descriptive. The idea was that one had only to put a few drops of this fluid into a petrol tank to put the vehicle out of action for ever. The latter chemical was supposed to be quite deadly. Scatter a few drops about any room, I was told, and the inhabitants would feel so sick that they would have to pack up work and might well be away for weeks. Its smell was much worse than that of sulphur dioxide, rotten eggs or a dead rat.

It was some weeks before I got round to trying out these prescriptions. Not feeling inclined to wreck my own car in trying out this fearful contaminant I bought a £5 one out of this bag of gold. The idea was that it would be ruined in a day or two if only a few drops of this stuff were put into the petrol tank and could then be thrown away. Actually, it remained with the section for about a year and eventually had to be retired only because somebody was thoughtless enough to drive it into a wall.

Joe was a little put out about my failure to incapacitate our £5 motorcar with this witches brew. He demanded to know what I had done about testing his 'Superscent.' The true answer was 'damn all' and Joe seemed to guess this. So I roared back to Room 173 with my tail between my legs, dug the sealed and unopened bottle of stink stuff out of the filing cabinet, handed it over to Gordon Norwood, and appointed him Group Leader for this particular project and Chief Chemist to the section with no additional pay.

Gordon accepted this, which is more than I would have done, and opted to take the stuff round to Thomassin's and try it out there. His reasoning was sound. These Clerkenwell premises. he pointed out, always stank to high heaven anyway, no doubt because there were many dead rats under the floorboards. Thomassin had become acclimatised to this and thrived on the atmosphere whereas nobody else could stand it for more than an hour or two. So if we could drive out Thomassin with our Superscent we could be assured of its potency.

At the risk of delaying production, I agreed to this plan. Norwood then surreptitiously scattered half the contents of the bottle around Thomassin's workshop when he wasn't looking and awaited developments. There were none. Thomassin noticed nothing amiss and Norwood himself had to admit that he found the atmosphere no worse than usual. So back came the bottle to Room 173. Just as a precaution, Gordon put it outside on the windowsill instead of back into the cupboard and then we forgot about it for a while.

Then we noticed that many of our visitors on entering the room would start sniffing and looking round the place suspiciously. Next a messenger came to see us and after doing this sniffing act nodded his head with satisfaction and said that this was the same as the other rooms on this side of the building and that settled the matter. C 4 had already been told about it and were getting somebody in to see to the drains. Not wishing to offend C 4, which section provided us with offices and things, we kept quiet, retrieved the bottle, and in due course dropped it into the Thames from Westminster Bridge. In the meantime, I had written an encouraging minute to Joe stating that we were now getting very satisfactory results with his Superscent and had been misled in the first place because we had not realised that if the stuff were introduced gently at first the victims would suffer little inconvenience and rapidly develop immunity. It was effective only when somebody came on it suddenly. It might, I suggested, prove to be valuable as a protective screen for places such as petrol depots which the enemy might try to occupy in case of invasion. The personnel there would become acclimatised to the smell and scarcely notice it whereas any raiders would be made sick and have to go away.

I was rather pleased about this one and thought MIR (c) had done some good work even though it was by accident. But back came a minute from Joe instructing me to cease work on this project, destroy any remaining liquid, and also destroy any documents or notes in connection with the experiments. Apparently it had been ruled from very high up that such a liquid as this could be classed as a Poison Gas and that its use was therefore prohibited by the Geneva Convention. Love's labour was again lost.

However, we were soon back again in the chemistry business. I was summoned by Joe to a meeting with Lord Rothschild — this one was Victor Rothschild — who was apparently a top line chemist and had offered his services to the War Office in this capacity. Joe therefore planned to start an MIR (c) Chemical Committee to be run by Rothschild and myself. Rothschild got busy, and the new Committee held its first meeting at the Imperial Institute on April 17, 1940.

It was an impressive body, Lord Rothschild was Chairman and the members were as follows: Dr F. Roffey (Ministry of Supply), Professor A. C. Egerton (Fuel Expert), Professor H.V.A. Briscoe (Physcial and Industrial Chemist) Dr H.J. Emelius (Physcial and Industrial Chenist), Professor I.M. Heilbron (Organic Chemist and Fuel Expert), and last and undoubtedly least Captain R.S. Macrae, (M.I. representative, War Office).

The Chairman explained that the Committee would be under the direct control of Lt-Colonel J.F.C. Holland who would be represented by me. We did not get off to a very good start, because somebody at once suggested that the committee was redundant, unnecessary and should be disbanded and would I please put forward this suggestion to Col. Holland. Later I did so and he threw the file at me, from

which I gathered he was not in favour of such a move. In the meantime, we got on with the meeting. The Chairman explained that
with the threat of invasion hanging over us the first item on our
agenda must be to find ready means of putting motor transport out of
action, perhaps by contaminating the petrol in the tank. It would also
be nice to be able to render unusable bulk supplies of petrol at depots,
garages and filling stations.

The committee regarded this problem as one rather beneath their
dignity. So far as putting motor transport out of action was concerned
every child knew how that could be done. It was merely a matter of
putting sugar in the tank, and not much was needed. This dissolved in
the petrol, thus affecting the mixture which reached the engine. In
effect, toffee was then formed on the cylinder walls so that the engine
soon stuck to a standstill. It then had to be dismantled and the toffee
cleaned out before it could be got going again. I had a sneaking
suspicion that Joe Holland's Motorists' Delight was merely a sugar
solution and that had not worked at all. So I was relieved when
other members of the committee expressed doubt and started talk
ing about mercuric salts and other more sophisticated chemicals.
Finally I was asked to arrange immediately for the carrying out of
trials. I could start off with sugar, but other concoctions would
be supplied to me. It would then be simply a matter of selecting the
most effective one.

At this time, MIR (c) was rather an insignificant section at the
War Office so far as the transport boys were concerned. No vehicles
were allotted to us and we had to wait in the queue for a pool car.
So we had been using our own private cars for the very considerable
amount of running about we had to do. It at once occured to me that
here was a great opportunity to right a wrong. Armed with the paperwork covering the formation of the Military Intelligence Chemical
Committee, as it was now called, which fairly bristled with High
Priority and Top Secret notices, I went along to see the Transport
people. I had first taken the precaution of writing a cunning minute
and getting Joe to sign it when he was too busy to read it. The gist of
it was that the CIGS through the GSO I of MIR had entrusted MIR (c)
with work of the highest possible priority concerning the im-
mobilisation of vehicles in the case of invasion. This work would
involve carrying out experiments with all classes of Army vehicle. As
a first move, please allocate immediately to MIR (c) an army car of
some standard type. The vehicle need not be a new one but must be in

69

good running order. It should be written off when allocated, as it would almost certainly be destroyed in the course of experiments.

This minute with the backing up documents worked like a charm. My minutes usually did, for I was getting quite good at hitting the right note with them. A most friendly Major dealt with the matter to such good effect that the very next day I was told that there was a car outside in the quadrangle to be handed over to me. Down I went, to be presented with a magnificent limousine which had just been thoroughly overhauled at Feltham. It was the kind of vehicle reserved for the use of Generals and was complete with glass partition, speaking tube, and all mod. cons. Millis was most impressed with this vehicle when I got him along to see it and found it difficult to understand how I had got hold of it. We agreed that it was a crying shame to think it would be a total wreck in a week or so and did discuss confining the work to our £5 motorcar and keeping this one for our own use. But we were frightened of getting found out. Anyhow I was able to console Millis by pointing out to him that now I had learned the knack I could get another easily enough when we had finished off this one and a ten ton lorry as well if he would like that.

We need not have worried. As we expected, our week's sugar ration had no effect at all on the running of the engine. I then started trying out the Chemical Committee's products At first I was reluctant to use this car for anything but local runs where I could abandon it when it passed out without great inconvenience. But gradually, as more and more concoctions were tried out in it with no ill effect whatsoever, I grew bolder and this vehicle acquired such a name for reliability that we came to use it for all long runs. When the Chemical Committee gave up in despair and decided that the only way to immoblise an engine was to introduce large quanties of abrasive into the oil in the sump our earlier chemical experts Schulman and Bauer took over with hoots of joy and kept on turning up at Room 173 with little bottles of stuff which they were certain must be the answer. Becoming carefree, I used to pour all these concoctions into the tank of the car at once and risk an explosion. It thrived on this treatment and actually ran better and better. Finally, I thought I must really bump it off, to which end with tears in my eyes I introduced into the crankcase a large quantity of the Chemical Committee's special abrasive which had a base of carborundum.

Two years later, this majestic vehicle which epitomised Old

England was still running. In spite of all the torture to which it had been submitted it had never faltered. I would have liked to acquire it and put it out to grass like an old horse, but there was no machinery for doing that. It must also be admitted that this car had its weakness in the form of the brakes, which is why I do not name the make. The fellow who designed its anchors must have got a decimal point wrong. The drums and shoes offered only half the area they should have done. To make matters worse it was a cable-operated job with undersized cables that stretched so quickly that it was impossible to keep them in adjustment without hourly attention. So throughout the life of this vehicle we had to proceed with great care. By standing up and putting all my weight on the brake pedal I could stop it in time provided the cables had been taken up recently. Millis was smaller and lighter and he worked it out that it took him 34% longer than it did me.

Between us we had rented a house at Mill Hill at this time as we had both got tired of living in caravans — about which more later. Of course we used this car to run from Mill Hill to the War Office every day. Earlier in the year, we had encountered a very nasty foggy period. On the way home at about 9 o'clock one evening — we always worked late — Millis complained that now we had done three circuits of Regent's Park how would it be if we found our way out and stopped at the 'Swiss Cottage' for a drink and perhaps a Welsh rarebit. This we managed in due course with Millis dismounting at regular intervals and guiding me.

Duly refreshed, an hour later we found our way to our motorcar and on walking round it I noticed something. 'Millis' I said in an awestruck voice, 'our machine is equipped with a foglight. All we have to do now is to find how to switch it on.' After hunting around for a while we found the required switch and set off. The effect was remarkable. Our foglamp seemed to make the fog disappear and we were able to motor along as comfortably as if it were a clear day. Arriving home in remarkably good time we discussed this phenomenon over another drink and tried to find an explanation. A couple of Scotches are known not to improve the eyesight, so it could not have been that. It also seemed unlikely that the Welsh rarebits could have had anything to do with it. So it simply must be the foglamp. I went out to have a look at it with the help of a torch, but could find no name or identification mark of any sort. The shape also was unorthodox. Again it looked as if the luck of MIR (c) was holding

71

and that we had stumbled across a war winner. If our army transport could rush about in thick fog as we had done whilst the enemy dare not move what an advantage we should have! Job No 1 the next morning was to remove and dismantle this foglamp directly we got to the War Office and find out how it worked.

Millis generally left it to me to drive this vehicle whilst he thought great thoughts. But for a change next day he announced 'I will drive' and proceeded to do so. All went well until we reached Haymarket. It is not a severe slope, but the drill with this motorcar was to stand on the brake pedal right at the top which should ensure that before reaching the bottom the vehicle would be under control. Millis forgot this, and to my horror I found that we were slowly but inexorably overtaking a truck in front and that nothing could be done about it as Millis was already standing up and putting all his weight on the brake pedal. In due course the overtaking operation was concluded; there was a crunching noise and a tinkle of broken glass. When we got out to inspect the damage it seemed to be confined to one object — this foglamp. It was crushed flat, so that it proved to be impossible to take it to pieces and even if this had not been so the design could not have been established from the remains. Our war winning weapon was irretrievably lost and ever afterwards I have believed in gremlins. No foglamp I have tried out since has given anything like the performance, and I am convinced that none ever will. Maybe I believe in fairies as well!

The M.I. Chemical Committee ran on for six months or so but it was never a success in spite of Lord Rothschild's valiant efforts to make it so. At every meeting the member who had maintained in the first place that there was no justification for our existence made out a better case so that we all became half-hearted. He wanted to know what on earth the War Office was doing trying to run chemical research when we had the Ministry of Supply with its Director of Scientific Research and a large staff of specialists well able to carry out this work. This question took a lot of answering. We played around for a while with ideas for contaminating petrol, sabotaging electric cables by spraying them with chemicals, and with producing more effective incendiary bombs. But nobody was very enthusiastic about anything except the Chairman and we made no progress. When the threat of invasion dropped off we just faded out.

One thing this Chemical Committee did do was to stimulate our attached chemists, Schulman and Bauer, into intensive action. They were very hurt at not being asked to join this committee, and I myself would have liked to see them on it. But I was assured that Cambridge and Imperial College would not mix too well at this time. So S & B had to content themselves with trying to beat Imperial College to it and produce the answers when they had failed to do so. They were unlucky, though. True, they concocted an unbelievable number of petrol contaminants, but none worked any better than did the Chemical Committee's submissions. Then they turned to incendiary bombs. In a great state of excitement, they came to me one day to inform me with bated breath that they had now succeeded in developing an incendiary bomb which would make the ordinary thermite affair look like a damp squib. This stuff was really terrifying. The heat produced was so intense that everything around was shrivelled up to nothing. They would be willing to give me a convincing demonstration if I could find some isolated site in the country preferably with a lake or pond, so that there was plenty of water available for dealing with fires. And full security measures must be observed. It just would not do for any outsider to witness this terrifying spectacle.

Nobby Clarke's brother had a farm, down in the Bedford area. He was most co-operative. Soon all arrangements were made and an official party attended there for the demonstration. S & B had intended to fire their incendiary bomb by remote control and thereby avoid the risk of getting shrivelled up. But they had now devised a delay action of some sort whereby they would be enabled to prepare the bomb at the pond's edge and then have time to retreat before it went off. Would we please keep well away; we could inspect the damage afterwards.

Bomb No 1 was made ready and started to fizzle. S & B retreated hurriedly, and we waited with our hearts thudding. The fizzing went on, and that was all. After a time, S & B emerged from cover, held a hasty conference, and tried Bomb No 2. Again we all shuddered for a while, and again nothing happened. Finally the whole thing had to be called off, and it was never called on again. Apparently the idea worked well enough in the laboratory on a very small scale but there was an inherent snag which made it unworkable in real life.

I was really sorry for Schulman and Bauer, for they were both patriots and enthusiasts and worked exceedingly hard for MIR (c). They were of great help to us over the development of delay mechanisms and in conducting the early work on the sticky bomb. For his pains, poor Bauer because of his name found himself in an internment camp at the Isle of Man soon after the war started and it took us a couple of months to get him released. He remained attached to us for a long while and then left us to join a research team at work on the atom bomb. I well remember how I took him to task for this and pointed out to him that if he would only use his head he would realise as I did that an atom bomb could never be made to work. It must be a law of nature that any reaction of this sort would automatically be damped out. If it were not it would develop into a chain reaction and we would all be damped out anyway. So why waste his time?

The Hiroshima event came along to show me how wrong I was, and Bauer made his name in the atomics field. Jack Schulman, to my great sorrow, died a few years back. He was a man I learnt to admire and whom I was proud to call a friend.

8

Empire Building

BY THE TIME the war had been running for three months, it was evident to me that MIR (c) must either get on or get out. We could not hope to survive as a kind of independent research and development department if we had only a staff of four, one little office, and limited facilities for getting experimental work carried out by outside contractors. We must grow up, and do it very rapidly indeed; otherwise we should soon be swamped. Millis could not see my point of view and got quite cross with me about it. Our job, he pointed out, was to design new weapons, not to produce them. We were nicely set up for doing that. So what was there to worry about? He could not understand that although we were getting popular in some directions we were getting unpopular in many more and that if we went on designing new weapons until the cows came home nobody was going to make them and they would be rejected as a matter of principle. I had a go at Joe about this, and wrote a marvellous paper under the heading: 'The need for MIR (c) to acquire its own Engineering Workshop so that it can deal effectively with the very heavy programme of research and development work to which it has been committed' — this being a side kick at Joe. He was quite sympathetic, but he was absolutely overburdened with work and I could not get him to give proper consideration to my project. To get rid of me he told me I could take some outside offices if I liked, so I closed for that.

In these days we did not get time to learn to know our opposite numbers in the many M.I. departments. But everyone I approached proved to be most friendly and helpful — much more so than my colleagues in civilian life. It was towards the end of January that I had started my campaign for a works and Joe told me to go and talk to a Major Crockett about it. I did, and he was very helpful. His assistant Captain Hutton told me he had an eye on the International Broadcasting Company at 35 Portland Place where there were excellent offices available and a really good workshop but that he could not do anything about it himself for the time being so I could have a go if I liked. I did like. Such an organisation seemed to fit in with my overall plan for making use of concerns which were rather unemployed because of the war. Obviously IBC was not going to be earning any money from pushing out programmes for advertisers. from Radio Normandie and Fécamp

Soon I was able to hire two very nicely furnished offices at 35 Portland Place and then to induce the IBC Chief Engineer, Norman Angier, to tackle some of our experimental work. Encouraged by this success, and the ease with which I had got C4 to approve this outside accommodation, I also knocked them down for an extra room in the air raid basement. A Major Kennedy who dealt with appointments also found for us a Captain Faber who joined us in May so that MIR (c) now had a total permanent staff of five plus various attached typists. I could never have achieved this impressive result all by myself. It became possible only because Joan Bright took pity on me and dropped the right words in the right ears. Rather unfairly, I banished Norwood and Faber to the basement where they could settle down to their telephoning without disturbing Millis and myself and for a few weeks we entered an era of comparative peace.

But my ambition could not be quelled for long. I was spending more and more time round at 35 Portland Place which was becoming my natural headquarters. I could work there much more comfortably than at the War Office and what is more use the place as a depot for our stores. Norman Angier I found to be a man after my own heart. We were complementary to each other. I was perhaps a bit stuffy and orthodox whereas he was a bohemian type. He couldn't care less, for instance, if I filled the place up with high explosives, which was handy. But I had to cajole him into giving our work priority although he had not much else to do and he hated the sight of my uniform. We worked together throughout the war and apart from one or two minor rows we got on extremely well — and still do.

I soon discovered that Norman had a gift for a) acquiring machine tools and b) acquiring staff. As Chief Engineer of IBC, his job was presumably to be in charge of the technical side of the broadcasting stations at Radio Normandie and Fécamp and also to record pro-

Group at The Firs, Whitchurch.
Left to right: Norman Angier, the Author, Millis Jefferis, Ralph Farrant.

A demonstration of M.D. devices to V.I.Ps.
Left to right: Norman Angier is signalling to the Author that it is all clear to fire a Kangaroo Mine. The Prof., Millis Jefferis, and the Prime Minister are waiting to see the result.

grammes at the London end. To enable him to do this he had elaborate recording equipment fitted up in studios and as mobile units. But as he had a passion for machine tools he had somehow or other induced his organisation to let him turn the entire basement of the premises into a very finely equipped workshop. Of course they had bags of money and could well afford this venture; but how Norman ever justified the expenditure I shall never know. He could talk the hind leg off other donkeys besides myself.

The staff attracted me even more than the machine tools. Norman himself would be an enormous asset. Over renting the offices and so forth I had to deal with Leslie Knight, who seemed to be remarkably competent as a kind of administrative officer. Then there were two chaps, Smith and Wilson, I rated as Design Officers who were called in on some of the experimental work being carried out for MIR (c) by IBC. They proved to be remarkably quick on the uptake and what impressed me was that having been advised of the requirements they would trot off to their respective dungeons and produce drawings after which they would go into the workshops and produce and assemble the required bits and pieces without outside aid. There was also a Leslie Gouldstone who had been the recording king but now that there was no more of this work to be done was making himself most useful by supervising the various machine hands and all assembly work.

The thought of how successful MIR (c) could be if I could only acquire this little lot kept me awake at nights. Hollow-eyed, I concocted a most elaborate minute for submission to Joe. It started off by saying that DMI (Director of Military Intelligence) had ordered that MIR (c) must immediately be expanded to enable the section to cope with the exceptional demand for its stores and to conduct additional high priority experimental work. The following action must therefore be taken: 1 The organisation known as the International Broadcasting Company had suitable premises adequately staffed and equipped at 35 Portland Place, W.1. They would like to help the war effort but at present had no way of doing so. They should therefore be requisitioned in their entirety under some amicable arrangement, 2, Would C4 please instruct the Ministry of Works to take the necessary action over requisitioning the premises, 3, Would the Staff Section please enrol all those at 35 Portland Place who wished for civilian employment with the War Office and endeavour to pay them at their present rates: 4, Would the Finance

Section please make available the funds necessary for this operation. Signed, J. F. C. Holland, Lt-Col. GSO1. MIR.

This minute really was a work of art and I was very proud of it. Beautifully typed by myself, I showed it to Millis after buying him a couple of drinks and urged him to take it to Joe Holland for signature as with a matter of this importance it would be improper for me to do so myself whilst he was around. Millis roared with laughter, congratulated me on my effort, but assured me that in no circumstances would he be willing to try to sell this idea to Joe. He was not very keen on the idea anyway and thought we were doing quite well as we were without looking for more responsibility. Also, he thought the risk of Joe throwing something at him might be very great. Sadly I put the minute in my pending tray and there it stayed.

The next thing that happened was that Joe thrust upon us Lt-Colonel Blacker, an Irish Officer complete with eyeglass and leggings and looking very smart indeed. Blacker at once turned on his charm, of which he had an unlimited store, and soon had both Millis and myself in thrall. He claimed to be the only privately established inventor of weapons in the country and that as an officer in the Territorial Army he was now looking for a job. Nobody seemed to want him very much so how about him being attached to our section? Joe Holland seemed to be in favour of the idea. So were we before he had finished. He produced a long list of weapons on which he was working. One, I remember, had the impressive name of 'Hunstopper' and consisted of a length of piping carrying a dozen cartridges which fired themselves somehow or other in sequence so that in effect this device was a very cheap and discardable machine gun. I liked this idea very much, and also a spring gun affair for firing quite a heavy missile from the shoulder.

But the one Millis fell for was the 'Blacker Bombard.' This was an anti-tank weapon which would fire a bomb containing a 10lb or 20lb charge against a tank. Where it was unorthodox was in that instead of firing the charge out of a gun barrel the gun barrel would actually be attached to the charge. In other words, the bomb would consist of a shaped head carrying the charge of high explosive and a tail tube with stabilising fins. This tube would serve as the gun barrel and would be fired off a spigot. Thus the firing unit could be kept quite compact as there would be no need for it to have an enormous barrel. The large bomb could be lobbed with reasonable accuracy as it had stabilising fins and could have a soft nose so that

78

it poulticed on to the target before it detonated to get the full effect. Poultice charges were almost a gospel with Sapper Millis which made this a winning point. But an even bigger winning point was that for the past two years the Ordnance Board had consistently turned down Blacker's idea. In Millis' eyes, this was certain proof that it must be a good idea for he maintained that he had never known them to be right yet. Maybe this was unjust, but we had had a little trouble with them over the 'W' Bomb.

The upshot of it all was that Millis agreed to experiment at once with the Blacker Bombard and instructed me to go round to IBC next morning and put some work in hand, which I did. Blacker was lovable but impatient. Every evening for a while, I had to run him round to 35 Portland Place so that he could see how the work was going on. He would hang around the office most of the day and then betake himself to outside the staff entrance a quarter of an hour or so before time. There he would march up and down collecting and solemnly returning the salutes of the soldiery. He was fully entitled to them and they were given unstintingly. I was always happy to salute him myself, for until one could notice the lack of red tabs and other paraphernalia everyone thought he must be at least the CIGS.

Myself I was concentrating on trying to perfect the Sticky Bomb at this time which meant that I had to be away a lot. Imperial Chemical Industries at Ardeer were being most co-operative over this and about once a week I had to visit their factory where Dr Weir and Dr White were having experiments carried out for me and were devising a new high explosive to meet this unusual requirement. By now I was becoming expert at making myself comfortable in army service. Flying being a bit unreliable, I used to catch the midnight train from St Pancras which got me to Ardeer quite early the next morning and repeat the performance for coming back. The only trouble was that even though I was a General Staff Officer, as a mere captain I qualified for only third-class travel. This meant I had to share a sleeping compartment with three others and that the chances of any of us getting a decent night's rest were remote for I snore horribly. By now, I had learnt that, even if one worked at the War Office, no priority treatment could be claimed. However it still often paid to study King's Regulations and have a look for loopholes. Sure enough, I discovered that although a captain was entitled to only third-class travel on the railways exceptions could be made. One such exception was that if the officer were carrying explosives of any kind he must travel first-class. This was a very simple answer. From then onwards, I made it a rule to have a couple of sticks of blasting gelatine in my suitcase whenever I had to travel by rail — which I was then able to do in the utmost luxury.

On returning from one of these comfortable visitations, I found the office empty but for Stewart Blacker. For Millis had disappeared for a few days to concentrate on the design on a one man submarine with a Commander Varley. Blacker had apparently been a bit bored during our absence and had as usual spent his time poking round the office reading all the paperwork he could find. After we had chatted for a while he said: 'Oh, by the way Bobby, I found your minute about requisitioning that IBC place in your tray so I took it along to Joe and got him to sign it. I hope that was all right.' Was it all right? I could hardly believe my eyes when I saw it.

The next day I got really busy, and thanked my lucky stars that Millis was still away so that he did not know what I was up to. All I had to do was to write minutes to the sections concerned on the following lines. 'It has been ruled by DMI and confirmed in a minute signed by the GSO of MIR that as a matter of urgency immediate action must be taken to acquire the organisation known as the International Broadcasting Corporation of 35 Portland Place, W.1. which is to become part of the War Office and be assimilated by MIR (c). The relevant extract from this minute concerning your section reads as folllows: 'Would C4 please instruct the Ministry of Works to take the necessary action over requisitioning the premises.'

I soon realised that I had missed my vocation and could have made a fortune as a confidence trickster. My operation was a spectacular success. All I had to do was to write these minutes and take them round to the sections concerned to get immediate and effective action. In under a fortnight, MIR (c) was the proud possessor of the entire premises of IBC at 35 Portland Place together with all the plant and equipment and staff. For I am glad to say that nobody really objected to being taken over in this rather high handed fashion. Naturally enough there were a few mild grumbles at first and I was a bit unpopular. But very soon without exception the IBC boys worked whole-heartedly for the department and all remained with it throughout the war.

Millis was at first a little displeased with me for having carried out this manoeuvre and even more displeased with Blacker for suborning Joe Holland into signing the necessary minute when he had refused to try to do that himself. In fact he boycotted 35 Portland Place for a while and based himself firmly at the War Office. But soon the lure of actually having his own workshop where he could get bits and pieces made by his own staff and altered as much as he liked was too much for him, and he spent more time at Portland Place than anywhere else. So did Blacker.

Neither of them knew that soon after my initial success I had nearly lost control of 35 Portland Place. Quintin Hogg, who was working with another MIR section, was looking for an office block of this sort and had been told about the possibilities of IBC at around the same time as myself. Working in the approved manner, he was well on the way to acquiring the place when he learnt that I had actually got it, which rather upset him. He came along to me with a proposal that his section should take over the building in its entirety and allow MIR (c) to use just the basement workshops. This idea did not appeal to me at all, and rather like Tweedledum and Tweedledee we started a battle. Probably he would have won in the end, because although we were both only captains he had more influence. But I was able to hold out long enough for him to find other offices which suited him better so all ended happily.

Joe Holland was exceedingly busy and it took me some time to induce him to come round to have a look at the War Office, Portland Place, which was now our official title. It took a lot to make Joe gasp, but he did. 'How on earth did you get hold of this lot, Bobby?' he enquired. 'Has Millis got Winston Churchill to back him or something?' When I told Joe that he had performed this feat all by himself by signing the minute submitted to him by Blacker he found it difficult to believe me. Then he sank into one of our very comfortable chairs, muttered something about never having heard of half colonels being as powerful as all that, said he was suffering a bit from shock, and was there a drink anywhere? There was, for by now we had everything laid on.

This was in July 1940. The following month we ran into trouble. The Ministry of Supply had always resented our not coming under their jurisdiction but when we were only small fry they had not bothered much about it. Finding us growing up with such remarkable speed they became alarmed, and the matter was raised with the War Office at the highest level. The VCIGS instructed the DMI to find out exactly what we were doing and why we were doing it. At this time, the DMI had acquired a Brigadier Wyndham to do a kind of

81

McKinsey act (although this was before McKinsey's time), study the activities of the elaborate network of sections which now came under his control, and make recommendations for co-ordinating them and improving their efficiency. Putting MIR (c) under the microscope was just the job for the Brigadier and I was summoned to his room at the War Office right away. A Guardsman with the reputation of being a fine soldier, he was not very sympathetic towards research sections getting mixed up with the Army and his idea seemed to be to abolish us right away. I assured him that if he did this it would cause great consternation in all directions because the vitally important work we were doing at 35 Portland Place could not readily be taken over by anyone else. With a slight snort, the Brigadier announced his intention of paying a state visit to our establishment to see for himself if there was any truth in my suggestion.

The situation was serious. We were working hard on a number of projects but our total staff including the workshop was only a dozen or so. One could not expect a layman visitor who looked round the place to be very impressed and I visualised the Brigadier returning to the War Office and writing a three-line minute which would result in our prompt disappearnce. Something had to be done about it, and by great good fortune I was given a couple of days in which to do it. The first thing was to get Millis out of the way, for I was sure he would disapprove of the plan I had in mind and anyhow it would have been wrong of me to get him mixed up with it. I persuaded him that it was essential for him to go up to ICI, Ardeer, right away to settle some design queries.

By this time, we were one small happy family at 35 Portland Place. I explained the position to the IBC staff and they all agreed that it would be a great mistake for us to let ourselves get abolished through failure on the part of the Brigadier to appreciate the value of our work. As they had all been closely connected with the entertainment world, the plan I put forward appealed to them very much indeed. Transport was sent off in all directions to obtain quantities of our devices from contractors. A supply of overall coats was acquired — some white and some blue. Leslie Gouldstone dug out of his stores a remarkable collection of meters and other electrical apparatus and turned one of the cellar rooms into what we were sure would pass as a most modern test laboratory. Other rooms were turned into assembly shops by the simple process of taking dozens of the various devices to pieces and putting the bits in boxes on the benches. Various

82

gauges, meters, and the odd microscope scattered about the place helped matters.

When the Brigadier arrived, he was taken on a carefully conducted tour. First we went through the machine shop, where blue overalled mechanics were working away turning handles and pulling levers, what appeared to be the results of their frenzied efforts taking the form of components piling up in boxes. Next we started on the various assembly rooms, where mixed bunches of people were deftly putting together devices and submitting them to peculiar tests. One of the great disadvantages of this basement engineering department which extended under two houses was that it consisted of a labyrinth of passages connecting rooms or cells of a variety of sizes. But on this occasion, the feature was a great advantage. There were alternative ways of getting from one section to another. Everywhere the Brigadier was taken he found the place fully occupied with people hard at work. Directly he left one room the inhabitants would pop out of it to take up new positions in another room, reaching it by a different route. We mixed up the teams a little, and changed the appearance of individuals. A change of overall coat from blue to white can make a wonderful difference, as can leaving it off altogether. Our two charladies who had been promoted to assembly hands for this occasion proved to be absolute artists at disguise, mainly through having a selection of coloured mob caps.

This act worked. The Brigadier, who I am still certain had been determined to close us down right away, had reluctantly to agree there was so much going on that it could not be stopped just like that. He would have to give this matter further consideration and discuss it with DMI. I would be informed of their decisions in due course. I had succeeded in curbing his impetuosity and convincing him of the fact that we could not conveniently be snuffed out right away. He was still anxious to detach us from the War Office, though, and a week or so later came up with the bright idea that we should be translated into Special Operations Research and come under the Ministry of Economic Warfare or the Foreign Office. As, to my certain knowledge, Special Operations already had about three research outfits of their own with which we were doing business this plan was a non-starter. No doubt any one of them would have been happy to absorb us and we could have lived happily ever after at one of the comfortable country mansions they had managed to acquire. But we did not want to be absorbed. Our value lay in our independence.

I was able to fight this one off fairly easily; but the Brigadier was undaunted and soon came back with the old plan that we should be taken over by the Ministry of Supply and put under the Director of Scientific Research — an even worse fate. In the meantime, though, I had not been idle. Fighting losing battles never did appeal to me and by now it was obvious that we could not hope to beat those who were determined to remove us from the War Office. Joe Holland was anxious enough to keep us, but without backing he was not powerful enough to do that. So we must find a new niche for ourselves altogether if we were to remain independent and not be swallowed up by some other research department. Winston Churchill was now Prime Minister. The Prof. with the official title of Scientific Adviser to the P.M. was his right hand man. The Prof. liked Millis in particular and the section in general. He would certainly not want to see us absorbed by some other department and of no further use to him. It should not be difficult to sell him the idea that he should contrive to take us over by some means or other. Although there was as yet no Ministry of Defence it existed on paper and had its Minister — the Prime Minister. Why should we not become a Ministry of Defence Department?

I was seeing quite a bit of the Prof. at this time, and things were going well for us. A note in my diary for July 28, 1940 reads: 'Successful trial of S.T. (Sticky) Bombs at Farnborough. P.M. very satisfied. For Sunday August 18, 1940 part of the entry reads: 'Gave demonstration of Blacker Bombard at Chequers. Used 23lb bomb. P.M. most impressed and gave the all clear to go ahead with this project. As First Lord of the Treasury, authorised us to spend £5,000 for a start.'

This, our first demonstration at Chequers, was rather fun. The threat of invasion was still hanging over us and causing the P.M. intense worry. His main cause for concern was that although we had the Home Forces and the Home Guard very ready and willing to repel an invader they had nothing to do it with. Tanks could just walk through them without hindrance. The accepted weapon for tank attack had been the Boyes rifle, but against the German tanks it was no more than its name suggested. Molotoff cocktails or phosphorus incendiary bombs were then supposed to be the thing, but they proved to be completely ineffective. The P.M. had been present at a demonstration at Hangmore Ranges, near Farnborough, where they had been tried out. They caught alight well enough, but caused the occupants of the tanks no inconvenience whatever. It says something for the sticky bomb that at this same demonstration we dare not try it out against inhabited tanks and had to content ourselves with blowing holes in scrapped ones.

Prof. had therefore advised the P.M. that so far as he could see MIR (c) were the only people who had come up with any kind of valid answer to this problem. The sticky bomb was certainly a runner. He considered the Blacker Bombard was another one. Why not let Millis Jefferis — this little Sapper major who had designed the 'W' Bomb for Royal Marine — come out to Chequers to demonstrate it? Why not, agreed the P.M., so it was fixed. And, as usual, it was fixed in a tremendous hurry. We were still in the experimental stage with this weapon, and the workshops at 35 Portland Place had to work 24 hour shifts before we got everything sorted out and could take to Chequers a weapon which we felt might work without blowing up and injuring the P.M. and his retinue.

A few weeks previously we had acquired a gunner in the form of a Major Ralph Farrant who had got bored with kicking his heels at a Special Service Training Centre in Scotland and had somehow contrived to get himself attached to us. He remained attached to us throughout the war and afterwards rose to the giddy rank of Major-General and President of the Ordnance Board. One might expect a genuine gunner to sneer a bit at the Blacker Bombard which looked nothing at all like a gun but rather like something thought up by Heath Robinson. But Ralph was not like that. He threw himself whole-heartedly into helping Blacker to perfect this weapon and taught himself how to fire it. Soon he was able to hit things with the 23lb bomb it threw, which was not at all easy. So of course we appointed him Chief Gunner for the Chequers demonstration and hoped for the best.

Ralph did not let us down. He selected as his target a tree which seemed to us to be an awful long way off, made careful preparations, and then waited for the VIPs to come along — which they did after lunch. Behind the P.M. and the Prof. stalked de Gaulle and Smuts, who were very frequent visitors to Chequers at this time. There followed a raft of Service and civilian officials, all of high rank. It was most impressive and both Millis and I were shaken at the thought of the awful anti-climax there would be if Ralph missed the tree. Norman Angier had built the spigot mortar, so everone agreed that it would be wise to let him check up on the siting. This he did, and somehow or other managed to fire the weapon whilst doing so and quite unexpectedly. The missile very nearly wiped out General de Gaulle and unkind people afterwards suggested that the P.M. had in some way bribed Norman to have a go at this. I am sure there was no truth in such an assertion. Anyhow the tree was hit, the demonstration was a roaring success, and it was most impressive to hear the P.M. say to Millis: 'As Prime Minister I instruct you to proceed with all speed with the development of this excellent weapon. As First Lord of the Treasury, I authorise expenditure of £5,000 on this work to tide you over until proper financial arrangements are made.'

Why I am confident that Norman had no malicious intent was because only a fortnight previously I had had a similar experience and nearly bowled over King Haakon — a kindly man I would not hurt for the world. Somebody had asked us to devise a Mobile Mine and this job got wished on me. The idea was to have a small self-propelled vehicle stuffed with high explosive which could be planted on the ground anywhere and then directed to a target perhaps 200 yards away by remote control and then detonated. We were not very clever at radio control at this time, so I opted for guiding this machine by cable control. We fitted the front wheels with solenoid operated brakes to serve as steering gear. The power unit had to be an electric motor supplied by batteries installed in the vehicle so all that was needed was a control unit with the necessary switchgear and and a drum carrying a multi-core cable which would automatically reel out when the machine went on its way. Close Switch A to start the motor, Press Button B or Button C to apply temporary braking to the near side or off side front wheel respectively, press Button D to explode the charge and what could be better than that?

I induced a firm called Brunton & Trier Ltd. at Putney to make this contrivance for me. They made a very good job of it, and I became quite clever — or thought I did — at manoeuvering the vehicle about their yard using the remote control. But we needed a much bigger and better testing ground than this and Roehampton Club very kindly put their golf course at our disposal as it was not busy at this time. When the Prof. advised the P.M. of the impending demonstration he said that much to his regret he would be unable to attend himself but that King Haakon would very much like to come along. So that was fixed, and in due course I stood behind the control box on the first tee, monarch of all I surveyed, surrounded by King Haakon and other notabilities. After giving a little lecture on the design of the equipment I ran the machine forwards for about 50 yards and then stopped it. To show how it could be manoeuvred, I explained, I now proposed to direct it round a bunker and bring it back a little way before despatching it to its far distant target. I directed it round the bunker all right, but then the device went berserk. The electrics must have gone a bit wrong. First the steering became ineffective. That did not matter much as all I had to do was to open the switch to stop the motor. But it refused to stop; apparently a relay had jammed. And of course the wretched machine now quite out of control must head for our party on the first tee. We waited to try to determine its course and then fled at the last moment. As luck would have it, or maybe because he was the tallest of us, the machine picked on King Haakon to aim at and he had to run the most — which he was well equipped to do. He escaped fairly easily and then to my intense relief the machine buried itself in a nearby bunker and passed out.

I was a little dejected about this. King Haakon and the rest of the VIPs were all exceedingly nice to me, urged me to go ahead with the development work, and asked to be invited to the next demonstration. But never again, I felt, was I likely to have the privilege of getting royalty on the run. I did in fact revise the electrics on this machine and dispense with this method of steering by braking which although it works well enough on tracked vehicles did not appear to me to lend itself to wheeled ones. It was a happy day for me when a Ministry of Supply department demanded to be allowed to take over this project from us. I believe they improved this Mobile Mine very successfully and that quite a number were used.

The next few months at Portland Place were hectic. We had an unbelievable number of projects on hand and everyone had to work desperately hard to make any progress with them. At intervals, Brigadier Wyndham would pop up with suggestions for transferring us from War Office control to the Ministry of Supply but each time I had only to see Prof. to get the proposal called off. For by now he was a very powerful string-puller. Then the air raids added to our troubles. Hours of working time were lost through various members of our small staff arriving late in the morning and having to leave early if they hoped to get home. Soon we were unable to get ahead with anything at all and in desperation I produced an evacuation scheme whereby we would transfer the whole shooting match to the country. It was opposed by the War Office who perhaps thought that a bomb might be a good way of getting rid of this unwanted child. Millis was dead against it too as he regarded it as running away.

All I could do was to make my plans and wait. Almost at once, our store at Hendon was completely destroyed by incendiary bombs and we lost almost our entire stock of devices which were due to go out to Military Missions in all parts of the world and in particular to a newly established one in Australia. Then, only a few weeks later, 35 Portland Place itself was hit and we were put completely out of action.

Fortunately in destroying the Hendon store the Germans had made my point for me and I had been given permission to find premises for us in the country. To this end, I kidnapped from the Ministry of Works — maybe it was still the Office of Works then — a long-suffering gentleman called Mr Rose who had been instrumental in requisitioning 35 Portland Place for us. He was induced to arm himself with a blank requisition warrant duly signed by some high authority and be attached to us until our problem was solved. When we could spare the time, which was nor often, Angier, Knight and myself would buzz off in different directions to see what we could find. I had ideas of taking over some golf club so that I could improve my game during my time off, if any. But none proved suitable. In the end, Angier and Knight found the answer in a property called 'The Firs' at Whitchurch, near Aylesbury, Bucks. It belonged to a Major Abrahams who was in residence there but owned another country property and had therefore perhaps indiscreetly put this one up for sale. He was a very big shot in the Red Cross and later became Sir Arthur Abrahams. The impeccable butler who had first shown us round the place had been under the impression that we were potential purchasers and advised him accordingly. It was therefore a bit of a shock to him when Mr Rose whipped out his requisitioning form and informed him that the place was ours.

Major Abrahams was a very patriotic gentleman. In spite of the rather fast one we had pulled on him he did everything he possibly could to welcome us to his house and make us comfortable there during the weeks when we were moving in and he was moving out. He and his wife almost came to regard this vanguard of MIR (c) as part of the family and insisted on us having our meals with them. We were all really sorry when they finally went off. The last to leave was their old father who had also been very kind to us. He had some trouble with his waterworks and it said much for his natural dignity when none of us laughed as he was solemnly placed in the back of his Rolls-Royce by the butler who then carefully deposited on the floor about a dozen jerries kept together by a golden cord.

The Firs was an ideal place for us. The large house could provide both offices and sleeping accommodation. There was extensive stabling, which could readily be converted into workshops. There were several cottages on the premises and, best of all, included in the property were levelled sites where buildings to serve as stores and so forth could be erected. There were also fields which could be used as firing ranges and where experimental demolition work could be carried out. Norman Angier & Co had certainly picked a winner.

Of course we ran into the usual bother directly we had secured The Firs. Various officials appeared and wanted to know what authority we had to take a place of this size. The arrangements must be cancelled right away and we must find something much smaller. But I was on a good wicket. In my evacuation scheme which had been reluctantly approved by the DMI, I had been careful to avoid any mention of the size of the premises required. And nothing was stated about this in Mr Rose's requisitioning paper. Nobody could shoot me down. As a precautionary measure I had to enlist the help of the Prof. and get him to intervene to save Mr Rose from getting into trouble. This battle was easily won.

We got going at Whitchurch in an incredibly short time, thanks to the efforts of all concerned. Gordon Norwood commandeered army lorries from one place and another and soon we had dug out all the plant and machinery from the wrecked workshops at 35 Portland Place and brought them out to The Firs. Here, aided by the bag of gold, we had been able to employ local labour to convert some of the stabling into workshops and install the plant. The electricity people supplied a whacking great transformer to give us power and the telephone people ran in new lines. The co-operation we secured was really remarkable and it was soon evident to me that all of my executive colleagues were blessed with some kind of mesmeric appeal.

9

More Empire Building

IT WAS SOME TIME before I could induce Millis to visit Whitchurch and inspect his new acquisition. He was very busy having meetings with top Service chiefs about one thing and another and anyway still did not approve of the move. However, he did come along in due course and was about as startled as Joe Holland had been when he first inspected MIR (c) at 35 Portland Place. He immediately decided he could get on with his work far better at Whitchurch than he could in London and instructed me to make arrangements to accommodate himself and his family. Then off he went.

When he popped up again a few days later it was evident that there was a lull in his development activities which he had decided to employ in getting The Firs organised. Millis was a genius, and like most genii was not a good organiser. Everything had gone remarkably quickly and smoothly up to now. In the house, we had converted some of the bedrooms into offices — a General Office, a large Drawing Office, a Front Office which I had allocated to Millis and myself, and three or four other offices for executives. We had created a Mess with a large lounge, a dining room and a bar. Yet we had retained sufficient bedrooms to accommodate about a dozen people.

This really was a remarkable performance considering that the transformation had been carried out in about a fortnight. Most of the credit for it went to Leslie Knight who had a gift for this sort of thing, but Gordon Norwood helped a lot. He specialised in making evacuation arrangements and worked on rather unorthodox lines. We had a very useful Irishman named Moogan working at Portland Place until it was bombed. Having eleven children, he could claim to be a production expert; but we did not employ him in that capacity.

90

His job was to keep the workshops clean, and he did it very well. We badly needed him at Whitchurch and I told Gordon Norwood to bring him out somehow or other. A couple of days later I was a little shattered when a large chauffeur driven Daimler swept into the drive at The Firs and out of it tumbled the entire Moogan family. Daimler Hire charged us extra for removing toffee from the inside of this magnificent vehicle and the local billeting officer nearly had a nervous breakdown trying to cope with this situation.

My role where hoisting our colours at The Firs was concerned was confined to agreeing all the plans of these two helpers; but I still felt entitled to share in this pride of creation, so to speak. When, therefore, Millis suddenly came up with schemes for reorganising everything I was exceedingly put out. For an officer who had served in India his attitude was surprising and I had to take off my service cap to him for being a genuine socialist. This was a shocking situation, he maintained. I had allocated the house to the officers who were to live there in the height of comfort whilst the workshop hands, who were the salt of the earth, were presumably billeted outside. This situation must immediately be reversed. The house must be given over entirely to the workshop staff and constitute a hostel for them. Tents could be pitched on the lawns to accommodate myself and some of the officers and the remainder could be billeted in the village. No wives were to be allowed on or near the premises. And by the way, that expensive furniture in the house must immediately be sent to store and replaced by some which I must obtain from the War Department or Office of Works.

Millis obviously felt very strongly about this, for I was quite unable to soften him up with a few drinks as I had previously been able to do when similar differences of opinion arose. Yet I knew that if I tried to implement his ideas the whole place would become a shambles in no time at all and it would become impossible to run it. Having tented offices might work all right for a Field Exercise but it certainly would not work for this permanent establishment. What is more, I had contrived to learn how such establishments as the one I now had in mind could be organised and turned into great successes and Millis had not.

My lesson had been learnt through having to visit our previous colleagues, the Cloak & Dagger Brigade. The first detachment had abandoned the St Ermins Hotel at St James's Park in favour of a foothold at Bletchley Park at Bletchley, Bucks. Bletchley Park was a super-secret station run by the Foreign Office, inhabited mainly by brilliant long-haired youths who contrived to break the enemy's codes every so often. It was our main underground communications centre handling all messages received from or despatched to our agents throughout Europe and the rest of the world, the actual transmitting and receiving apparatus being located in another area. Although not a brilliant long-haired youth, my wife contrived to get a job with this outfit, which oddly enough involved her in handling messages from secret agents which frequently included reports about operations where the effectiveness or otherwise of MIR (c) weapons were given. I would never have believed that any woman could be so security-minded. It was not until after the war that I learnt that she had handled messages saying what wonderful work had been done with our various weapons and in particular the limpet. Although to have known we were doing so well would have made a new man of me, not a squeak did I get out of her.

The Cloak & Dagger department concerned was regarded by Bletchley Park as a kind of illegitimate child for which accommodation must be found. It owned a couple of Nissen huts only. But the fellow who was running it, a Commander Langley who was one of the finest men I have ever met, knew his stuff. Surrounding his department with a cloud of secrecy he christened it the Signals Development Branch and would admit to no address but a Room number in the War Office. He sent circulars to almost every branch of every Service explaining his hush-hush activities and telling them the code names to be used if they wanted to order materials from him.

Soon Langley acquired his own establishment in the form of Aston House, a very nice mansion indeed at Stevenage. He was a wonderful organiser, and in no time at all aided by his second-in-command, Colonel Wood, he and his quite large staff were so nicely bedded down at Aston House that they might have been living there since the year dot. What is more, they were doing a lot of work as well. It was at once obvious to me that as an Empire builder I was not in the same class as Langley and that I would be well advised to take lessons from him. Of course he had one enormous advantage over me — all the money in the world to play with. At the time they left us at the War Office when we had been sharing a common bag of gold, these Cloak and Dagger boys had been under the Foreign Office. Then they became Ministry of Economic Warfare under Mr Dalton. Either way they had no money problems. Any sum they cared to

Trials of the "Great Eastern": 1. Blast off. 2. Bridge in position ready for tanks to make the crossing. 3. Recovering the section of bridge which spans the river so that another demonstration can be given.

Demonstrations at 'The Firs'. 1. Millis Jefferis inspects the 'Great Eastern' ramp while in the background the building section completes the construction of another target. 2. The Author and Sir Malcolm Campbell at a tank plough demonstration. 3. Mine clearing tank. ESM Warne and Capt. Rosling are standing on the superstructure.

mention was dished out to them in cash, and no questions asked.

The service personnel and all other staff were paid weekly in cash whatever salary was fixed by the Commanding Officer. No Treasury approval was required. And what is more, these lucky people had to pay no income tax at all on their earnings. They were so hush-hush that so far as the country was concerned they just did not exist. It gave me some satisfaction that I did manage to cash in on this one. Working with the long-haired cipher breaker boys at Bletchley Park my wife came under the same heading and officially ceased to exist, although I am glad to say she did not do so in practice. How nice it would be if the same rules applied now and I could tell the Income Tax man to take a big jump!

There was, I soon discovered, a lot in this security angle. Langley had surrounded his establishment with barbed wire and Sentry Boxes complete with armed soldiers. It really was most impressive. Even when I arrived in my appropriated General's car properly uniformed it took me about half an hour to gain admission to Aston House. The guard would ring through to the house and the officer of the guard would in due course arrive in a Jeep to inspect me. After frisking me for concealed weapons he would solemnly escort me to the house and that would be that.

Langley got really upset if anyone tried to vary this drill. I received a furious note from him when an enterprising officer whom I had sent to Aston House to collect some high explosive for me decided that as last time it had taken him an hour or so to gain admission he would this time make out an order for himself on the appropriate War Office form for these stores then walk in through an open window. Did I not realise, said Langley in the rocket he sent me, that such actions as this could completely destroy his carefully built up security screen?

I apologised humbly, and promptly ran into more trouble. I had sent to Aston Park, Nobby Clarke, who by now was employed by the Admiralty as an Assistant Naval Designer on the First Lord's instructions so that he could try to build the trench tunnelling machine referred to in the 'W' Bomb chapter. His brief was to sort out a little Limpet trouble we were having there. Nobby never did stand on ceremony. After waiting five minutes or so at the Guard Post he wandered off and contrived to avoid all security measures and get himself into the house and Langley's presence in another five minutes flat. Nobby relished this kind of exercise and specialised in it later on when he joined the Cloak and Dagger experts himself — first at this station E.S.6 and later as O.C. of one at Hertford. But although Langley belonged to the same Senior Service he would not wear this one at all. Next day I received a note from him deploring this conduct on the part of an officer for whom I was responsible. In future, he said, would I please send some officer with some sense of responsibility to Aston House on these missions. If I again sent Captain Clarke he might be admitted to the grounds of Aston House to carry out such work as the testing of Limpets but in no circumstances would he be allowed inside the house and he could not be served with meals. Langley went off a few months later to take a more active part in the war at sea and Nobby then did get into the house for meals. In fact he lived there for several months, having been taken on the strength by Commander Langley's successor — Colonel Wood.

As I say, I learnt a lot from Langley. This security racket was a good one: at once it made the establishment look vitally important. But Langley had introduced other useful side effects. He had established a proper Mess on shipboard lines. Every evening his officers had to wash and polish themselves and present themselves at the appointed hour for drinks and dinner. All the formalities were faithfully observed including Mr Vice President proposing the health of His Majesty and the passing of the port the right way round. Obviously this was the kind of place to which one could with confidence invite the biggest VIPs in the world from the P.M. downwards. I must try to organise The Firs at Whitchirch on similar lines.

It proved to be quite difficult to do that. I managed to talk Millis out of his tents and for the time being out of getting rid of the furniture, for which we were paying a rental of only £200 a year. He beat me over this one in the end, but not until a couple of years later when the establishment had been so upgraded that the Office of Works had to dish us out with high grade furniture such as they normally kept for Buckingham Palace.

My real troubles, though, were with Brigadier Wyndham who was now more than ever determined to get rid of MIR (c). He regarded this as his life's work, and I had to admire him for the way he stuck at it. I regarded it as my job to keep the place going somehow or other and so we entered into battle, with myself on the losing side. A mere Captain is at a disadvantage when dealing with a Brigadier. Millis as a Major would have been a shade better off, but I had great difficulty in getting his support. He had no ideas whatsoever about building up an organisation of some sort and really did not particularly want one. He merely wanted to design special weapons. If to this end the Powers-that-Be thought he would be better employed at Woolwich or in China for that matter that would be quite all right by him. As an Army officer all his life he was used to being posted to some other place directly he had settled down somewhere and rather approved of the process. It saved one from getting into a rut. Perhaps it would be a pity if they packed us up and we lost The Firs, but I had nothing to worry about. They would certainly find me another job.

Brigadier Wyndham had by now almost concluded arrangements whereby MIR (c) was to be taken over by the Ministry of Supply and come under the control of the Senior Military Adviser there and the Director of Military Administration. There could be no more certain death. All the orthodox design departments and in particular the Armaments Design Department at Fort Halstead were under this control. They were all exceedingly jealous of us and anxious to dispose of us. Already the high-ups at the MOS had told Brigadier Wyndham that they regarded The Firs which I had worked so hard to get as being quite unsuitable premises for us.

The Brigadier when he came to inspect the place heartily agreed with them and for good measure stated that we must also give up 35 Portland Place and move to two offices in Westminster Bridge House. The outlook was indeed gloomy. The only fortunate thing was that as we were now in effect a shuttlecock being played with between the War Office and the Ministry of Supply nobody was at the moment in a position to sign a piece of paper deciding our fate. One great advantage of government organisations is that few people in them have the authority to do anything drastic and anyhow they hesitate to do it without first consulting a lot of other people. It was one thing for the Brigadier to make a plan and quite another for him to get it approved. I was given ample time in which to get it sabotaged.

Of course I went to the Prof., who was now sitting very pretty indeed as Scientific Adviser to the Prime Minister and in a position to exercise very considerable authority. He was surprised to learn that we were in trouble, for although Millis had been seeing him quite a lot he had not bothered to mention it. I painted a dark picture, with Millis as the centrepiece. Here, I said, was an officer whom all agreed was exceptionally brilliant over armaments design. I considered

95

myself very lucky to be associated with him and to have been able to assist in the good work by creating the organisation he must have if he were to be fully successful.

The orthodox design people were exceedingly jealous of Millis and were determined to do him down. They planned to abolish us. If this happened, I pointed out to the Prof., the Prime Minister and himself would find this talented officer who had already produced for them the 'W' Bomb, the 29 mm Spigot Mortar, and the Sticky Bomb would be utterly stifled and of no further use to them. For us to be put under the MOS would be the end. This move must be stopped. The only possible answer was to translate MIR (c) in to a special department under the direct control of the Prime Minister, such control of course to be exercised through the Prof.

I must say for the Prof. that once one got him wound up he went like mad. On later occasions I found this rather a handicap because if anybody suggested to him that Millis was being badly treated in some way or other he would immediately set about pinning down the criminals and getting them fired or removed to other posts. In this he was quite ruthless. On this occasion, however, I was very satisfied and felt like somebody who presses a button to launch a battleship. Whilst I waited, the Prof. went to discuss this matter with the P.M. The next day he saw Sir Andrew Duncan, the Minister of Supply, and General Ismay, secretary of the War Cabinet. The whole thing was wrapped up in no time at all. We were to become M.D.I., which being translated meant the first Ministry of Defence department to be created. As I have said, there was no such Ministry at this time but there was a Minister — the Prime Minister having assumed this post amongst others.

On November 1, 1940, I received pieces of paper giving me official notification of this change, but naturally it took some time to implement it. However, the pressure was off and for the next month or so we had an exceedingly good time. Brigadier Wyndham retired hurt. The Ministry of Supply came into the picture now, but only because they had been advised by their Minister that in future they must be responsible for the administration of M.D.1. They were, however, to have no control over the department as that was to be vested in the War Cabinet.

Winston Churchill considered this matter important enough to merit a mention in Vol 2 of his *History of the Second World War* entitled *Their Finest Hour*. He writes:

'This was therefore no time to proceed by ordinary channels in devising expedients. In order to secure quick action, free from departmental processes, upon any bright idea or gadget, I decided to keep under my own hand as Minister of Defence the experimental establishment formed by Major Jefferis at Whitchurch. While engaged upon the fluvial mines in 1939 I had had useful contacts with this brilliant officer, whose ingenious inventive mind proved, as will be seen, fruitful during the whole war. Lindemann was in close touch with him and me. I used their brains and my power. Major Jefferis and others connected with him were at work upon a bomb which could be thrown at a tank, perhaps from a window, and would stick upon it. The impact of very high explosive in actual contact with a steel plate is particularly effective. We had the picture in mind that devoted soldiers or civilians would run close up to a tank and even thrust the bomb upon it, though its explosion cost them their lives. There were undoubtedly many who would have done it. I thought also that the bomb fixed on a rod might be fired with a reduced charge from rifles.'

General (Pug) Ismay in his book gives much the same version. He says:

'Another of my foster children was one of Churchill's pet creations. He maintained that during the first World War the War Office had been dismally slow and unimaginative in addressing their minds to the provision of special mechanical devices to meet the conditions of static warfare on the Western Front, and in particular he had never forgotten the official obstruction which had caused such inordinate delay in the production of his dream child, the tank.

Accordingly, as soon as he became Prime Minister he insisted on having a small experimental establishment of his own, which was to work in closest touch with Professor Lindemann. Major Jefferis, whose inventive genius had come to Churchill's notice, was placed in charge, and I was instructed to take him "under my protection" lest the Ordnance Board and the Ministry of Supply, who were unlikely to approve of freelances, should make things difficult for him. Jefferis, with continuous support and encouragement from "The Prof." and the Prime Minister himself did valuable work, but his start was not a happy one. He was trying his hand at producing a small bomb which could at short range be thrown at a tank and stick to it, thus ensuring a powerful explosion when it detonated. Unfortunately his first trial bomb failed to stick, and was about as effective as a damp squib. I was sorry to think of Jefferis' disappointment, but I much enjoyed the receipt later in the day of a minute warning me that "any chortling by officials who have been slothful in pushing the bomb" would be viewed with great disfavour! How to convey this warning to the persons for whom it was intended, or even to identify them, were puzzles which I failed to solve. But anyway the Sticky Bomb eventually proved completely successful, as did other inventions of the ingenious Jefferis.

'Needless to say, the supervision of the experimental section under Jefferis was only one of the many responsibilities which the Prof. undertook on behalf of the Prime Minister, but it was certainly one that he found very attractive.'

This story about the Sticky Bomb is a good one but not quite fair to it. Only at a minor try-out did we have this flop. A note in my diary for January 30, 1940 says 'Sticky Bomb tests at Farnborough entirely satisfactory.' On June 1 the P.M. wrote a note instructing us to go right ahead with the Sticky Bomb but it was not until October 2 that he wrote one of his shortest minutes on record. On 10 Downing Street notepaper it said under the heading Sticky Bomb 'Make one million' and was signed WSC. This worked and we did.

There followed a period which was rather confusing. Having been given the green light we started to build up The Firs like mad. By the end of November 1940 we were pretty well organised. I have notes that on November 25 the Workshops were at it all night on some rocket project Millis had suddenly thought up. Again on December 19 the Workshops, Drawing Office and General Office worked all night. After that there was always something happening and, like the Windmill Theatre, we never closed.

The new set-up completely baffled the Ministry of Supply, For them to be told that they must give us everything we wanted and look after our wellbeing without having any say at all in what we did naturally caused great feelings. It fell to my lot to introduce myself to the Director of Military Administration, Brigadier O.Y. G. Hogg, and tell him what we wanted. He put me on to the officers in charge of his various departments. Some of them were kind to me and some were not, but in the very nature of things none could be very helpful.

It was easy enough to get the service personnel transferred to the Ministry pay list and after a bit of haggling they accepted the civilian staff as well for the time being. But when it came to trying to get help over extending the buildings at Whitchurch as a matter of some urgency I ran into real trouble. The retired dyed-in-the-wool colonel who had been brought back to run this department was not standing for any nonsense from upstarts like me, whether backed by the Prime Minister or not. I must submit my applications in writing and they would be dealt with in due course. If he approved them, then they would be submitted to the Office of Works who would prepare plans and estimates which would then come back to him so that he could apply for Treasury approval for the expenditure. To talk about starting this work right away was complete and utter nonsense. I'd be lucky if it was started in three months. And what was this note he had received from the Brigadier stating that I had builders working overtime at The Firs installing benches and that kind of thing. This was a waste of money and must stop immediately. And now would I please get to hell out of his office and in future keep out of it.

The same kind of thing happened when I tried to get transport in a hurry from the Ministry, for we badly needed trucks and drivers apart from motorcars to collect and deliver the devices which were now being turned out for us in great quantity. Finally Millis, who had turned a complete somersault, decided that it was vital for The Firs quickly to be converted into a sizeable research organisation so that he could run a number of projects at once, that I was making poor headway in this direction, and that he must see the Prof. about it.

Actually it was not until this stage that General "Pug" Ismay came into it. The P.M. said to the Prof. 'See Pug about it' and that was that. Pug really was a marvellous fellow with an absolute gift for inducing people to do what they were most reluctant to do without upsetting them or hurting their feelings. Suddenly I was *persona grata* at the MOS and even the previously indignant colonel received me politely. Things started to move. Immediately we were allocated transport and RASC drivers. Instead of our accounts having to go through the normal channels and be approved by a raft of people a special No 2 account was opened for me at my own bank and my signature alone was good for any amount. As very nearly one million pounds passed through this account at Aylesbury, I feel the Midland bank should let me off bank charges for life — but they don't!

The other great concession made to us was that, instead of having to go through the usual MOS drill when placing contracts, which called for getting several estimates and approvals from higher up, we were permitted under our own power to issue an Intimation to Proceed order to a contractor and then leave it to the special finance department concerned to sort things out. They were not permitted to query such orders whatever they might feel about them which hurt them a bit at first. But we soon got on very well with them.

A great deal of credit must go to the DMA, Brigadier Hogg, for the way in which he helped us. At first he was inclined to treat me with some suspicion and I believe he thought that the creation of M.D.1. by the P.M. was just one of those things which would soon fizzle out if left alone. However, when Pug had worked on him he became really keen on Whitchurch and soon regarded it as his pet establishment. From time to time I broke most of his very good rules but he never tried to put me on the mat and was always exceedingly nice about it. At Whitchurch we came to look forward to his visits, especially when he was accompanied by his wife who was affectionately known to us as the Red Queen because she looked like Tenniel's drawing of her.

All this was a great help, but we were still not going fast enough. It was vital for us to have a large stores and transport centre actually on the premises, and so far as I was concerned the alternative suggestion that we should hire a barn some miles away was out. In due course, Office of Works officials came along to consider the matter and promised to get plans and estimates prepared in a month or so. I discussed this little problem with Gordon Norwood who suggested that the only possible answer was for us to start our own building department. I told him to go ahead, and the very next day this new venture was started. The building department proved to be invaluable in a very short time and finished up by dealing with all the very extensive constructional work that had to be carried out at The Firs without outside aid of any sort. The department employed over 30 hands in the end and had its own carpenter's shop, concrete mixers and so forth. In my view it was one of Gordon's greatest achievements.

A bit of fiddling had to be done. With my new powers I could sign a cheque each week for the wages of the existing staff as approved by the MOS. But obviously I should have been asking for trouble if I suddenly engaged a dozen builders without authority and paid them just like that. The MOS was already playing quite nicely over this staff engagement business and took only a fortnight or so to approve our proposals instead of the customary couple of months and I was most anxious not to upset them and queer the pitch. The answer should have been the bag of gold, but unfortunately that had gone. For I had to own up to having it when we had the new deal and were severed from the War Office. A sad little note in my diary for January 5 1941 says 'Balance of £677.1.8 in Macrae's private account transferred to his official No 2 account at Midland Bank, Aylesbury.'

Remembering my good and fortunately placed friends at Aston House I at once went over to have a talk with them. We were, I pointed out, supplying them with all our devices such as booby traps and limpets, free of charge. As they had bags of money, would they mind paying for some of these. They said not a bit, and I walked off with £500 in cash in payment for 500 limpets for which they did not want a receipt. This started off my new bag of gold very nicely and enabled us to take on new staff right away and pay them until they could be taken on the strength in the proper manner. I should add that I kept most careful accounts covering these highly illegal transactions and still have them.

By the end of the year, we were really in business at The Firs. The experimental workshop was running full blast, we had completed a temporary stores, and trucks were whistling in and out with our products. The Prof. made his first visit to The Firs on December 17, 1940. He was duly impressed, and from then on, except when he was away, he called on us at least once a week and sometimes more often.

10

We Dig Ourselves In

DURING THE FIRST six months of 1941 we dug ourselves into The Firs most successfully. It was not easy, though, in spite of the priority we had acquired. Millis, bless his heart, took everything for granted. It was simple enough to get a place of this sort running, so why need I waste my time on it? He wanted me on development work and not as some kind of Administration Officer. I must find somebody right away to take this job over from me so that I could get on with something that mattered. Almost anyone would do.

Being a genius, and having up to now been looked after by the Army who had told him what to do and in its own good time had helped him to do it, Millis had no idea at all of the need to fight civilian battles and really never understood this. Having been brought up in a hard school, I did. I would not have minded being able to shake off this newly acquired responsibility and going back to the design work that I really liked. No, maybe that is not quite truthful for I was by now feeling a bit important and ambitious and wanted to build up the finest special weapons development department in the world. Incidentally, I believe this object was achieved in the end although of course I was merely second-in-command of the team that did the job.

I can honestly say that if Millis could have secured the services of a Commander Langley or somebody of his calibre to get the place organised I would have accepted the situation very readily and gone back to design work entirely. But such organisers were just not available. Millis got the DMA, Brigadier Hogg, to come out to Whitchurch to discuss this matter with him and say would he please post to the establishment some officer, perhaps a Major but a Captain might do, who could take over these simple duties from me. But

102

although he too was a dyed-in-the-wool army officer, Brigadier Hogg as DMA at the Ministry of Supply had learnt his lessons and he knew as well as I did that unless somebody as experienced as myself were at the Whitchurch wheel the ship would soon go on the rocks. So he talked Millis out of this one, which I think was pretty noble of him. For at this time, M.D.1. was just a headache he had acquired as I was myself, and he would have had every excuse for encouraging its self destruction. It was not until later on that he came to love us.

So on we went. Having learnt the drill, on our being created M.D.1 I had of course drawn up the structure of our new establishment and submitted it to the Prof. who had to put it forward to the Ministry of Supply. Having studied King's Regulations and other works, my course was clear. As a mere Section of a War Office department, our top man could be only a Major or GSO 2 and his 2 i/c could be no more than a Captain or GSO 3. But now we were to be a separate establishment, things were different. We would be entitled to a Superintendent, with the rank of Lt-Colonel or the equivalent. The Deputy Superintendent would be a Major, and that would be me. The prospect was attractive. But this thing had to be carefully handled.

I wrote a most impressive minute putting forward these suggestions for Professor Lindemann to approve and forward to the Minister of Supply, Sir Andrew Duncan. Having got Millis to sign this document when he was thinking of something else I sent it up to town by special messenger. This was just as well, for the very next day when I was not looking Millis and Norman Angier evolved an entirely different and I believe quite unacceptable scheme which I had great difficulty in preventing them from putting forward. It cost me a lot in whisky to scotch this one.

All this activity took place in January 1941, but it was not until April 4, 1941 that our new establishment was approved. And in the meantime there were endless meetings with Ministry of Supply and Treasury officials who were not at all keen on implementing this stupid idea of the P.M. At intervals, I had to appeal to The Prof. and General Ismay to intervene, but it all came right in the end. We received our bit of paper stating that M.D.1. had been classed as an establishment under a Superintendent. Major Jefferis was appointed Superintendent and promoted to Lt-Colonel. Captain Macrae was appointed Deputy Superintendent and promoted to Major. Major

Farrant was appointed Assistant Director and would retain his rank of Major. Lieutenant Faber was appointed Experimental Officer, and soon afterwards he was promoted to Captain. The civilian establishment was dealt with in a separate minute and Norman Angier was created an Assistant Director.

It was all most satisfactory. We at once threw a party to celebrate the occasion and there was much cheering for Millis when he turned up in his newly adjusted uniform and it was found that, in a moment of mental aberration, Ruth had added his pips above the crowns instead of below them.

This delay in getting the establishment through did not really hamper us at all except that we had to wait to get our increased pay. We had scored a notable victory in that on January 3 we had been informed by the War Office that our range of booby trap mechanisms — the Pull, Pressure and Release Switches — had now been approved, would be listed in the Ordnance Vocabulary as approved stores right away, and we were to be responsible for production. Would we please arrange for the manufacture of these devices in very large quantities.

As by now we had everything pretty well laid on, this was not so difficult as it sounded. It became merely a matter of sending out these Intimations to Proceed to contractors who were already teed up to do the job and anxious to do it. But we rapidly ran into a bottleneck. All approved Army stores had to be inspected by CIA, being short for the Chief Inspector of Armaments. All large contractors had their appointed CIA inspectors already installed on the premises, so for them this was no problem. But the small firms we wanted to use had no such facilities. For CIA to find inspectors and appoint them to these firms would take months. There were a few travelling inspectors, but not nearly enough to deal with out work. There was only one answer, we must run our own inspectorate.

Such talk was pure heresy. In no circumstances could the War Department accept stores that were not passed by CIA so that was that — for a day or two. Then frantic signals were sent to us by the War Office departments concerned. Where were the M.D.1. stores ordered for this country or that? It was vitally important that we should meet our delivery forecasts. Again we explained our little problem and put forward our solution — this time through the Prof. Reluctantly it was accepted, and within a week or two we had our own inspectors covering every firm manufacturing our devices.

This was not quite so clever as it looked as the need had been fore-seen and when an uncle of Ruth Jefferis had called to see Millis at 35 Portland Place some time in December 1940 he suddenly found himself appointed my Chief Inspector at half pay (from the bag of gold of course) until his full time services were required — which proved to be quite soon. Mr Keelan, who before he thought he had retired was with the Indian railways, served us well and faithfully and finished up with about a dozen inspectors under him.

Being able to break with tradition in this way gave us enormous advantages. For the official Design Department to produce an in-spection drill covering such devices as these would take months and to get the bugs out of their specifications would take many more months. The trouble was that the job of improving the specification would be given to some draughtsman who knew nothing whatever about the mechanism concerned or any troubles that had been experienced in designing it. All he could do was to run through the drawings for every component, decide what tolerances could be permitted in each case, and issue inspection instructions accordingly. He could not hope to be right. As a result, thousands of perfectly satisfactory units could fail inspection and be scrapped merely because some dimension proved to be a little above or a little below the prescribed limit regardless of whether or not this affected the performance at all. On the other hand, devices with some vital flaw could be passed as perfect merely because the inspection drill made no mention of looking for this flaw.

We made a rule that only the designer of the device could draw up the inspection drill in consultation with the Chief Draughtsman. For instance, I drew up those for the booby traps. We would specify what gauges were needed and have a trial set made in the workshops. Mr Keelan would then work through a batch of the mechanisms concerned to see how things went and would comment on any draw-backs he found. When all was agreed he would go through the drill with each of his inspectors and that would be that.

Of course from time to time we would get loud appeals from some contractor to the effect that the inspector had turned down a vast batch of his product for no good reason and he might then enlist the help of the inspector in asking for acceptance to be granted in this particular case. Again, no individual could authorise any departure from the drill: that could be done only by the three people who had formulated it. We were always very fair about this and if we considered it possible to make some relaxation so that the faulty batch became acceptable we would do just that and adjust the inspection drill accordingly. This led us into trouble at times because if the firm concerned had a CIA inspector as well as an M.D.1. inspector and the same kind of situation arose, as could well happen, he could lodge no similar appeal and it could take him months to get the case investigated. This fact amongst others made us extremely unpopular for a while, but we fixed things in the end by affiliating the M.D.1. inspectorate with CIA so that in theory at least they owned it.

Another example of how we had a great advantage over the orthodox departments was over the matter of publications. When they produced some new device, which in the normal way would not be often, some long suffering fellow at the War Office would get the job of including a description of it in the Manual of Infantry Weapons which was supposed to tell the soldiers all they needed to know about such things. Although there were exceptions, such descriptions were generally very sketchy ones which did not give the information that was really wanted and were accompanied by illustrations that meant nothing at all. We decided to produce our own descriptive leaflets for all the stores we produced and this time nobody minded at all.

As Gordon and I were both journalists this was just our cup of tea. From my days on 'The Motor' I remembered how well a mechanism could be shown in an exploded drawing as compared with an ordinary one and soon ran to earth an expert in this line called Everest who had worked for me before. With his help, we completed a full range of leaflets covering our devices which in due course came to be regarded by the War Office as classic examples of how this job should be done.

Let me make it clear that we did not claim to be better and brighter than the other fellows over this kind of thing. We just happened to have the luck, the opportunities, and the right kind of experience to enable us to take advantage of most situations. We were also reasonably far sighted. The attacks to get us out of 35 Portland Place were renewed with even greater intensity after we had established ourselves at The Firs. What possible justification had we for keeping on the place when half of it had been bombed away? I argued and argued, and found it exceedingly difficult to get any support over this one. Millis said he would be quite content with an office in Great Westminster House which he would probably never use anyway.

Time and time again I received instructions to vacate 35 Portland Place by a certain date and was most encouraged to find that when I failed to comply with them nobody seemed to notice. It was in my view essential for M.D.1. to have a firmly established base of its own in London and not just an office in some government building. Stuck out in the country, communications could be a problem. Our London office must be a highly efficient communications centre always manned by a duty officer. I planned to make it so

The plan was implemented and proved to be a roaring success. The Ministry of Supply were not very good on telephones, and anyhow I was reluctant to approach them about this matter of improving the service at 35 Portland Place as this might well lead them to discover that we were not supposed to be there. Gordon Norwood then performed a miracle. In some incredible way he managed to persuade the Signals boys at the War Office that, although we no longer belonged there, as we came under the War Cabinet it was their responsibility to see that we had the best telephone communications system in the country. I rather suspect that here he enlisted the help of various GSO 1s at the War Office who were constantly trying to ring us about getting supplies and were finding it most difficult to get hold of us. I would not like to say that Gordon had contrived to make this more difficult than it should be, but such a thing could happen!

In no time at all, we had at 35 Portland Place a vast switchboard manned by two operators with special lines giving us direct connection to the War Office and many of its out-stations, the War Cabinet and a few other places. But most important of all we had two direct lines to The Firs at Whitchurch so fiddled that they could be used just like ordinary extensions — which was not the case with normal special lines. We had telephones with scramblers at both Portland Place and The Firs and the system was 100 per cent perfect. During working hours, we could from Whitchurch get in touch with any London number in about ten seconds flat. At night time, the special lines were left plugged through so that in effect our Whitchurch operators could go direct through Langham exchange instead of via our Whitchurch lines.

This really was a wonderful set up and I am quite sure that it was invaluable to the department. Without it, we should have been severely handicapped. It made life easier in the village for us too because as our installation did not come under the Post Office we

107

could and did run extension lines wherever we liked without having to make any applications. I ran my own to my billet at the far end of the village and very handy it was.

By this time we had enough officers complete with secretaries to enable us to man the Portland Place office for six days a week, each team having to serve only the one duty day per week. I drew up a duty roster and we all came into it except of course Millis. Anyone else who had business in London could put down his or her name on the list for the duty car which left Whitchurch for Portland Place every morning and returned every evening. Officers who wanted to visit us at Whitchurch could report at Portland Place in the evening and be taken out there instead of having to make their own way.

Once this system was working, everyone fell for it including Millis; and again it proved to be an invaluable one. It was carried on throughout and after the war. Needless to say, directly it was in operation nobody had the pluck to try to turn us out from Portland Place even when it got bombed a bit more.

This bombing gave me my one and only chance during the war to pose as a hero. I was extremely allergic to air raids, and — not to put too fine a point on it — they frightened me to death. The position was made worse by Millis, with whom I seemed frequently to be caught in blitzes. Like Winston Churchill he seemed to revel in them and nothing pleased him more than to strut down the middle of some London street when alarming whistling noises and bangs were going on all around. My first idea on such occasions was to put on my tin hat and my next to dive into the nearest doorway hoping to find shelter. But Millis would have none of this. No tin hat — no shelter. The trouble was that I did not have the pluck to break away and had to march along beside him trying to keep cheerful.

I could never understand these brave fellows. Ralph Farrant was much the same. He would announce with satisfaction that he would be going up to town in the duty car in the morning and proposed to spend the night in London and get a first hand view of the blitz. I must say I myself contrived to get back to Whitchurch at nights whenever I could although I did stay in town and sleep in the Portland Place shelter when duty really called. There was only one exception to this arrangement. The Polish Embassy owned the house next door to 35 Portland Place and for air raid shelter purposes the two premises had been joined together at the basement level. One night when compelled to stay the night at Portland Place I chose my

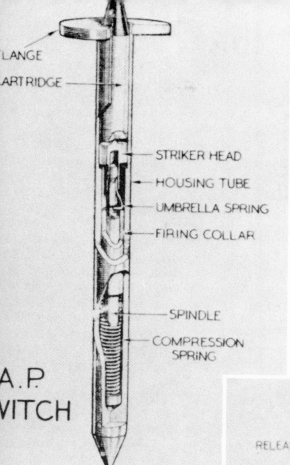

FLANGE

CARTRIDGE

STRIKER HEAD

HOUSING TUBE

UMBRELLA SPRING

FIRING COLLAR

SPINDLE

COMPRESSION SPRING

A.P. SWITCH

Some M.D.1. Toys:

Left: The AP Switch. Buried in sand or soft soil it was invisible to the naked eye and had a demoralising effect on enemy troops. It was armed with a standard .303 cartridge and steel bullet which usually managed to hit the most vulnerable parts.

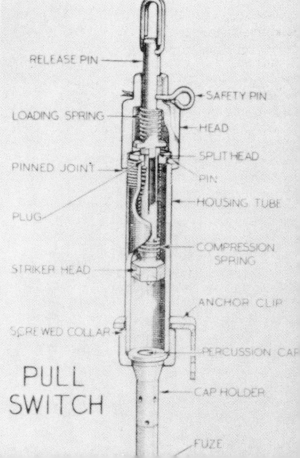

RELEASE PIN

SAFETY PIN

LOADING SPRING

HEAD

SPLIT HEAD

PINNED JOINT

PIN

HOUSING TUBE

PLUG

COMPRESSION SPRING

STRIKER HEAD

ANCHOR CLIP

SCREWED COLLAR

PERCUSSION CAP

CAP HOLDER

FUZE

PULL SWITCH

Right: The Pull Switch. This had a wide range of uses when coupled to a release or trip wire; it would detonate mines or initiate signal flares.

Some M.D.1. Toys:

Left: The Pressure switch. Designed primarily for use in blowing up railway lines, the pressure switch could be used for any booby trap where pressure on the device could cause firing.

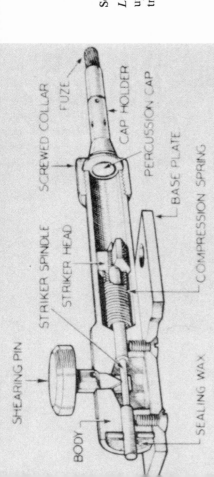

PRESSURE SWITCH

RELEASE

Right: The Release Switch. A disturbing application of this device was its use for booby trapping seats of all kinds.

shelter and bedded myself down as best I could, having a most unpleasant and alarming night. Next morning on waking up I happened to pull aside the tarpaulin partition and saw in the next door cubicle a wonderful vision in the form of a beautiful — presumably Polish — lady who looked rather like Greta Garbo but was wearing less. She promptly vanished, but I was sure it was no illusion.

What I had missed really worried me. Instead of lying on my uncomfortable little bunk listening to bangs and shivering I could have been having an interesting chat with this lady who might perhaps have filled in the time by teaching me Polish. On thinking this matter over, I decided to break my cowardly habit of going back to Whitchurch that night and have another try at this air raid shelter. The idea was a flop. I found nobody else there and the raid was a worse one than usual.

About this hero business at Portland Place, this is how it happened. The date is engraved on my heart — April 17, 1941 — as well as in my diary. It was my day as duty officer at Portland Place and I was accompanied by my faithful P.A., Anne Hall. To her I was dictating resounding minutes to the Ministry of Supply about Sticky Bombs or something when an air raid warning went. Daylight raids were not much, so we took little notice. Then came one of those whistling noises which get louder so that one knows something is more than likely to happen. This magnificent front office at Portland Place was equipped with an enormous desk, which was one thing I greatly liked about it. The instinct for self-preservation being strong upon me, I dived for the large compartment under this desk. On the way, quite by mistake I grabbed Anne Hall's leg — a thing I would never have dreamed of doing in the normal way — so that she perforce was brought into my sanctuary with me. There was then a bang, and large chunks of glass did whizz about the room, which I admit might have done us a bit of no good if we had been in our previous places.

Anne then assured everyone that by my prompt action I had saved her life, which was complete nonsense. However, I was able to bask in this false glory for a while although it soon faded out.

The blitz brought out some wonderful characteristics in people. At Portland Place we had our example in Mrs Walters, a charlady we had inherited from the IBC. However severe the night air raids, she always turned up at the right time in the mornings for duty. When the daylight raids were really bad and even staunch people like Millis and Ralph Farrant gave the impression that they felt perhaps a shade jittery, in would come Mrs Walters with a tray of cups of tea held in rock steady hands and wish us all a quite unperturbed good morning. She put me for one to shame, for she was by no means a robust woman. To our very great sorrow, she died of cancer soon after the war ended although we did our best to save her. She was a fine woman.

After all these musical interludes about Portland Place I must get on with the story. By the end of January 1941 we were fully operative at The Firs, and working most nights. I see from my diary that on January 4 we were loading up trucks all night to take our stores to the docks to catch a ship for Australia. Soon another lot had to go off to Bombay and then there was a top priority shipment to the Middle East. Gordon Norwood and SQMS Bidgood between them got the job of organising these convoys and leading them to their destinations and very well they did it. Finally they were made 'Prov and Mov' meaning provision and movement and given their own headquarters at the stores and transport centre that had been built by Gordon's gang. There they lived happily for some time, adding to the social life of the community by at intervals turning the carpenter's shop into a dance hall and running a Woodchopper's Ball.

In January a team of Office of Works experts — I believe they were by now promoted to Ministry of Works ones — arrived at The Firs, made a lot of notes of our requirements, and went away again. For a long time there was no result at all, and then a solitary builder fellow appeared to tell us he had been briefed to start work on the stores building we wanted, approval for it having now been secured from the various authorities concerned. We showed him the quite nice building we had put up ourselves whilst waiting and sent him away.

Naturally enough, this started a full scale row. Paper work fairly flew around between the Ministry of Supply and the Ministry of Works and a couple of months later we received a series of most frightful rockets. But by this time we had done a whole lot more building under our own power and the complainants found it quite impossible to keep up with us. They gave up, and in time we all became good friends.

During this year, the establishment expanded at an enormous rate. First the Prof. and then the P.M. had been sold on the idea of creating M.D.1. solely on the grounds that this would give them their own establishment for the high speed development of special weapons and war devices. So at first we had to concentrate on setting ourselves up in such a way that we could do this with 100 per cent efficiency. First we got the experimental workshops going, equipping them with machines some of which had been rescued from 35 Portland Place and others which had been extracted from a surprised Machine Tool Control on instructions from Sir Harold Brown. The main drawing office was started at the same time. It was very fully equipped and its strength of two draughtsmen was soon stepped up to six.

But the cleverest thing we did was to start individual design units. Norman Angier, as I have said, had a gift for surrounding himself with an excellent staff, all of whom I had been lucky enough to collect and bring to Whitchurch. Amongst them were two characters known as Smith and Wilson, respectively. They were both a little pale at first through having lived so long in these Portland Place cellars. Smith, who was the senior, was a kind of foreman but usually I found him at Portland Place making some exquisite piece of mechanism all by himself. Wilson lived in a cell about six feet square and at first reminded me forcibly of a fish in an aquarium. In this cell he just had room for a drawing-board on which he produced really beautiful work remarkably quickly.

It was at once evident that both these gentlemen although they had no engineering qualifications whatsoever were born designers of mechanisms. They were therefore set up at Whitchurch in a hastily converted loft above the workshops which they immediately filled with most expensive equipment and instruments which we had difficulty in getting. They were authorised to order any materials they wanted and did so. Each was given an assistant and they constituted our first two design teams. Later we had four.

Nothing could have paid off better. Smith, or Wilson, would be advised that for some new weapon we wanted some new kind of fuse which would behave as no fuse had ever done before. He would ponder on this problem for a day and then the priority ordering department we had created would receive chits marked 'Urgent.' In a surprisingly short time, we would discover that M.D.1. had a fuse dropping test tower similar to the one at Woolwich, a centrifuge rather better than the one they had, and a couple of the latest stroboscopes. Maybe a fortnight later, the partners concerned would pop up with half a dozen samples of the required fuse, which they had made themselves and subjected to their own tests, complete with drawings, asking that they should be given field trials. This we could arrange, for at once we had requisitioned a couple of adjoining fields from a farmer and converted them into firing ranges.

Smith and Wilson really were a wonderful pair, and if we had combed the country and roped in people with all the qualifications in the world we could not have found their equals. I am glad to say that when some time after the war M.D.1. was being closed down and I was faced with the task of trying to find suitable posts for such valuable members of the team as this I was able to convince the Ministry of Supply that the unqualified Smith and Wilson were more than well worth having and fix good appointments for them at the Rocket Research Establishment at nearby Westcott.

Soon we discovered another bottleneck. Many of the devices on which we were working had to be filled with high explosive. In a week or so we would rush through the design of some new type of bomb or shell or grenade and knock up half a dozen prototypes for trials. These would then have to go to an ordnance factory such as Chorley for filling and, as they were very busy churning out stuff for operational use, it would generally be a month or so before they came back again and we could carry out our trials. ICI could do us a little better, but not much because they too were working flat out. Norman Angier settled this one in characteristic fashion. Out in the grounds by the tennis lawns we had a nice summerhouse with a thatched roof. Amongst the staff we had a professional hairdresser named Mr Bridle who like all hairdressers had made his business pay not by cutting hair but by mixing up concoctions, putting them into bottles and selling them to the customers.

Bridle was doing some useful but unimportant job in the stores or somewhere like that during the daytime and cutting our hair in the evenings. Norman soon had him out of that and contrived to get somebody at Chorley to give him a quick course in the manufacture and handling of both high and low explosives. Then he was installed in the summer house and at once we were able to carry out our own explosive filling and save weeks of delay in producing these weapons for field trials. What was most surprising of all was that although Mr Bridle appeared to be a quiet and cautious kind of fellow who would treat even a small firework with great respect he showed no signs of fear whatever in his new profession and the thought that a slight mistake on his part might blow not only himself but also the rest of us to kingdom come never seemed to enter his head.

We kept very quiet about our summer house high explosive filling department for we were all aware of the fact that it did not comply in any way at all with the very strict regulations governing the running of places of this sort, Norman having acquired a book on the subject. But somehow or other Brigadier Hogg heard about it and came roaring out to Whitchurch to investigate. This was most unfortunate. I had just about succeeded in gaining the confidence of the Brigadier, who did not get on at all well with Millis and would deal only with me. And of course to keep his good will was all important, for as the Director of Military Administration of the Ministry of Supply he could make things either easy or difficult for us. As an Ordnance officer brought up at Woolwich he was naturally appalled at this summer house filling shed and ordered me to close it down immediately.

Millis was away at the time, but when he got back to The Firs and I told him what had happened he immediately countermanded the Brigadier's order and told me to keep the filling shed going. I could see a full scale row blowing up with the Ministry of Supply over this and, although by enlisting the help of The Prof. we should undoubtedly win it, life would afterwards be made very difficult for me. So next day I went up to London to see first The Prof. and then the Brigadier. To the latter I delivered a very tactful message from the Prof. which I had invented in place of the forceful one he had given to me. It was to the effect that he was aware of this illicit high explosive filling station but quite thought that it was for use only in a case of emergency when some trial was being carried out that could not be delayed. He was surprised to learn that it was now in full time operation, but this was apparently due to the fact that he had been urging us to speed up experimental work on new types of charges. The P.M. would be very concerned if this work were delayed so, although the Brigadier's decision to close the place down was undoubtedly the correct one, if he could see his way to allowing it to carry on until these particular experiments had been completed that would be much appreciated. In the meantime, the Prof. would like to suggest that I should seek authority from the Brigadier to put in hand at once the building of a proper high explosive filling shed which would fully comply with the regulations as it was now clear that it was essential for M.D.1. to have such facilities.

This worked like a charm. The Brigadier readily fell in with both suggestions and I was back in favour again. And a year later I was able to show him round our nice new high explosive and incendiary

113

filling sheds which complied with all the safety regulations and looked most impressive. For good measure, I then sat him down in the summer house, which was now again serving its proper purpose.

By now we had our firing range properly laid out and, somehow or other through one of his IBC contacts, Norman Angier had secured a chronoscope although there were very few about. This instrument was for measuring the velocity of the rounds fired. We also constructed a couple of large swimming pools which had to be reserved not for bathers but for underwater experiments with various devices. Next came a magazine for the storage of explosives which had to comply with even more regulations than did the filling sheds and finally we had to link up the various premises with roadways. When this work was completed, we could claim without fear of contradiction that we had the finest and best equipped armaments development and research station in the country.

Whilst all this important experimental side was being developed we still had to expand our facilities for storing and handling the M.D.1. devices which were now being demanded in ever increasing numbers. Millis now had no use at all for this side of things and neither had the Prof. and I could quite see their point. It was that our job was to design and develop as many new weapons as possible, not to produce them in quantity. So why not hand over to the Ministry of Supply all this troublesome business of controlling the manufacture, inspection and supply of our accepted devices and put the premises and staff concerned to some more useful purpose.

This was all very well, but I was the fellow who had contrived to get the M.D.1. establishment built up very rapidly indeed and I knew quite well why I had succeeded. It was not because we were making our name as designers of new weapons. It was because the weapons we had designed were now in very great demand and we controlled their supply. Our bottomless banking account, our increased staff, and our excellent transport and communications systems were due almost entirely to this fact. Prof. or no Prof., we could not have secured them otherwise. So only over my dead body and those of the 'Prov and Mov' boys would I let this one go. I was being patriotic as well because it would have been quite impossible for the Ministry of Supply to take over from us without a bad and possibly disasterous break in production. We were operating on entirely different lines from them and to get our contractors to work in their ways would take months if not years.

I won over this one merely by keeping quiet, thereby avoiding being ordered to close down this side of things. And soon my position was strengthened. We discovered that it was one thing to develop a new device to the prototype stage and quite another to get it into production. This arose because we had just perfected a most ingenious delay action fuse thought up by Millis which I shall describe later on. We produced samples, we produced detailed drawings of all components together with the necessary specifications and turned over the whole lot to the Ministry of Supply. They could find no contractor willing to tackle the job, which was admittedly a tricky one involving amongst other things turning a 'neck' in a lead rod to very fine limits. The design, we were informed, was an impracticable one and we had better scrap it and try again.

There was only one answer to this problem. We started our own factory, snatching a dozen automatic machines and a raft of other machine tools from under somebody's nose and putting Leslie Gouldstone in charge of the outfit. Quite soon this particular device was being turned out in considerable quantity and, having learnt our lesson, from then onwards whenever we produced a new mechanism we would always put it into production ourselves. On occasion we would content ourselves with turning out just a few thousand units to show that the job could be done and then handing over the tooling to some contractor. But sometimes we would decide to undertake the whole of the production ourselves, perhaps ordering some of the components from outside contractors.

We staffed this factory at first by recruiting hands in nearby villages and collecting them with a couple of buses. Later on, the Ministry of Labour sent us a dozen or so little Welsh girls. More stables were hurriedly converted into a hostel for them and a welfare officer named Miss Wond — of course always called Fairy Wand — was appointed to look after them and see they did not get into trouble. They just hated it at the start and were longing to get back to Wales. But soon they all fell in love with Leslie Gouldstone and got to like Miss Wond as well. From then onwards they settled down happily and worked themselves almost to death. They all cried their eyes out when the war was over and they had to be sent back home. I did the same!

Having this factory really set the seal on our success. We were now a going concern, and nothing and nobody could stop us. If we had chosen just to carry on supplying our devices to centres all over the

115

world and gear up the factory to churn out fuses of one sort and another at an even higher rate our existence would have been amply justified. There was no longer any actual need for us to devise more new weapons although that was the purpose for which we had been created. But of course none of us looked at things in this way. Although they were at the start unsympathetic to these bread and butter projects, both the Prof. and Millis came to realise their value as a solid background to our organisation. By all means keep them running, it was agreed, but let them run themselves. The rest of us must concentrate on new developments. So far as I was concerned I really must drop all this and get back to design work.

Needless to say I did nothing of the sort. But the departments really did run themselves now and all I had to do was to hold a watching brief over them and retain nominal control. To do this was essential, because Millis, in addition to continuing to regard himself as the world's great organiser, was very easily influenced by would-be reformers especially if they were technicians. To build up such an organisation as this with the staff available is a very tricky business. There must always be clashes of personalities and the aim must be to keep the clashers separate so far as possible. One has to switch people from one job to another until a balance is struck. And once it is struck it is fatal to upset it.

Time and again, after he had been worked on, Millis would come up with some plan for re-organising the whole place based on the fact that somebody had taken a dislike to somebody else and had convinced him that the man or woman concerned was no good at the job. The fellow in charge of the workshops must go. Why not put the factory manager in his place. Who was to run the factory? How about giving the job to that new Captain who was being posted to us next week? Oh, and would I please get rid of the Quartermaster Sergeant who was running the transport section? Admittedly he was doing the job all right but some of the women did not like him. It would be easy enough to get a replacement.

It was easy enough to understand Millis' mentality. He had spent the whole of his life in the Army where anyone was supposed to be able to do any job and there were few specialists. It never occurred to him that I had put A in charge of the experimental workshops because he was experienced in running such places and B in charge of the factory because he was not only a first class production man but also very good at getting the best out of the hands. What I found

116

more difficult to understand was the mentality of some of the people who suggested these reforms to him merely as a kind of whim. One attached scientist whose reform plan was readily adopted by Millis and then shot down by me rounded on me and accused me of being a weakling striving to remain popular with everybody and frightened of upsetting anybody. There was truth in his assertion, for one simply had to remain popular to run a mixed bag of this sort and make it work. Anyhow I was not frightened of upsetting this particular scientist.

To be fair to Millis, although in my absence he would sometimes go to the length of drafting orders changing everything around, he would never actually publish them without first telling me about them and I never failed to talk him out of these ideas. This was because I was down on the establishment list which I had prepared and got accepted by the Ministry of Supply not only as Deputy Superintendent but as the Administrative Officer of the outfit. Millis had no authority to make changes of this sort unless he changed me first, which he once did seriously consider trying to do. But his better nature prevailed and I honestly think it was in his own best interests for it to do so.

Remembering the lesson I had learnt from Langley at Station E. S. 6, as soon as I could collect enough soldiers I surrounded the premises with barbed wire, shut all gates and had guards on duty day and night. Later we were given a detachment of Military Police for these duties and soon built quarters for them. There is no question at all that this added greatly to our status and impressed the high ranking officers of all three services who were now flocking out to see us every day.

It was not possible to hold formal mess dinners on the E. S. 6, lines because most of the officers were working all kinds of hours so that we could have no fixed meal times. However, we did ourselves very well, Leslie Knight having stolen from the Langham Hotel their chief barman Ted Funnell who made an excellent caterer.

We built a large canteen and later on added to it a theatre complete with all the necessary trappings where we gave cinema shows twice a week. Here we were lucky in recruiting for the administration staff Oswald Bussell, a very experienced producer in the amateur theatrical world. Our stage performances were considered to be pretty good.

This might sound as if we were paying more attention to play than

117

to work, but this was not so. Everyone on the station without exception worked exceedingly hard. Usually by the time they had knocked off in the evening it would be far too late for them to go to a cinema at Aylesbury so it was essential for us to provide what entertainment we could for them. I must say that whilst they could be a bit awkward over some matters the Ministry of Supply and Ministry of Works gave us their fullest co-operation over getting this side of things going. No doubt they had been faced with the same problems as ourselves at other isolated outstations and knew this was the only answer.

The entire digging-in operation was completed before the end of 1941 although it took us another year to complete the set-up. So in two years we had contrived to turn the little three man section with which we started at the War Office into a large and wonderfully well-equipped research and development station of a quasi-military nature with a staff numbering over 250. We were a completely self-contained community but not a closed shop one. For other service departments dealing with experimental work soon learnt that at Whitchurch we could offer them help and facilities which they could obtain nowhere else. The Royal Navy invaded us in a big way, but the Royal Air Force were close runners-up. And scarcely a day passed without some new faces appearing amongst us. This was all good for trade.

II

Some Special Weapons

WE COULD NOW claim to be by royal appointment sole suppliers of nasty booby traps to the British Army and Allies if any. They have been described in a previous chapter. It was the 'W' Bomb that first made us famous although the Limpet was a close runner-up. Next came the Blacker Bombard now called the 29 mm Spigot Mortar and the Sticky Bomb now called the S.T. Grenade and later christened the Grenade No. 74 in that order. The Ordnance experts who compiled their famous vocabulary of stores had no flair for titles. Our Pull, Pressure and Release Switches, so named because this precisely defined their functions, were renamed Switches 1, 2 and 3, which meant nothing to anybody. Fortunately the Limpet and Clam were permitted to retain their identities which consoled me a little.

After the successful demonstration of the Blacker Bombard at Chequers when we were instructed by the P.M. to get on with making the weapon we ran into a lot of trouble. Having opposed the adoption of this weapon for many years, the Ordnance Board was not going to give way as easily as all that. Every move we made to finalise the design and get it adopted was bitterly opposed. We also had quite a bit of work to do to perfect the two types of round we proposed to fire from this spigot — an H.E. round which would poultice itself against a tank and blow a hole in the plating and an A.P. (anti-personnel) round which would do enemy troops a bit of no good.

It was for this job that our summer house filling shed was started. But experiments did not go at all well at first. I have a note that on April 29 1941, a highly successful demonstration of the 29 mm Spigot Mortar was given, which would seem to be appropriate. But on June 30 there was a demonstration at Shoeburyness which was a complete flop. According to the report on this matter, the Director of Ammunition

Production who was present at first refused to allow Ralph Farrant to fire live A.P. ammunition because it had not been inspected by CIA. When he was at last allowed to proceed Ralph must have been shaking with rage, for he missed the tank target with his next three shots and then hit the wrong one with his fourth. That failed to hole the plate and so did a Sticky Bomb which was applied to it for good measure. It was not a good day for M.D.I.

On March 26, the P.M. had ruled that we must make or get made a first batch of 2,500 29mm spigot mortars complete with ammunition at the earliest possible moment. He had good reason for his anxiety. There was still fear of invasion, and there was no question that if this happened the Germans would land tanks. To meet this eventuality, we had Home Forces and the Home Guard distributed round the country. But unfortunately the Home Guard had no weapons whatsoever that they could use against tanks and if any appeared they would have to run for it — a prospect they found discouraging. If only to boost up their morale, it was essential to give them something with which they could make a stand.

Of course the theory held by those who were opposed to the adoption of the Blacker Bombard was that there were other hand weapons which would do the job, but they could not get away with this one. Having almost invented the tank himself, the P.M. knew as much if not more about what it could do and what could be done to it than did the fellows on the Ordnance Board and so did the Prof. They had both attended demonstrations of anti-tank weapons at Farnborough and found them most depressing. Tanks — and not heavily armoured ones at that — would trundle round whilst marksmen took pot shots at them with Boyes rifles quite without effect. There had been a lot of talk about the deadliness of the latest version of the Molotov cocktail made up by some chemical firm and large stacks of these bottles were laid out ready for use. There was some concern that, if the tank drivers could not pull up quickly enough and hop out, they were likely to be frizzled to death, but after looking at the bottles they said they would be happy to take a chance.

The demonstration of this phosphorous grenade was an utter and complete flop and, having had our own setbacks, we could sympathise with those who put on the show. That particular weapon was out and nothing would bring it back. What was called the Smith gun designed by the owner of some big toy business showed up a little better but the round it fired was not really heavy enough. What it boiled down to was that, short of a field gun which could hardly be made standard equipment for the Home Guard, there was nothing at all to stop a tank and the only new weapons in the running were the Blacker Bombard and the Sticky Bomb — both from the M.D.1. stable.

The decision was that I should be left to hold the Sticky Bomb baby and try to keep a roof over our heads whilst Millis, Ralph and Norman roared round forming a consortium of spigot mortar makers and enlisting the invaluable help of ICI over the manufacture and filling of the rounds. They did an excellent job of work and it was not all that long before almost every Home Guard unit had its spigot mortar to give it confidence. Poor Blacker who had been fighting for all these years to get his weapon adopted got rather squashed out of the project once it reached this stage. He was a charming fellow whom I liked and admired and I always got on with him extremely well. But there was no question that other people — and in particular the three musketeers described — could find him intensely irritating.

On my desk one morning I found a minute to Brigadier Hogg signed by Millis asking for Lt-Colonel Blacker to be removed from M.D.1. and posted elsewhere. I tore it up, but this gave me the unhappy job of trying to get rid of Blacker without hurting his feelings. I managed well enough and we remained good friends right up to the time of his death some years after the war ended. I used to make a point of inviting him out to Whitchurch every so often and his visits were always a great success now that he had no say in what was done about his Bombard. I was delighted when after the war the Royal Commission on Awards to Inventors voted him a very large sum indeed mainly on the strength of this Bombard invention. It is not all that often that such justice is done.

Earlier on, I described the first fruitless experiments with the Sticky Bomb at Cambridge when like Harlequins, Schulman and Bauer hurled rubber sausages at walls with no effect. When Millis handed this little problem over to me I at first thought I was on an easy one. But I soon changed my mind. The specification was for a bomb or grenade which one could hurl at a target, which would squash against that target so that the contact area was considerable, which would stick to the target, and which would then go bang and blow a hole in it. This sounded quite simple, but it wasn't.

Starting from scratch, the Cambridge sausages were no good at all on three counts; 1. they could not be thrown with accuracy; 2. the rubber solution used as the adhesive was not good enough or sticky enough, and 3, even if this device hit the target, stuck to it, and exploded it would still be ineffectual because with such a small area of contact it would do no damage.

If I had needed driving to drink, trying to get some sense into this Sticky Bomb would have done it. First I had to make up my mind where to start. It seemed to me that the first requirement was a matter of ballistics. If soldiers had to throw these things at tanks it was essential that they should have a reasonable chance of hitting them even if they were not professional cricketers. Therefore a ball was the ideal shape. But if a ball were covered with sticky goo it would not be possible to throw it. So that one was out. It would be essential to have a sticky-free handle by which the thing would be thrown.

I nearly got on to a winner then. I made a triangular bag shaped like a brickbat out of buckram with a handle at the apex. The idea was that if it could be thrown so that it would land flat on the target it would offer a wonderful surface contact area. It had to be thrown from some twenty yards away, and I have found that even one of these juggler fellows could not throw a contraption of this sort with any accuracy. After some experiment, my helpers and I decided that the odds were all against us and that if one out of twenty of our brickbats hit the target and laid flat against it we should be lucky. Design abandoned!

Back we went to the cricket ball with a handle — except that we made it about the size of a large grape fruit. Practising with wooden dummies, we found that this device could be thrown with reasonable accuracy. This was better, but we still had to make the missile first stick to its target and then poultice on to it in some way. The answer to the poulticing problem at first appeared to be to use a flabby fabric bag filled with an almost liquid explosive. But this did not work. It proved to be impossible to throw such a device with any accuracy and back we were at the brickbat stage.

All right, the sphere must retain its shape when it was thrown but collapse when it hit the target and poultice on to it. The answer might be a glass flask. We acquired a lot of glass flasks, filled them with porridge, and did our throwing tests. This was a whole lot better, but of course when the flask smashed the stuff splattered out all over the place and much of it was lost. Put a sock on it was the answer, and this is what we did. The Sticky Bomb was at last taking shape.

A Mr Hugo Wood of Leeds proved able and willing to produce smashable glass flasks to our specification in any required quantity and that was a good start. But we still had the problem of finding a suitable adhesive.Experiments in this connection were running in parallel. Almost every known kind of sticky stuff from Seccotine and rubber solution upwards had been tried and found wanting. For not only had this adhesive to hold something weighing about a pound for at least several seconds: it also must never dry up. Some of the promising concoctions we tried worked well at the start but after a week or so had dried out and were no good at all.

To-day one could walk into any ironmonger's shop and buy a tube of adhesive which would do such a job as this perfectly well. But this was not the case in 1940. Somebody suggested birdlime — I think it was Schulman at Cambridge — and this certainly performed better than anything else to date. It was still not good enough, though. The thing to do seemed to be to go to see these birdlime makers and ask them if they could improve on their product a bit. The tin of stuff I had simply had a large 'K' on the lid and the address was given as Stockport. Millis, the Prof., Joe Holland and Uncle Tom Cobley and all were now on my tail over this little matter asking what had gone wrong with me and why I was not getting better results. On impulse I took myself to Euston and caught a train to Stockport.

On arrival, it proved not difficult to trace the birdlime makers. The 'K' was significant, for they were named Kaye Brothers Ltd. A taxi took me there, and I received my next setback at once. It was Wakes Week and the place was virtually closed down. However, a Mr Dexter, the Works Manager, was there and to him I explained my problem. He promised to deal with it and he did. Soon afterwards there appeared at Room 173 the War Office, a Mr Sinclair, who was the Managing Director of the company, and his Chief Chemist, Mr Hartley. They offered their fullest co-operation over this matter and they certainly gave it. Hartley spent hours mixing up evil-smelling brews in his cauldrons like an old witch. Every few days, either he would come down to London with his latest samples or I would go to Stockport and try them out there.

It was a long and arduous business, but we won in the end. There were other little problems to be solved, but the adhesive one had been settled. If you have a vast toffee apple, which is more or less what this was, you cannot carry it about in the nude, as it were, unless you want to stick to it yourself. It must have a cover. This cover must be quickly detachable when the weapon is to be thrown and cannot be something which is solemnly stripped off. We made a metal cover consisting of two hemispheres hinged together with a spring-loaded hinge. It was kept closed by a tear-off clip which held it in place round the neck of the glass flask. A number of little rubber spikes fitted to the insides of the covers so that the toffee apple was securely located, but as they were only in point contact with it there was no risk of the cover not springing open and coming free. This was about the only part of the design which gave no trouble at all.

By this time I rather fancied myself over the design of release mechanisms and produced a very clever handle which, when a safety pin had been removed and the grenade was thrown, flew apart to release a striker and initiate firing. This worked perfectly well, but I was now so frightened of the Sticky Bomb gremlins that I dared not adopt it. Instead I used a version of the old Mills grenade release which had served me so well for my bomb dropping gear in the First World War. It was merely a plastic handle with an outside lever. The lever was retained by a safety pin. When this had been removed, the device was safe as houses whilst it was gripped in the hand. But when it was thrown the lever flew off under the influence of a spring to release a striker and start things going. A cap was fired which lighted a five-second fuse. At the end of the five seconds a detonator went off and through a primer exploded the maincharge consisting of 1 lb of a special high explosive devised for us by ICI.

My diary makes sad reading for a while where the Sticky Bomb is concerned. There is an entry of December 27, 1939 merely stating that work was going on on the Sticky Bomb. On January 2, Kay's come into the picture and the triangular model is mentioned. On January 30 1940 Sticky Bomb tests at Farnborough were satisfactory enough for the P.M. to want us to go ahead, but it was not until June 1 that he put this instruction in writing. Then there are innumerable entries about further tests being unsuccessful, interspersed with terse notes stating 'Macrae on S.T. grenade drawings or trials.'

At last we got the thing right, or right enough, and it was then that our real troubles started. From the point of view of the Ordnance Board the device was a Heath Robinson affair which broke all the rules of the game and just could not be permitted. To carry high explosives in a glass flask was all wrong but, if it were done, there was a regulation stating that the thickness of the glass must be about four times that which we were using so that it would be virtually unbreakable. The new explosive produced by ICI had not been tested and

124

Some M.D.I. Toys:

Left: The L Delay. This device was invaluable in sabotage work needing delayed action fuses. Activated by the stretching of a lead element until it broke, these fuses could be supplied in timings from anything between one hour and one month.

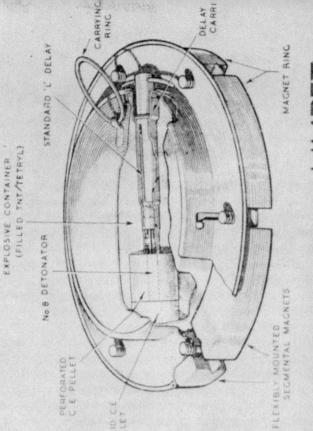

EXPLOSIVE CONTAINER
(FILLED TNT/TETRYL)

STANDARD 'L' DELAY

CARRYING
RING

DELAY
CARRI

MAGNET RING

No 8 DETONATOR

PERFORATED
C.E PELLET

SOLID C.E
PELLET

FLEXIBLY MOUNTED
SEGMENTAL MAGNETS

No 8 DETONATOR OR FUSE

SPRING HOLDER

CAP
HOLDER

CAP

SPRING ANCHOR

STRIKER PIN

STRIKER HEAD

TENSION SPRING

OUTER TUBE

SAFETY CLIP

3 DAYS
LATER

TAB

STARTING PIN

METAL ELEMENT

L. DELAY

Right: The Limpet. This was carried on a belt strapped to the diver from which he could remove it and place it on the side of a ship. Powerful magnets kept it there until after a predetermined time it was detonated and blew a large hole in the vessel.

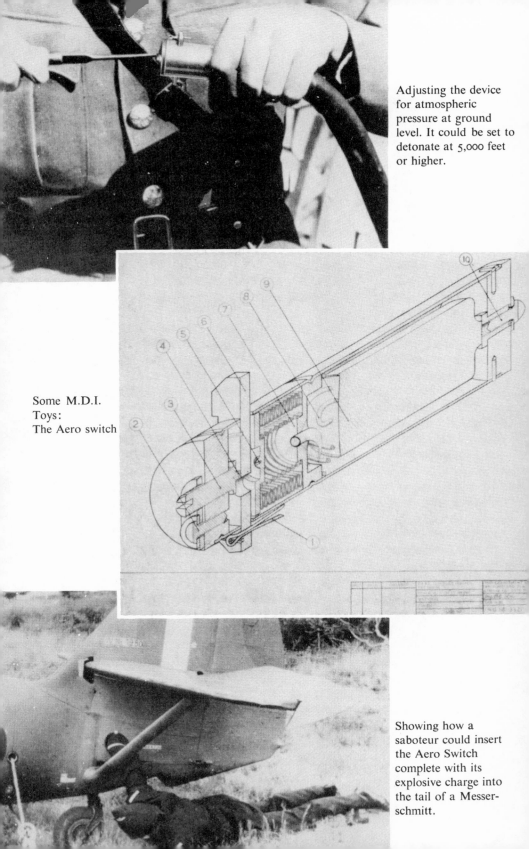

Adjusting the device for atmospheric pressure at ground level. It could be set to detonate at 5,000 feet or higher.

Some M.D.I. Toys:
The Aero switch

Showing how a saboteur could insert the Aero Switch complete with its explosive charge into the tail of a Messerschmitt.

approved by the appropriate departments so its use could not be allowed.

Gradually we got these points cleared but new objections were then raised. To make this grenade a service issue would be quite impossible because there could be no way of packing it so that it would withstand the specified rough usage treatment which called for the containers being dropped from a great height without the contents suffering damage. As a matter of fact we designed special metal boxes which very nearly enabled the grenades to stand this racket but not quite.

Time went on, and official approval for this comic weapon just could not be obtained. By now, the P.M. was getting really cross and finally the Prof. got a note out of him scribbled in his own hand on 10 Downing Street notepaper merely saying: 'Sticky Bomb. Make one million. WSC.'

Armed with this little bit of paper, I next day visited the Ministry of Supply and put the cat amongst the pigeons. The Director of Armaments Production at once had to call a full dress meeting with representatives of the Ordnance Board, the Chief Inspector of Armaments and Heaven knows how many other experts present. The decision was unanimous, except for me. As a weapon, the Sticky Bomb was not approved and never would be. To arrange for its manufacture would be exceedingly difficult and could not be done without interfering with vitally important production work. If it were made in no circumstances would it be acceptable to the Services. So let's call the whole thing off!

This was all very well, but the DAP was as frightened of the P.M. as I was. Waving my little bit of paper, I pointed out that M.D.1. came directly under the War Cabinet and the P.M. and that it was quite impossible for me to query a definite instruction of this sort. If the Ministry felt unable to undertake production of the weapon would they please authorise M.D.1. to do that? M.D.1. was of course now an approved production department and well able to undertake this work.

I think everyone was rather relieved at this suggestion which got DAP off the hooks. But it was pointed out that even if the grenades were made they would still be unacceptable to the Army and could be issued only to the Home Guard. That suited me all right. My job was to produce the grenades and it would be up to the P.M. and the Prof. to argue about who could have them.

By now, our contractors' service was operating so well that it was no trouble at all to arrange this production work. One firm made the handles, another the metal covers, another the glass flasks, and another the wool socks. Yet another made the metal carrying containers. All these components were shot up to Kay's at Stockport where they were assembled and inspected by the two resident inspectors we based there. The socks were then treated with the adhesive, the grenades packed in their metal containers, and these complete outfits were sent off to ICI at Ardeer where the high explosive filling was carried out and the detonator units were included in the containers. Final inspection was carried out at Ardeer and a percentage of the grenades was proofed there.

The fact that we had got into production with the S.T. grenade quite smartly and with apparent ease irritated the opposition and they soon gave us battle. First, our completed grenades were classed as dangerous and must not be admitted to any Ordnance Store. This made things awkward, although we could and did make deliveries ourselves to special units of one sort or another to which we were supplying M.D.1. stores. But we were not going to be allowed to get away with this one. On March 6, 1941 the Ordnance Board issued an edict that production of the S.T. grenade must be suspended. No good reasons were given, and of course this started a war. On March 13 the P.M. demanded an enquiry into this matter, and I was summoned by the Director General of Munitions Production, Sir Harold Brown, to talk to him about it. Naturally he was rather put out.

Nothing much happened until The Prof. called a meeting about the S.T. grenade at the Cabinet Offices at which Millis and Lord Melchett as well as myself were asked to attend. Melchett was by now our very good friend. He was most indignant at the hold up. He had discovered that Woolwich had been instructed to get in touch with Ardeer about the special explosive for the Sticky Bomb over a month back but had failed to do so. To suggest that said special explosive, devised for this job by his two experts, Dr Weir and Dr White, was unsafe was utter nonsense. It was based on the nitro-glycerine they had been supplying to the world for years and could not possibly be faulted.

The Prof. got busy after this meeting, and on April 29 1941 we had to give a special demonstration of the S.T. grenade at Bisley. At last our luck had changed, and it was highly successful. The Secretary of State for War, who was present, at once ruled that production of the S.T. grenade must be resumed and also that it should be issued to the Army as well as the Home Guard.

The Ordnance Board and Chief Inspector of Armaments refused to admit defeat for some time. On two more occasions, instructions were given for S.T. grenade production to be suspended and another order was planned stating that existing stocks of these grenades in Ordnance Depots were classed as dangerous and must be destroyed. A sorrowful CIA Colonel got on to me to ask me if I realised the awful responsibility I was shouldering in this light-hearted manner in supplying the weapon to the Army when it was utterly unsafe and likely to kill the users. I said I did, and was prepared to accept it because to date I had in demonstrations used more S.T. grenades than anyone else and was still very much alive and kicking.

A terrific uproar occurred when at last a case of grenades was found in which the neck of one of the glass flasks had cracked and a little of the explosive had leaked out. Some expert at once had ideas about this. Should any of this explosive get on to one of the hinges of the box, he maintained, there was every chance that when it was opened friction would cause an explosion and the whole thing would go up, probably setting off something else as well. Everything was stopped again and we were back to square one. ICI then solemnly took a dozen of the standard boxes, smeared the hinges liberally with their explosive, and fixed up apparatus to open and shut the lids of the boxes ad infinitum. When this performance had gone on for a week or so without anything going bang, CIA had to admit that the risk was not so great as supposed and off we went again.

This private guerilla war went on until July 12, 1941 when in a late news broadcast the BBC gave a wonderful story about how the Sticky Bomb was proving to be the only effective weapon for the infantryman against tanks, and the Press made much of it the next day. This settled the matter, and I am sure the P.M. and The Prof. did a bit of chortling as well as ourselves.

From then onwards we had to concentrate for a while on stepping up production of the S.T. grenade and also in training the troops in how to use it. We made some practice grenades out of wood the same shape as the grenade itself and so weighted that when thrown they behaved in the same manner. Once the soldiers had got the hang of this throwing, which they did quite quickly, we would give them for practice the sticky bombs themselves filled with an inert substance and minus the detonator assemblies. After they had learnt how to use these they were all ready to go.

I put Captain Faber in charge of these training operations and he had to travel all over the country to do it, roping in helpers wherever he could find them. He took to it like a duck to water and soon became the most experienced S.T. grenade thrower in the world. I was not nearly so good at it, but if both Faber and Bidgood, the other acknowledged expert, were away giving demonstrations and VIPs turned up at Whitchurch wanting to be shown how the Sticky Bomb worked I had to provide the entertainment. We had a special demolition area on the ranges and all I had to do was pop into my little slit trench and hurl the grenades at the sheets of armour plate which we used for targets, ducking down just before the bang came so that I was perfectly safe.

Faber spoilt all this. One morning when he was temporarily back at Whitchurch he was nosing through a pile of papers I had sent him when he came across several reports saying how remarkably successful the Australians had been lately with our Sticky Bombs in knocking out enemy tanks through having developed a new technique for using them. Instead of throwing the grenades from a safe distance in the approved manner and risking them missing the target or not sticking to it well enough, they would find themselves a nice ditch at the side of the road and wait with their grenade at the ready. When an enemy tank came along they would pop out when it was abreast of them so that they could not easily be spotted by anyone, slam the Sticky Bomb on to the tank, and go away. They had found by experiment that they had to be only a few yards away from the device when it detonated to be quite safe provided—and this was a big 'provided'—they retired in the opposite direction to the way the handle was pointing. If they chose the wrong direction the handle would be shot through them like a bullet.

This idea delighted Faber, who was by now getting bored with throwing the grenades and craved a bit of excitement. With my permission, he said, he proposed to try this new technique on the ranges right away and would I like to come and watch? This put me in a nasty spot. In theory it was my duty to forbid the experiment for it would break all the rules and, if anything went wrong and Faber got hurt, I should be in real trouble. Also even at this stage it had occurred to me that if Faber made this idea work and in future demonstrated the weapon in this manner I should be forced to do the same and give up the safety of my little slit trench. The prospect did not appeal to me.

However, progress must not be thwarted so the experiment was made. Faber was dead right instead of being dead. I was the same, for from then on I had to demonstrate his way. The first time I tried it I was shaking like a leaf and when the bang came I felt sure that must be the end of me. But encouraged by Faber I soon got the hang of the thing and I must say it made the demonstration much more impressive than before. The thing to do was to stroll casually up to the target and wallop the grenade on to it very heartily indeed. At first this was a bad moment because nobody likes to take liberties such as this with a pound of high explosive. However ICI had done their stuff properly. They said there was no chance of this explosive going off on impact and this proved to be true. The next care was to see that the handle was not pointing towards the audience and the third to see that it was not liable to move through insecure fixing. The operator must then release the firing lever in such a manner that when it flew off it did not hit him in the eye, turn around, and march off in leisurely fashion. In the five seconds available one could travel five yards which was enough There would be a considerable draught when the grenade exploded but nothing worse. One would rapidly earn a reputation for being as cool as a cucumber and frightfully brave, which was most satisfying. So were the large holes which this way we always managed to blow in the plates, where previously we could have failures.

For quite a time all went smoothly with the Sticky Bomb which had now been officially adopted by the Ordnance people in spite of their previous threats and rechristened the Grenade No 74 — which again meant nothing much to anybody. Orders were stepped up and everything went well. For some time past I had been working with Wilson on a Mk II Sticky Bomb which was to set the seal of respectability on this hitherto Heath Robinson device. The glass flask so abhorred by the Ordnance Board was to go. In its place we had a plastic one. It took us some weeks and many trials to find the most suitable plastic for it and the most suitable thickness and the result was another row with CIA later on. Some expert there at once pronounced this plastic to be incompatible with the explosive and predicted that in consequence the grenades were likely to go off by themselves if left in store for any length of time, Of course we had been careful after deciding on our plastic to ask ICI to try it for compatibility with their explosive and after doing this very thoroughly they had given it a clean bill of health. This was reluctantly accepted by CIA, but only after they had managed to get production stopped for a week whilst they thought over the matter.

The Mk II No 74 grenade offered other little advantages. By using a plastic flask we could adopt a much more secure method of fixing the handle. The metal cover was also made so that it could be freed more quickly and easily and the detonator unit was cleaned up. Finally after passing all tests with flying colours the No 74 Grenade Mk II was given full approval by the Ordnance Board and CIA, was put into full scale production, and became a service issue.

That seemed to be the happy ending to all the troubles we had had with this peculiar weapon, but it wasn't. With all its faults, the Mk I had never injured its user. There were many stories flying around about some soldier taking a big back swing with his grenade after releasing the firing lever and getting the thing stuck to his back where it exploded and blew him to pieces, but this was all nonsense. There was no case on record of any accident of this or any other kind. But now there was. Out of the blue, signals started to come in saying that Grenades No 74 were causing accidents through prematuring and that one man had already been killed.

This was really bad. I received the news just as a covey of Generals was about to descend on Whitchurch for a demonstration of our weapons. As usual, the Sticky Bomb was one of the star turns in this programme and to cancel this item would certainly cause comment and speculation that would be bad for M.D.I. I cursed Faber and toyed with the idea of going back into my slit trench until I realised that if the grenade decided to go bang directly the firing lever was released I should be no better off. So I had the bar illegally opened, fortified myself with a number of gins and Frenches, and got on with it. Everything went normally and I need not have worried.

Courts of Enquiry had to be held into these happenings and once again production of the device was suspended. Wilson and I chased around like scalded cats trying to find out what had gone wrong and which Mark it had gone wrong with. As always in these cases, the reports were vague and contradictory. However it did seem that Mark II was the model most likely to be at fault and that there had been a few occasions when one had gone off almost instantaneously. Could the wrong fuse have been used? A hasty visit to Ardeer proved that this was impossible.

A test rig was set up and hundreds of both Mk I and Mk II detonator units were tried out and timed on it. They all behaved perfectly. We tried out hundreds more detonator units and at last found the trouble. Fortunately it was confined to the Mk II grenades with their improved type of detonator unit in which we used a 1.7 grain detonator instead of a cap — a change we were making in all our devices. The reason for it was that a cap has to be hit quite smartly whereas the detonator can be fired with a comparatively gentle prick from a needle. There had been cases of Sticky Bombs misfiring through the operator releasing the lever slowly instead of letting it fly off, thus reducing the blow imparted by the striker. With this new arrangement, however slowly the lever was released, firing would still take place.

Of course the new design had been thoroughly tested not only by ourselves but also by CIA before it was approved and it was not thought that anything could go wrong here. But something did go wrong. The detonator was fixed in a holder to which was attached the short length of slow burning fuse required by means of crimping. A No 8 detonator was crimped to the other end of the fuse. In theory a perfect joint was made in both cases. In practice, something had gone out of adjustment in one of the crimping tools so that in the assembly instead of the holder and detonator tube closely embracing the fuse a gap could be left. Through these gaps the 1.7 grain detonator, which is quite a fierce little fellow, could throw a spark which would fire the No 8 detonator instantaneously instead of through the medium of the slow burning fuse. This was not likely to happen, but unfortunately it did happen on a few occasions. What was particularly annoying was that if we had stuck to the Mk I design instead of trying to improve on it this trouble would not have occured. For we soon found that even if the crimping were faulty a cap would not throw a spark in the same way as the detonator. The answer was easy. Inspection was tightened up so that no more faulty crimping could get through whilst as an insurance policy we added a little rubber sleeve to seal both joints.

All we had to do then was to withdraw all detonator units issued with the Mk II grenades and replace them with these new ones. As a routine matter, the rejected units were inspected before they were reconditioned and it was found that out of the many thousands produced only a hundred or so suffered from the fault. But that was quite enough to do the damage. However, this proved to be the death of the last of the Sticky Bomb gremlins and after that all went well. The Sticky Bomb continued to serve as the only effective anti-tank weapon for the infantryman until later on M.D.1. produced the PIAT. Apart from being issued to the Home Guard, hundreds of thousands of Grenades No 74 were supplied to our forces and allied ones throughout the world. I think it fair to say that, although the 'W' Bomb started us off and the Blacker Bombard put us on the map, it was the Sticky Bomb that first brought us fame and forced the Powers that Be to admit that our existence was justified.

I 2

More Trials and Tribulations

ONE OF THE delights of running an establishment such as M.D.1. is that you never know what is going to get up and hit you. We appeared to have run into an era of calm once the Sticky Bomb was safely launched. The day to day little difficulties one must always expect to crop up in an outfit of this sort had all been happily smoothed out to date. We were all as busy as bees, which was just what was wanted. The name of M.D.1. was now firmly established and the future seemed to be assured.

Having a bit more time on my hands, I had offered to help Millis and Ralph over some 29 mm spigot mortar difficulties and, after going to Bristol to sort out a problem concerned with the tails of the H.E. rounds coming adrift when they should not, I joined them at ICI, Buxton, for the first firing trials with live ammunition. They went well. All appeared to be peace and joy. We returned to Whitchurch in happy mood.

Millis went off to town the next day on the duty car. He returned in the evening to inform me that he had had a talk with Lord Beaverbrook and Sir William Rootes who in addition to being Minister of Aircraft Production was now serving as a kind of Defence Overlord at the Ministry of Supply, and agreed to transfer M.D.1. to them from the Ministry of Defence — just like that. This was most disconcerting and I could have been knocked down without a feather. I did seriously wonder if Millis had gone off his rocker. I had fought like a demon and in a most unscrupulous manner to prevent us from being taken over by the MOS and I had won. We were nicely set up on a high priority basis under the Prof. and the P.M. himself. Now Millis was suddenly offering the whole thing to MOS on a plate — and for no ascertainable reason whatever.

Three days later, on August 11, 1941, a letter arrived from Beaverbrook and company confirming the verbal arrangements that Jefferis had made with them. This was really awful. I was quite certain that if the MOS got hold of M.D.1. we would soon be completely emasculated and probably either integrated with the orthodox design department or abolished. Either way we should become quite useless for the purpose we had been created — to serve as a high speed weapons design department. It was not until after the war was over that, through Winston Churchill and the Prof. being pushed out of power, the MOS was able to grab us, absorb us and then abolish us, to prove my point. But I knew I was right.

In the meantime, what was to be done? I had my worst row with Millis and I am afraid accused him of acting blindly, stupidly and in a manner unfair to all of us. I felt badly enough about the possible effect of his action on the establishment but I felt worse over its effect on the feelings of The Prof. He had been extraordinarily good to us in general and to Millis in particular. He had contrived to get the P.M. to back us to the hilt under his direction. It was well known to everybody but Millis that, whereas the Prof. was said to be the P.M's right hand man, Beaverbrook too was very much in favour and the two were jealous of each other. Millis had not even warned the Prof. about his sudden move. What a slap in the face it would be giving him if it went through.

Millis' answer to this one was that having acquired one fairy godmother he saw no reason why he should not change her for a better one should he feel so inclined and would I please see Rootes to-morrow and give him the fullest information about M.D.1. and its activities for at present he knew little about us. I had to do that. Millis then, after a further meeting with Rootes, saw General Ismay who said he thought that the War Cabinet would not object to our transfer to Beaverbrook if Millis really wanted that. Still the Prof. had been told nothing about all this.

Brigadier Hogg, the DMA, who was now my good friend, came into the picture. He had heard the news and had learnt that if the deal went through we would come under the Director of Artillery, which would be most inappropriate. He was recommending that if this happened I should be promoted and given more control over the department as he was convinced that Jefferis was not the man for this job and should concentrate on his experimental work. This was very nice of him, but it was not what I wanted at all.

On August 18, 1941 the Prof., just back from the U.S.A., obviously hurt but not so indignant as he might have been, telephoned me to ask what was all this about Millis having agreed to go over to Beaverbrook without even mentioning the matter to him. According to the MOS, Millis was jumping for joy over this new arrangement. Why was this? Would I please see him about this matter at once? He was not at all sure that he would approve the transfer.

The next day, the Senior Military Adviser to the MOS. came out to Whitchurch to talk to Millis about this transfer. Millis urged him to arrange right away for all our production facilities to be taken over from us by other Ministry departments so that we could return to pure experimental work. I was in despair. Even though events had proved my policy to be the right one, Millis now seemed determined to reject it and break up our little empire.

He then went off to Scotland and the next day I was on the mat in front of the Prof. He said he could not understand the situation at all, which did not surprise me because neither could I. He said he was pretty annoyed about it. The first he had heard about it was from Beaverbrook when he was in America. However, Beaverbrook had assured him that he would not take over M.D.1. without the Prof's agreement. The Prof. then phoned Lord Melchett to get his views on the matter. Melchett said he was sure Millis did not want the transfer. But General Ismay, who was telephoned next, said he was sure Millis did want it. It was all most confusing. All I could do was to pull out all the stops I could and oppose the change most bitterly. On his return to Whitchurch I told Millis I had done that, and he did not seem to mind.

Nothing happened for a week. Then the Prof. summoned me to the Cabinet offices again, told me the transfer of M.D.1. to Beaverbrook was definitely off, and showed me correspondence which confirmed this. Evidently he had had to work quite hard on the P.M. to get this result and promise to prove to him what good work we were doing by staging a demonstrstion of our special weapons and devices at some ranges near Chequers at a week-end. Could I fix up all this by next Sunday? It was now Wednesday. I said I could and got busy.

Having for some time been staging demonstrations of this sort I was by now getting quite good at the job. I prepared a programme for approval by the Prof. and then issued the necessary orders. It was a pity the P.M. could not come to Whitchurch where we had everything set because that would have saved us a lot of trouble. But the Prof. assured us that every minute of his Sunday was fully accounted for and

134

he just could not spare the extra hour needed to make the journey.

This programme and orders may be of interest, so it is published in an Appendix. The demonstration, I am glad to say, literally went with a bang. Everything worked well and smoothly, and there was not a single hitch. The P.M. was very satisfied indeed and so was the Prof. We were all pleased that we had not let him down, and awaited the results with interest.

On the following Saturday the Prof., who was now Lord Cherwell, came out to Whitchurch to talk to me about the matter, for Millis was away in Scotland. The Prof. explained that although previously the MOS had been content to house and feed us and exercise no control over us, now that Millis had stirred things up they were not willing to go on doing that. The line they were taking was that the Superintendent of the establishment had asked to be taken entirely under their wing and they agreed to that. If that were called off they felt disinclined to continue to be responsible for adminstering M.D.1. The 64,000 dollar question was: 'Where did we get the money from to pay the bills if the MOS would not continue to provide it?'

I had an idea which I still think was a brilliant one. We belonged to the Ministry of Defence and were its first and so far its only department. Why should not this Ministry be responsible for us? True there was as yet no such Ministry but only the Minister — the P.M. But as the First Lord of the Treasury he could vote a large sum to get the Ministry established. I said I would be happy to organise this little matter for the P.M. if I were given the all clear because I was confident I could do that. The Prof. was quite interested and agreed to talk to the P.M. about the idea. But he wanted an alternative suggestion so I said why not let me have a go at the War Office. True they had been un-flatteringly anxious to get rid of us earlier on. But now we were rather successful they might welcome us back.

The Prof. gave me the go ahead to approach the W.O. but, being by now an experienced diplomat and anxious to avoid any accusation of conspiracy, I got him to get Millis on the telephone there and then and secure his approval for the move. However, on return from Scotland Millis got his own back by promptly making a date to meet Oliver Lucas who was Billy Roote's second-in-command at the MOS.

Three days later the Prof. telephoned me to say that the P.M. had now very definitely turned down the suggestion that M.D.1. should be transferred to Beaverbrook. This was very satisfactory. Would I please come to see him the next day, which of course I did. He said he was putting forward to the P.M. my idea of getting the Ministry of Defence started but in the meantime he would like me to approach the War Office. I went right off to talk to the finance boys then having first enlisted the help of the GSO's of various departments which were either desperately anxious to get supplies from us or keenly interested in some of our development work. I had no trouble at all. The finance chiefs said that if the MOS did not want to go on paying us they would be happy to take over and give us all the money we needed.

Millis seemed to have fallen in love with Billy Rootes. He saw him again a couple of days later and promised him he would try to persuade the Prof. to let M.D.1. go over to him and Beaverbrook. Then, taking Ralph Farrant with him and wisely leaving me out, he did see the Prof. and apparently secured his agreement to the move As a result, I was ordered to see Rootes and Lucas and tell them all about M.D.1.because I was the only fellow in a position to do that.

I did not get on at all well with them — I could not expect to as they both knew I was opposing the transfer as hard as I could. Rootes confirmed that Millis had come to him begging to be taken over and that he had agreed to the move. When it had been effected, he said, I must understand that M.D.1. would have to be run on strictly orthodox lines. Our production work would be taken over by other MOS departments and we would work in collaboration with the official research and development departments.

This was just what I feared and, when I got back to Whitchurch, I tried to explain once again to Millis that if he insisted on going ahead with this plan we might just as well close down M.D.1. right away and save ourselves trouble. I also assured him that under the new set-up he would certainly not be free to develop whatever new weapons he liked without restrictions. With his fertile brain he was coming up with a new idea of some sort about once a week if not more often. When this happened he did not need to seek permission from anyone to try it out and he had top priority at Whitchurch for doing so.

Did he think that would happen when we belonged to the MOS? Every time he wanted to start a new project he would have to go and see the Director of Artillery — who incidentally did not like him very much — or one of his deputies to get permission to go ahead with it. More than likely it would often be refused, or given only low priority. Whitchurch would be closed down quite soon as there would be no justification for keeping the place open if we were no longer in the production business. Then Millis would be told to get his new weapons developed by the Armaments Design Dept. at Fort Halstead, our avowed enemies. He would be exceedingly lucky if they agreed to co-operate and luckier still if he got any results in six months instead of the average of six days which it now took us to try out his ideas.

Of course I should have tried this line before. At last I had made an impression. It was then I began to see why Millis had made this odd move of asking Beaverbrook to take us over. He just did not want the responsibility of being the head of a quite large organisation and mistakenly thought that in this way he could get rid of it and go back to the carefree way of working he had when we were only MIR (c). Of course in actual fact he had to carry no responsibility at all for the running of M.D.1. because I did that, but outside the organisation only very few people, such as the Prof. and Brigadier Hogg, knew it. It was only because Millis had such a terrific personality that I had been able to build up M.D.1. around him and I certainly could not have built it around myself. The fact remained that he was the titular head of the place and did not want to be that.

I now knew what it must feel like to be a theatrical producer who had found an unwilling star and forced him to fame. And the thought did worry me a bit because, whereas I had succeeded in making myself happy, it was obvious that I had done the opposite for Millis. However, personal feelings must be set aside because we were fighting a war and there was no question whatever that M.D.1. was making a most valuable contribution to the war effort. Whether he liked it or not, Millis was now so placed that he could use his great talent for inventing war devices to the full, which of course was what he really wanted to do. So I explained all this to my conscience and carried on.

Next day we had a meeting at Whitchurch to discuss policy. It was attended by Millis, Ralph Farrant, Norman Angier and myself. Millis came out quite openly with his wish to make the establishment very much smaller and confine its activities to development work. But now Ralph and Norman came over to my side. They both agreed that, if we were unable to stand still, we must expand rather than contract and that, if we did the latter and went over to the MOS on the lines Millis wanted, my prediction that we would soon disappear as an independent organisation would come true.

There was then a lull for nearly a fortnight. Millis had been definitely bloody but unbowed at our meeting and needed a little time

137

to recover. Then off he went to see Lucas and General Jacob, of the War Cabinet, who was deputising for General Ismay. The result was that Lucas decided to visit Whitchurch himself to inspect the establishment and I was instructed to put up the best possible show for him. He turned up three days later, arriving at 10.30 am and leaving at 12 noon. He seemed to be completely uninterested in everything. I was quite capable of sabotaging any demonstration and showing him the place at its worst if the need arose but it did not.

I was delighted when the Prof. rang me to say that Lucas had written a stinking report on M.D.1. for submission to Beaverbrook more or less suggesting that the establishment was doing no work of any value and was not worth having. The Prof. naturally took a different view of the situation. Beaverbrook would no doubt pass on this to the P.M. who, in spite of the recent successful demonstration, might take notice of it for he had never visited The Firs himself. The Prof. would then get a black mark, for he had been put in control of M.D.1. and was ultimately responsible for its success or failure. There was only one answer, he told me. Beaverbrook must be shown what M.D.1. was doing. He would get the P.M. to bring him and Lucas to another demonstration at Princes Risborough if I could run one. Could I make it to-morrow, Saturday?

Of course I said 'Yes' although it was rather short notice. M.D.1. then got exceedingly busy. Officers were called in from all directions, Ralph Farrant being fished off a train at Bristol and brought back by road. The ranges were requisitioned and troops found to man them. Targets were erected, guns and ammunition prepared, and impressive copies of my programme were made by the ever willing drawing office. We worked through the night.

Then I received a message to say that Lucas had asked for the demonstration to be postponed until Monday, This was a little frustrating. Hard on its heels came Mercury in the form of the Prof's Personal Assistant, James Tuck, who was to join us later. His message was that this demonstration would be a matter of life or death for M.D.1. which is what I had guessed anyhow. It seemed that the report written by Lucas was even more damning than the Prof. had given me to believe. In brief, it said that in his opinion our work was of no value at all, the weapons we had designed were useless, and that the establishment was badly run — obviously a dig at me.

I soon discovered that Lucas had a nasty suspicious mind, and that was why he had postponed the demonstration. He insisted that at it we must use only guns, ammunition and devices supplied from Ordnance stores. The inference was that we would use only our own stores, give them a 100 per cent inspection, and make absolutely sure that everything was perfect. This was precisely what I had arranged and I had had people working all night on this particular job. I began to think Lucas and I should swap jobs as we seemed to think a bit alike.

The demonstration took place in due course on the Monday. I cannot do better than quote the entry in my diary. It reads: 'Very successful demo. indeed at Risboro. P.M., Beaverbrook, Cherwell, C-in-C HF (Commander in Chief Home Forces, General Alanbrooke, D of A (Director of Artillery, General Clarke,) Lucas, etc., present. Lucas had to climb right down. Bombard, MkI and MkII STs demonstrated — also Jefferis Shoulder Gun. D of A laid on a Hawkins Grenade demo. to follow. Flop. Macrae asked D of A about Mk II ST. Told to submit it to Ordnance Board. Woodhall CSD (Chief Superintendent of Design), who was there, asked for it to go through him.

'Jefferis, Farrant, Macrae, Angier and Faber had meeting in afternoon. Farrant threatened to resign if Jefferis could not be persuaded that we could not continue to contemplate working under Lucas. Jefferis persuaded. Proposals drafted for submission to Cherwell.'

The next day, Millis and I went to see the Prof. and I again put forward my proposals for M.D.1. to be run entirely by the Ministry of Defence. They were sympathetically received. But two days later the Prof. advised me that the P.M. had turned down this idea and said we must stay under MOS. It was one of his mistakes. The Ministry of Defence had to be brought into full being after the war and it would have been useful to plant the acorn then.

I was advised that a contract for another half million Sticky Bombs was being placed, which seemed to indicate that Lucas was a bit wrong in suggesting that our work was of no value and that the weapons we designed were useless. After that there was a fearful anti-climax. Day after day we were expecting news of some sort but nothing whatever happened. In the meantime we were going from success to success. All of us were rushing round the country trying to catch up on the time we had lost doing this political work and running special demonstrations. I had to dash up to Glasgow to demonstrate our gear to a Special Forces unit before they sailed off to somewhere or other with it because everyone else was away.

More trials and demonstrations were being fixed every day. The 29 mm Spigot Mortar was to be demonstrated at Bisley in a very big way indeed to a vast collection of Army VIPs. This was arranged through the War Office. Then Lucas came into the picture. By now he did not like us at all. He ruled that some Ministry of Supply department should give the demonstration. The show was off one day and on the next. We were in on it one day and out the next. At last on Tuesday December 9, 1941 the demonstration was held. M.D.1. was permitted to take no part in it officially, but unofficially at the request of the War Office we had provided most of the ammunition because the MOS had slipped up on the job. We were allowed to have Captain Faber there as an observer and the Prof. decided to attend. Lucas could not stop that.

Next day I had phone calls from first the Prof. and Lord Melchett to tell me that the demonstration had been a roaring success. That was good. It encouraged Melchett to see the Chief of the Imperial General Staff at the War Office and tell him that M.D.1. was doing such good work that he should oppose any move to curb our activities. But no such move seemed to be going on now. On Monday, December 15, Millis and I went over to Marlow, where the Prof. had one of his headquarters, at his request to discuss with him starting work on several new projects. It rather looked as if we were back to normal. We then had satisfactory tests at Bisley of Millis's new shoulder gun, to be described later, and at Aldershot Norman Angier successfully demonstrated our new hollow charges, also to be described later. We had a happy Christmas although we had to keep going flat out all the time.

Evidently the Prof. had quite forgiven Millis for thinking of disaffection for, in the Birthday Honours List, it was stated that he had been awarded a CBE — which is quite a good one to get. I had known all about this because the Prof. had asked me to write the citation some time back — in fact just about the time the Beaverbrook trouble started. So it was pretty decent of the Prof. to let the recommendation go through. In due course, we gave a party in Aylesbury in honour of Lt-Colonel M.R. Jefferis, CBE, MC and, Mrs Jefferis which was attended by all the officers and senior

140

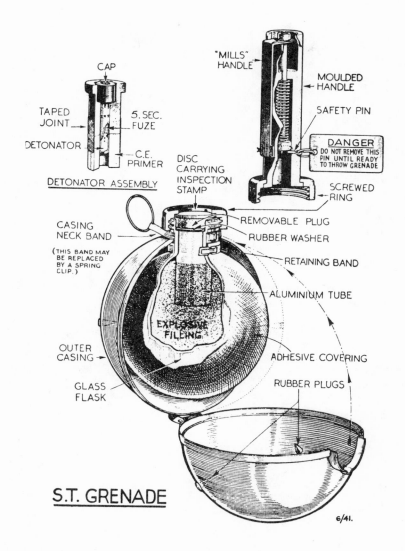

CAP

TAPED JOINT

DETONATOR

5. SEC. FUZE

C.E. PRIMER

DETONATOR ASSEMBLY

"MILLS" HANDLE

MOULDED HANDLE

SAFETY PIN

DANGER
DO NOT REMOVE THIS PIN UNTIL READY TO THROW GRENADE

SCREWED RING

DISC CARRYING INSPECTION STAMP

CASING NECK BAND

(THIS BAND MAY BE REPLACED BY A SPRING CLIP.)

REMOVABLE PLUG

RUBBER WASHER

RETAINING BAND

ALUMINIUM TUBE

EXPLOSIVE FILLING

OUTER CASING

ADHESIVE COVERING

GLASS FLASK

RUBBER PLUGS

S.T. GRENADE

6/41.

This exploded drawing of the Sticky Bomb is of the MK I version, using an explosive container made of glass, whereas the MK II and MK III versions used a plastic moulding. Modifications were also introduced in the firing mechanism to obviate the possibility of misfiring.

A War Office photograph of the P.I.A.T. in action. The tank has received a direct hit, and is "brewing up". *Left:* P.I.A.T. gunner on the Fifth Army front.

executives at The Firs together with Lt-Colonel Blacker and Captain Clarke.

Time marched on and nothing happened on the political front. Millis was bringing Lord Melchett more closely into our activities and having contrived for him as ICI to make all the ammunition for the 29 mm spigot mortar he had now brought him in on the new Shoulder Gun which looked like being a winner. Melchett was so impressed with M.D.1. that he came up with a plan for turning us into a civilian establishment and making us one of ICI's Research and Development places. This way too we should have lost our independence so I disliked the idea, but it did not come to anything.

On March 15 1942 the Prof. told me that my plan to have M.D.1. taken over by the Ministry of Defence was being given favourable consideration again although it had previously been rejected by the P.M. Nothing came of this, however, and there were signs that the MOS takeover bidding was about to start up again. By now I was getting tired of living on the edge of a precipice and decided I must give the situation more thought. The vulnerability of M.D.1. was all too obvious. When we had been made an establishment I quite thought that we would be as safe as houses. But I now realised that in government circles establishments counted for very little and could be tossed about between the various Ministries like ping pong balls. A careful study of the rules of the game showed me that to attain any degree of security M.D.1. must be upgraded and become a Directorate — a Grade B one for a start. So I got out a plan on these lines and presented it to the Prof. He fell for this one immediately, and on March 17, 1942 I had to see Sir Edward Bridges, secretary of the War Cabinet and Sir William Douglas, secretary of the Ministry of Supply and put my proposals to them. The Prof. then talked to Sir Andrew Duncan, Minister of Supply, and told me afterwards that he had sold him the idea.

I said nothing to Millis about this for a day or two in case it started him off on the Beaverbrook trail again. But I did tell him the whole story when a suitable opportunity arose. Surprisingly enough he seemed to be fully in favour of the idea. Maybe this was because I told him that if it went through he would become Director M.D.1. and be promoted to the rank of Brigadier. Millis was not in any way ambitious and so far as I know never in his life made a move to promote his own interests. But for anyone who was spending his whole life in the Army to be promoted from Lt-Colonel to Brigadier just like that could not fail to be an attraction.

A fortnight later, the Prof. told me that Duncan had now rather turned against the Directorate idea and that to strengthen his own hand he had asked the P.M. to write an official minute stating that he, the Prof., was to control M.D.1. For although the P.M. had asked him to do this, the fact had never been put in writing. This was a good move. Next the Prof. told me that he had persuaded the P.M. to write to Duncan asking him to make M.D.1. a Directorate.

However, more internal arguments went on and it was not until April 10 that the Prof. was able to tell me that both Duncan and Rootes had at last agreed to our becoming a Directorate and were delaying the issue of an official notification to this effect only because they did not like to issue it without first showing it to Lucas, who was away.

At last, on April 27, 1942, the Prof. came to Whitchurch to see me and show me the new deal papers signed by Duncan and Bridges. A summary of the decisions was as follows:

1. M.D.1. to become a Directorate Grade B.
2. Jefferis to be promoted to the rank of Brigadier and appointed Director.
3. Lord Cherwell to be in control of M.D.1. We were to report only to him and he would pass on information to Duncan when necessary.
4. Instead of having to deal with a number of different branches at the Ministry of Supply the Deputy Director of Technical Administration, Major Sumner, would now handle all our business for us. (This was a great blessing from my point of view.)
5. In future we could deal direct with the Ministry of Works over building matters and need not go through the Ministry of Supply.
6. We were authorised to continue with our production work but should consult the MOS over the placing of outside contracts.
7. Other upgradings would be considered.

There was no doubt about it, the Prof. had done a good job of work here. The immediate result so far as I was concerned was that Brigadier Hogg summoned me to see him. He had of course heard about this Directorate move earlier on although he did not know that I was responsible for making it and had assured me it would never go through. Now he had a copy of this official order from

Duncan in front of him and was very put out. What obviously annoyed him was that Millis, whom he never liked, was suddenly to be jumped up to equal rank with himself. However, he said that what he wanted to see me about was the other upgradings referred to in the paper. He could deal only with the military side, but what he proposed was to make me Deputy Director with the rank of full Colonel and leave the other officers as they were.

Now this would not do at all. I must admit that the idea of getting my red tabs and additional pay was attractive. But as the instigator of this new deal I could not possibly put myself in the position of being the only one to get promotion out of it apart from Millis. Being put in such a position would make me extremely unpopular with those who might consider they had been done down and make it very difficult for me to go on running the place by kindness rather than discipline — which was the only way I could do it. I pointed out to the Brigadier that with the present establishment we had a Superintentendent (Millis), a Deputy Superintendent (me) and two Assistant Superintendents (Ralph Farrant and Norman Angier.) Although in theory I should as Deputy Superintendent be one rank above the Assistant Superintendents I was not and did not want to be. So how about in the new set-up promoting me to Lt-Colonel only and doing the same with Ralph Farrant so that the status quo was preserved. As Norman Angier was a civilian, rank did not come into it for him but being made an Assistant Director would give him the same promotion as it would give us.

To my surprise, Hogg would not listen to this suggestion at all. He said that in no circumstances would he agree to Farrant's promotion and that he proposed to go ahead on the lines he had told me. Millis's promotion to Brigadier came through on May 12 and then there was silence from Hogg's office until I heard from him that after considering my request he had decided to promote me only to Lt-Colonel and make me the Assistant Director. He could not promote Major Farrant, who would have to be Deputy Assistant Director. It began to look as if my machinations were doing nobody but Millis any good which I supposed served me right. I wrote to the Brigadier telling him that I could not accept promotion if it were not given to Farrant as well and received a curt note in reply telling me I would have no choice in the matter.

There was a lull for over a month. Then Hogg came out to Whitchurch to discuss the matter with me and I managed to get the

Prof. to be present. Hogg stuck to his guns, and in fact fired anti-personnel rounds from them. I was to be the only Assistant Director. Ralph Farrant was to be a Deputy Assistant Director and Norman Angier was to be called the Superintendent. Even the Prof. failed to move him and could only ask him to defer taking action.

Action was deferred all right for three weeks. Then came Hogg's notice regarding military promotions. I was appointed Assistant Director, M.D.1. with the rank of Lt-Colonel. Major Farrant was appointed Deputy Assistant Director and retained the rank of Major. Captain Clarke (who was now with M.D.1.) was promoted to the rank of Major. Captain Faber was to be Staff Captain.

I did not show this piece of paper to anybody but handed it to Millis. As I expected, he was furious and said he would not accept these rulings. Farrant must be promoted. I offered to say nothing about my promotion for the time being and give him a chance to sort things out. Off he went the next day to contrive a high powered meeting with General Jacob at the War Cabinet, Sir William Douglas and Brigadier Hogg. I should never have allowed Millis to negotiate on his own. He returned to Whitchurch with the air of a man who had won a great victory and explained to Farrant, Angier and myself that he had agreed we should all be on a level and called Assistant Controllers, none of us getting any promotion at all. He was most surprised when all three of us turned on him and told him he had made a mess of the whole business, Mark you, Ralph and I had to be a bit careful because a Brigadier is a long way above mere Majors.

The next day, the three of us bludgeoned Millis into writing to Douglas saying he had decided against this idea of having three Assistant Controllers and must have instead a Deputy Director and two Assistant Directors as first suggested. We got the Prof. to approve this letter to give it a bit of weight and I delivered it to Douglas myself. He listened to all my arguments after reading it and then said as the whole matter had been settled it could not be re-opened so I had better tear up the letter. I said that as the Prof. had approved it, I could not do that and went away.

Fortunately, Brigadier Hogg had that very day published my promotion in his Part 2 orders and it could of course not be rescinded so this threw the whole matter into the melting-pot again. A day or two later, the civilian side of the MOS notified me of Norman Angier's appointment as Assistant Director. That left only Ralph Farrant to be dealt with, for Hogg still refused to promote him. All

I could do was to start a separate campaign over this issue, enlisting the help of the Prof. He finally went to the P.M. about it and Ralph got his promotion by the end of the year.

At last all our establishment problems were solved and we could get down to work again. There was no way in which Millis could upset the applecart any more and so far as I know he did not try to do so. We remained a Grade B Directorate until 1945 and were then translated into a Grade A one through a curious happening. General Hobart, said to be the only General to be twice bowler-hatted and who had been brought back by the P.M., had created the 59th Armoured Division consisting of 'funnies' — queer machines of all kinds for use in the coming invasion. Naturally we had contributed to his collection, notably with a rocket-operated tank bridge thought up by Nobby Clarke. We also had tank ploughs and a few other pieces of equipment on the stocks at Whitchurch.

As Whitchurch was now running on rails and could do without me, I thought it about time I had a look at the war and persuaded Joe Holland, who was now Engineer-in-Chief at the War Office, to recommend me to Hobart as his CREME (Commander, Royal Electrical and Mechanical Engineers) although that was not my corps.

The last time I had asked Joe Holland for a transfer was in my early days at the War Office when the Lt-Colonel who was heading a Military Mission to Singapore said he would like me as his second-in-command — which meant promotion from Captain to Major. When I approached Joe about this he was indignant. 'I thought better of you, Bobby,' he said. 'You are doing an honest job of work here and now you are suggesting going into retirement for the remainder of the war. I know somebody has to go to live peacefully in Singapore but I would rather it were not you. You content yourself with providing the Mission with your booby traps and things.'

Joe was perfectly right to stop me going, but his reason was wrong. Those who accompanied this ill-fated Military Mission went into retirement all right, or most of them did. The Japs arrived there at the same time that they did and promptly put them in the bag.

On this later occasion, Joe entirely agreed that it was time I stopped trying to blow myself up and had a go at the enemy. He gave me the recommendation and I think I might have got the job, for Millis would have waved me good-bye quite cheerfully. But the Prof. got wind of this and stopped the move. He now had the idea that what he regarded as his own pet establishment would fall to pieces without me, which was very flattering.

To return to General Hobart, he was a great martinet. I was present at his base at Orfordness on several occasions when he was about to make an inspection. The tension was terrific. Officers would stand around restlessly. Then about four outriders on motorcycles would appear followed by a fleet of cars. When they stopped, the General would descend from one of them with his Chief of Staff on his right and some other high ranking officer on his left. They would march forward in line in a most aggressive manner and the inspection would begin.

One day, General Hobart elected to visit Whitchurch to talk to Millis and inspect some of our 'funnies'. His cavalcade arrived late and he was in a bad temper. Generals were now ten a penny so far as I was concerned so I had made no special arrangements for his reception. In fact I had forgotten to advise the guard he was coming, so he was held up a few minutes at the gate until I got him cleared. He then bawled out Millis on the grounds that as a mere Brigadier he was not paying proper respect to a Major-General and a bad time was had by all.

Millis seemed to take this to heart a bit, although I accepted the blame, and complained to the Prof. about it. The Prof. went right up in the air. His pet had been grossly insulted and he would not not stand for it. If Generals were going to override Millis then the only answer was to make him a General too, but he did not know how to go about it. Had I any suggestions?

I had. Having studied Kings Regulations and other similar works during the past years the problem was no problem at all to me. All that had to be done, I told the Prof., was to upgrade M.D.1. from a Grade B Directorate to a Grade A one. The director then automatically became a Major-General. The Prof. thought this was a fine idea, and asked me to prepare the necessary paperwork right away. This time he encountered little opposition having induced the P.M. to to write a minute supporting the plan and in hardly any time at all Ruth was busy sewing crossed swords and pips, again the wrong way up, on Millis's uniforms and I was acquiring a red hatband and red tabs. For this time I did not argue about my promotion. I was told that as Deputy Director of a Grade A Directorate I should be a Brigadier and would be made one in due course. But the war finished first.

13

Some Little Weapons

Let it not be thought that the political activities discussed in the preceding chapter hindered our other work. This was not so. Hardly a day passed without our starting on some new project. I will describe later on a selection of the weapons large and small which we perfected. But first let me tell the story of the 'L' Delay which was conceived back at the War Office long before our Whitchurch troubles began and on the strength of which we were able to start our factory.

There was an urgent demand for a small delay action fuse for demolition work, booby traps and that sort of thing. It must be simple and small. Clockwork mechanisms were ruled out first because they were too elaborate and secondly because clocks are liable to stop, especially if they are roughly treated. The only device of this sort on the market at the start of the war was one called a Time Pencil produced by our Cloak and Dagger friends in great quantity. This Time Pencil was nice and small — about the size of a present day ball-point pen. And it did work to some extent. But it was a very dodgy device indeed and one had to be very brave to use it.

It consisted of a tube holding a spring loaded striker which when released would hit a cap and fire it to initiate detonation. The striker was anchored to the top end of the tube by means of a thin steel wire Running alongside this wire was a fragile glass capsule containing cupric chloride or some acid or other. When this top end of the tube was squashed between finger and thumb — and it was very thin so as to be readily squashable — the capsule was broken and the released fluid would start to attack the steel wire and eventually weaken it to such an extent that it would break and the device would fire. The trouble was that how long this process would take was almost anybody's guess.

No attempt could be made to calibrate these time fuses in hours.

147

They could only be identified with colour bands which indicated that they should go off within a few hours, a fair number of hours, or a lot of hours. And the situation was complicated by the fact that they had a terrific temperature coefficient. In very hot weather a theoretically long delay fuse might go off in a few minutes. In very cold weather it might not go off at all.

A safety pin was provided to interfere with the striker and the idea was that, when using the fuse, the tube should be squashed and then one waited a while before withdrawing the safety pin in case the wire went too quickly. The fact remained that this safety pin had to be withdrawn sooner or later and this operation was not a popular one, particularly with me. One might choose just the wrong moment and get blown up.

Undoubtedly these Time Pencils did good work and I am not running them down in any way at all. But there seemed to be room for improvement here. For that matter, there was room for improvement in the delay fuses used in aircraft bombs which worked in rather similar fashion and relied on acetone eating through a celluloid disc. This was just the kind of problem which appealed to Millis and he decided to give it thought. Quite quickly he came up with an answer which nobody else would have thought of in years. It was a true inspiration. He had read somewhere that lead covered cables were troublesome because the lead crept and increased in length. He decided that this phenomenon was worth investigating and hied himself off to the Non-Ferrous Metals Research Association headquarters at Euston where he found a Dr. McKeown very ready to talk to him.

Of course it was a bit shattering for a fellow who had devoted a lot of time to trying to produce lead which would not creep to be asked to produce some that did — and did it with some degree of regularity. But McKeown faced up to the situation and soon found that if he used lead from Broken Hills Mines with a 5 per cent tellurium content for making lead rods and took trouble to see that the grain ran the right way he could get a reasonably good reproducible performance from it. The next thing to do was to find the best way of making use of this discovery. One could arrange for one or more lead pins to be subjected to a shearing load which would cut them through in time. Or the lead might be subjected to tension and pulled until it broke. The question was who could be found to experiment with this idea, for BNFRA were not laid out for doing this sort of thing. And here we were lucky. It was just at this time that I had been able to enlist the help of the IBC workshops and when I offered the job to Norman Angier he was delighted. This was just the odd type of thing which appealed to him.

The road was long and weary. Various designs were tried out, and to do this we had to equip the place with a number of test rigs fitted with electric clocks. The trouble here is that, if you want a seven day delay, it takes seven days to test it. We had moved out to Whitchurch before we brought the experiments to a satisfactory conclusion. In the meantime, though, this brain wave of Millis had been put to good use for releasing sinkers on our 'W' bombs and replaced a soluble pellet.

The sinker was merely anchored to the body of the bomb at its base by three of our little lead rods which were poked through horizontally disposed holes in a ring which surrounded the sinker to engage holes in the sinker itself and then locked in place. The weight of the sinker took the bomb to the bottom of the river where it settled. But the mine itself having positive buoyance was anxious to rise again and this put a strain on the lead rods. Gradually they would bend until the mine was permitted to come adrift. As the temperature of the water was reasonably constant it was not difficult to design the device to give release in round about the time required, which might be of the order of one hour.

In the end, for the pencil-sized fuse, we had to choose between three designs. The most promising seemed to be one in which we had a little lead dumbbell made by turning down a neck in our special one quarter inch diameter lead rod. Brass holders were pinned to each end of the dumbbell. The top one was secured to an outer tube whilst the bottom one had attached to it a tension spring which was stretched and terminated in another brass holder which could be secured to the tube. A striker pin ran from the centre of the bottom lead holder part of the way down the tube. When the lead was subjected to tension through the influence of the spring it would gradually stretch at the neck until breaking point was reached. The striker would then be pulled down by the spring to pass through a hole in the bottom spring holder and fire a cap unit which was crimped in to the bottom of the tube.

There had to be a starting-pin, one that would keep the lead from being subjected to any load at all until it was withdrawn. That was easy enough. It could run through transverse holes in the outer tube

149

and one through the bottom lead holder. However, it would be unfortunate if something went wrong — the lead element being accidentally omitted or something of that sort — so that when the pin was pulled out the device at once fired. But we got over that one by devising a shaped pin which, when pulled, would at the start of its travel allow the load to be applied to the lead but would be trapped and would not be released if the bottom lead holder shifted at all. A safety feature of this sort had to be included in all our booby traps.

After a great deal of experimental work, we got this device working quite well. We wanted to make a series of these delays offering timings ranging from one hour to one month. The delay period could be varied in two ways — by altering the size of the neck portion of the lead or by altering the tension of the spring. It was not difficult to establish the most suitable values here but there was another problem. Like the Time Pencil, but not to the same extent, our lead delay fuse was seriously affected by temperature. All we could do here was to find out what the variations were through the temperature range, label each delay 'I hour at 70 degrees F or 30 days at 70 degrees F as the case might be, and supply a table showing how these and the other delays in the range would behave at other temperatures. We maintained that if the user were a good guesser or carried a pocket computer he should be able to pick the winning fuse for his operation every time.

By now, the requirement for a new delay had quickly become very urgent. Unfortunately although we had decided to favour the design described we had continued to experiment with the other two, the idea being that a stage might eventually be reached when we could pick the winner. I ruled that we could wait no longer and must settle the matter that very day; therefore the only answer was to go ahead and adopt this first design, forgetting the others.

This was the first row I had with Norman although not quite the last. But once he had given way, he played the game and went flat out to try to meet my programme. Later on, we did experiment a bit more with the other two versions and found that they were not so good as the one we had chosen so that put the matter right. We now concentrated on turning out small batches of these delays by hand for officials trials and getting out production drawings. In due course the design was accepted and we were asked to supply these delay fuses — we now called them 'L' Delays — in large numbers.

None of our own contractors was equipped to turn out a tricky device of this sort so we asked the MOS for help, providing them with samples, drawings and all relevant information. Several weeks later they came back with the sad news they could find no firm at all willing to tackle this job and ruled that the design was an impracticable one. Naturally we were not standing for that. We said that if nobody else could be found to produce this 'L' delay in quantity we would do the job ourselves, and proceeded to get on with it. Automatic lathes and second operation machines were acquired and installed very quickly. Benches sprang up, and elaborate inspection and test equipment was rigged up. Some local labour was recruited and our factory was in being.

We then had to admit that things were not all they seemed and that there was some justification for the MOS failing to find a manufacturer for our device. Innumerable problems arose. To turn down the neck in the lead rod to within the essential limits of plus or minus one tenth of one thousandth of an inch was not all that difficult to do slowly, which is why we had had no trouble on this score when making our samples. But to turn these units out quickly was quite another matter. Once they had been turned out, the trouble was how to gauge them for accuracy. And then this matter of spring loading was absolutely critical and nobody could be found who could supply us with springs of guaranteed loadings — for example a tension spring which when extended to a length of exactly four inches would offer a pull of exactly six ounces. It just could not be done.

I could now quite understand why no firm wanted this job — they just would not have the technicians who could solve these problems. We had them. Norman Angier, who headed the team, was pretty hot at this sort of thing. Leslie Gouldstone proved to be an absolute genius at contriving clever fixtures for both the manufacture and testing of the devices. Norman's brother Eric, who was also with us, could make any piece of machinery almost sit up and beg for work whilst a draughtsman we acquired, Jimmy Bacon, knew all about cam design for the automatics. Added to that, we had Smith and Wilson both anxious and able to help when help was needed. I kept out of this one and managed to get Millis to do the same. Such work was above our fighting class.

Little CAV second operation machines were used for turning the lead necks. Moving the cross slide one way brought in a steel tool for a comparatively rough cut: moving it the other way brought in a diamond tool for the finishing cut. The entire operation took no

151

more than 10 seconds and provided the machine was allowed to warm up for five minutes before work was started the necessary accuracy was achieved. But the next thing was to measure this lead neck to make certain it had been achieved.

By now the MOS was trying to help us by sending out expert advisers to talk to us about our problems. The gauging boys shook their heads sadly. There was only one possible way to inspect and check these units they told us and that was with comparators. With these instruments, which have to be used in a darkened room, a greatly magnified outline of the device to be checked is thrown on a screen. There are other outlines showing the extent to which an increase or decrease of the critical dimensions can be permitted, in fact one can have several such outlines if desired. A magnified image of the component under inspection is then offered up to them and it is not difficult to see if it comes within the limits.

We started three or four little girls with these comparators. They did the job all right, but tended to go mad after staring at the things for an hour or so. Their output was hopeless. It looked as if we should need about 50 little girls with comparators to keep up with five little girls on the lead-turning machines. Norman was in despair. He rang up the MOS experts to say how about orthodox 'Go' and 'No Go' gauges. They assured him that they would be of no use at all for this purpose when we were dealing with a soft metal such as lead and required such great accuracy.

This encouraged Norman a bit, for he had never known Ministry experts to be right to date. He went off and bought some Brown and Sharpe micrometers and had them fitted with great big dials calibrated in tens of thousandths of an inch. Two of these instruments were placed on a stand by each lead-turning machine and set and locked in place by Leslie Gouldstone. On completing a lead unit, the operator would merely offer it up very gently to the 'Go' and 'No Go' gauges and if it failed either she just threw it into a disposal bin. This extra operation added only five seconds to the time cycle for this particular job and we had an inspected unit. The comparator girls were delighted to be put on other work. And the method was such a success that we practically never had a 'L' Delay bad time performance through the lead not being to size.

We did run into another problem with the lead, though. It had to be pinned to the top holder, which meant drilling through holder and lead. As production was stepped up and we had more little girls engaged on drilling and pinning, discrepancies in performance started to crop up and more and more units had to be scrapped through the 5 per cent test failures. For always we tested 5 per cent of each batch produced and if they did not pass the tests the entire batch was condemned.

This trouble was traced quite quickly. Drilling the lead could work harden it so that it took longer to stretch and break. The solution was merely a matter of laying down a drilling drill. The speed of the drill had to be just right and the operator had to take three bites at the cherry.

I believe it was Leslie Gouldstone who solved the spring problem, but one of the others may have helped him. His argument was that if it is difficult to obtain springs that comply to our specification, why bother about it? The object of the exercise is to ensure that when the starting pin of the device is pulled out the prescribed load will be applied to the lead. Easy! All that is necessary is to have a little length to spare in the outer tube, arrange for a rod carrying the pre-scribed weight to screw into the bottom spring holder, set up the unit so that the weight extends the spring to its limit, and then secure the holder to the outer tube. If a six ounce weight is used, the spring load on the lead when the starting pin is removed must be six ounces and no more or no less.

He was dead right, of course. And he devised a nice little floating crimping fixture which registered with the spring holder inside the tube. When the weight had settled down, all the operator had to do was to pull a lever to anchor the spring holder in place. Leslie was great on crimping and put the whole thing together this way.

There was one other problem to be solved. BNFRA could supply us with this special lead rod which would give a stable performance but could not guarantee what that performance would be. With one batch of rods, for instance, if the lead were necked down to say one eighth of an inch and a spring loading of eight ounces were used the delay time at 70F might be three hours — with another batch it might be two hours or four hours. I never quite understood how they got over this one. All I know is that Norman Angier did a lot of mathematical work and came up with a collection of tables, graphs and what nots. After that it was all simple. When a new batch of lead arrived, Leslie would allocate it a number, pinch a couple of rods out of the stack, and retire with them to his strictly private testing sanctum. Here he would perform certain mystic rites and from the information thus obtained would be able to list precisely what spring loadings and neck sizes were needed to produce delays of the required timings from this batch of lead. All that remained was for him to decide what he would first make from it — that could be perhaps 1,000 7-day delays for a start — and then go round altering the settings of the lead-turning machines and gauges and adjusting the weights on the assembly fixtures.

This 'L' Delay was a startling success. The Ordnance Board adopted it, called it Switch No 9, and ruled that it was the only type of delay to be used in future for demolition work. Although we produced over five million of these devices at Whitchurch — we remained the sole producers throughout the war — and they were used everywhere in the world, there was not a single report of a failure with them or an accident. Maybe I should qualify that. With our first issues we were using ordinary percussion caps and there were one or two misfires. After we changed over to 1.7 grain detonators with needle strikers — a system developed by M.D.1. and then used in all our booby trap devices — we had no cases at all of misfiring.

There is a sad end to this story. When the war was over and at last M.D.1. was to be closed down, there were such large stocks of 'L' Delays that it was obvious that nobody would want any more for a while. But they would in a few years' time. I pointed this out to the Ministry of Supply and also pointed out that, whereas we had the complete set-up and know-how for making these devices, nobody else had a clue as to how to go about the job. Would they therefore please either keep the Whitchurch factory in being — by now I had it doing work for industry and running at a profit — or transfer all the equipment to the works of one of their approved contractors. Leslie Gouldstone would then show them how the job was done.

I had no influence at all with the MOS at this stage and neither had the Prof., for he was out of office. My pleas were disregarded and the whole of this special equipment was loaded into trucks and thrown on the scrap heap. About three years later the Ministry — or it may have been the War Office again by then — decided to re-start manufacture of 'L' Delays. They placed a contract with a firm who had to start from scratch as we had done. After a long time they got into some sort of production but they were working on quite the wrong lines and the devices they made proved to be unsatisfactory. I suppose it did not matter much because at this time nobody wanted delay

154

action fuses. But this stupidity must have cost the taxpayer hundreds of thousands of pounds and it resulted in the Services being deprived of one of the most successful war devices ever to be made.

Oddly enough, our next best seller was the Clam — my pocket version of the Limpet. It seemed to fascinate people. When I gave Joe Holland one of the first samples he refused to part with it and was always planking it on to metal objects in his office. For the Cloak and Dagger boys it was God's Gift from Heaven. They could carry these things in their pockets and just stick them on to something they would like to blow up. Although the explosive content was only around 8 ounces, ICI produced some very high speed stuff for us and the design was such that the explosive was almost in contact with the target over a considerable area. A Clam could put any motor vehicle engine out of commission or an aero engine for that matter. But its success was dependant on the use of the 'L' Delay which was made part of it. If operators had had to use it with a Time Pencil they would not have been so enthusiastic about it. My diary is full of notes of people squealing for Clams. The Russians had nearly a million of them and were always asking for more. The total number of Clams made under M.D.1. surveillance during the war was over two and a half million.

Our Aero Switch was another roaring success. Nobby Clarke when he was at the Station XVII got the idea for this one and came over to Whitchurch to see me about it. What was wanted was a small sabotage device which could be inserted into a German bomber by some brave fellow and would explode when the aircraft reached a certain height and cripple it. I called in Smith and Wilson on this one. A week later I found that in their design den they had installed a couple of vacuum pumps and other paraphernalia and were busy playing with expanding metal bellows. The final device was extremely neat and efficient. Inside a tubular plastic container they had an exhausted metal bellows with a compression spring inside. At atmospheric pressure this would be in the fully collapsed state. At reduced atmospheric pressure, the bellows would expand. At their centre was a platinum contact which would eventually meet another one to complete an electrical circuit.

The unit included a small dry battery and the usual explosive train — an electrical 'puffer' inserted in a No 8 detonator with a primer for luck. Attached to this was a rubber tube containing about 1lb of plastic explosive. Satisfactory operation was dependant on

155

ensuring that a fair degree of travel was needed to close the contacts, for it was not possible or rather practicable to make the device adjustable so that the operator could set it to zero to suit an airport which might be well above sea level. We decided that the minimum 'safe' height for the device to function was 10,000 feet and this called for a travel of three-sixteenths of an inch before the contacts met. I do not know how Smith and Wilson worked all this out but they did.

As we always looked after the welfare of our saboteurs we added the usual safety pin, which in this case took the form of a plastic strip with a slot down its middle, the strip passing through slots in the outer casing to interpose itself between the contacts. If the bellows had sprung a leak or something of that sort the contact affixed to them would enter this slot and prevent the safety strip from being withdrawn. So the saboteur was on a pretty good wicket.

Nobby Clarke's contribution to this sabotage device was to insist that it should have a flexible sausage of explosive. At his Station XVII at Hertford his job was to train saboteurs and he gave great thought to their modus operandi. In this instance he had worked out that such a weapon as this could not be conveniently concealed in the pocket but could without comment be carried in the trousers. He was wrong about the 'without comment' and there was always considerable ribaldry when he demonstrated this method to his pupils. But actually it was sound common sense and I believe they all adopted it.

In due course we went into production at Whitchurch with this Aero Switch and made and issued many thousands of them. Later by special request we managed to get the operational height down to 5,000 feet without sacrificing the saboteur's safety. The usual drill was to make a slit in the wing fabric of a German bomber and pop this thing inside so that in due course the wing would be wrecked and the bomber likewise. It was very satisfying for me one day to receive a signal via the Air Ministry saying that the previous night the entire Luftwaffe bombing fleet about to set out for London had been grounded whilst a search was carried out for this sabotage weapon which had already caused them too many casualties. When I next saw my wife I told her this with great pride, only to be informed that she knew all about it because she had handled the message at Bletchley Park but was not permitted to tell me about it.

The trouble about making special weapons of this sort and dishing them out to countries all over the world is that when the war is over you cannot get them back again. So sooner or later some unauthorised person is likely to use them. It has been proved that Limpets have been used to sink Israeli ships. Israeli aircraft have also been sabotaged through mysterious explosions. The experts have maintained that the Arabs are not competent to manufacture an atmospheric switch of any sort for this purpose but I am afraid they must be competent to find aero switches. We had to send so many to the Middle East.

There was always a great demand for anti-personnel devices and right from the start Millis had played around with what he called a pedestrian dart. This contrivance was quite small and consisted in the main of a cone-shaped metal body carrying a little high explosive and means for setting it off when the device was trodden on. The idea was to scatter these things from aircraft when they were supposed to embed themselves in tracks and lurk there unobserved until enemies trod upon them. The embedding was the trouble. The device had to to be designed so that it would fly straight like a dart and enter the ground just far enough without breaking up when dropped from a height.

Testing the experimental models was troublesome because it meant going up in aeroplanes which were not easy to get because they were all on war work. This problem Millis threw over to me and I threw it over to Gordon Norwood. He solved it quite simply by hiring Battersea gasholder, the top of which is 320 feet above ground level. Armed with a lot of these darts we set off one bright morning and ascended this gas holder. I was relieved to find that there was a lift to take us up to the top, but by the time it decanted me there I found I had lost my head for heights, if any.

It seemed safe enough when one was standing in the middle of the large steel circular platform which constituted the top. It was when I peered over the slender railing that ran round the edge that I felt dizzy. The thought of having to lean over this rail with arm outstretched dropping darts was distinctly unattractive to me and I was wondering how to get out of it with dignity. But I need not have worried. Gordon scampered about pitching these things overboard, and nearly going overboard himself in his anxiety to see them land, without any sign of concern. The explanation, I found, was that one of his hobbies was mountaineering.

This pedestrian dart never came to anything in the end, mainly because the A.P. switch I described earlier on served the same purpose more effectively and could be installed by anyone without an aeroplane. But the A.P. switch was too humane a weapon for our bloodthirsty warriors, who maintained that shooting a man through the foot did not put him out of action for long enough. The argument that he might well be shot through other places in addition was not accepted. What was wanted was a little mine filled with high explosive which would blow up the unfortunate soldier who trod on it.

I learnt about this requirement through reading 'Ordnance Board Proceedings' — an excellent periodical which purported to give reports on the Board's deliberations and in which was published minutes from all departments concerned when there was any discussion about some weapon or device. Needless to say, almost every issue of 'O.B.Procs' was soon carrying special features signed D.M.D.1. or more frequently D.D. M.D.1. But its real value to us was that we could learn what the other design departments were setting out to do and jump in ahead of them if we felt so inclined. It was rather like stealing candy from a kid, but we felt it was up to us to make the best use of ourselves and our unique facilities.

For many weeks now there had been lengthy discussions going on in this publication about what form this little anti-personnel mine should take and how it should be made. Every so often the official design department would pop up with another prototype which somebody would say was no good. The next effort might be all right but the MOS would say that it was a difficult production job and it would be six months before they could turn any out. These reflections would be interspersed with pleading or angry minutes from War Office sections and commanders in the field stating that the need for these anti-personnel mines was now a very great one and when could they have some?

As the booby trap king this requirement was right up my street and with the experience I had now gained I was able to knock out a suitable design right away. Within a week we were trying out live prototypes. They worked perfectly, and this was another case in which no modifications were called for even though these mines were eventually produced in millions.

The difficulty with all such things as this which probably had to be laid in a hurry was to make them completely safe for the layer. One way of doing this was to have an arming pin which could be removed by pulling a wire, the installer standing well away in case something was wrong and the mine went off. But I favoured the A.P. switch idea although I had not thought of this myself. With this, the spikes could be bashed into the ground regardless and the device was absolutely safe right up to the moment when the cartridge was carefully lowered into it. So what I wanted was a simple mine which could be put down in complete safety and become alive only when some firing mechanism was inserted.

As it would be necessary to make holes in the ground and ground augurs for making 2 inch diameter holes were in good supply I decided to have a container of this size and about 4 inches deep. It could be a tin canister with a lid or a plastic moulding but tooling up for producing such things took time. Besides, I was feeling adventurous. I decided to use cardboard, knowing that this would shock the Ordnance Board and CIA to the core — which it certainly did.

A firm called Bradstreet's which was already making cardboard packing tubes for us turned out in a couple of days some excellent little cardboard containers. They had a closed top with a hole in the centre, leading to a thin paper tube closed at the end disposed on the axis line. There was a recess at the bottom to take a plain disc which served as a closure after filling. Filling was merely a matter of dropping a standard C.E. pellet over this little tube, and then topping up with pentolite — after which the closure was put in place.

That was the mine part of the job, all ready to go. Next came the initiator. I had an idea here which I hardly dared mention and which I knew would cause trouble with the O.B. A number 8 detonator, which is a little tube one eighth of an inch in diameter by two inches long with some sensitive gubbins at the bottom of it, was what was wanted. But something had to set this off. From my study of the O.B. Procs., I knew the opposition were faced with the same problem and were trying to solve it by designing a complex trigger operated spring mechanism which would fire a percussion cap in the orthodox way. The complexity was necessary in this case because just treading on a striker and driving it into a cap this way would not fire it. A percussion cap has to be smacked — and smacked quite hard.

Here we had a big advantage. As I have mentioned, we had by now a little 1.7 grain detonator supplied to us by ICI which took up no room at all and would fire without fail when a needle was driven into it quite gently. Now this little detonator was of just the right diameter to fit the No 8 detonator and it occured to me that if we could put it there for a start we should have the neatest and smallest initiating unit yet devised with the added advantage that it could be fired so easily. But in the Ordnance world even to contemplate fixing something inside a No 8 detonator would be utter heresy. No 8 detonators, it was laid down in the safety regulations, were highly sensitive devices which must be treated with the greatest respect. Give them even a slight tap and they might go off all by themselves. This was true.

Wilson heartily agreed with me about the danger of tinkering with No 8 detonators and then set about doing just that in an intelligent manner. He anticipated the atomics boys with their now famous remote handling equipment by constructing some very simple apparatus and totally enclosing it in a large box made of thick perspex. He would insert the detonator into a special holder, close the box press button A, and a neat cannelure would be made in it one quarter of an inch below the top. He would then open the box, insert one of these 1.7 grain detonators into the tube so that it sat on the cannelure, close the box, press button B, and this time the top of the tube would be headed over to finish the job. A touch of special paint had to be added to make the device 100 per cent waterproof but this was done by hand.

The whole point was that doing it this way this dangerous operation could be carried out in complete safety. If a detonator went off during treatment that did not matter at all. Wilson had of course made his box strong enough to stand this kind of thing and fired detonators in it right at the start to make sure.

So that was that part of the job done, and it was probably the most important part. For without this contribution from Wilson the 'M' Mine would have lost some of its attractive simplicity. For a striker mechanism I adapted an idea I had seen somewhere or other. I started with a peg turned from quarter inch plastic rod. It was two inches long and one end was rounded. A one sixteenth inch blind hole was drilled into it from the other end. Into this hole went first a little compression spring and then a striker — a rod with a needle point end. This striker rod was necked down at one point. A transverse hole was drilled through the peg so positioned that the striker was held in the cocked position by two little ball bearings engaging the neck. These ball bearings were prevented from springing out by a plastic ring of 1 inch diameter and one quarter inch deep which fitted over the peg and could slide on it. They engaged a concave groove in this ring. Finally, this tiny striker mechanism weighing less than one ounce was fitted into the mine by putting the end of the peg into the quarter inch hole in the cardboard tube and lowering it until the flange rested on the top surface. The igniter unit would of course have been dropped into the tube first.

When the peg, which was hardly noticeable if the mine were properly installed and covered with a fine layer of earth, was trodden upon it would be forced down, the balls would come clear of the flange, the striker would be released, the 1.7 grain detonator of the igniter unit would be pierced and that would be that. The load required to force down the peg depended on the depth on the internal groove in the flange. We made it 1 lb so that a mouse would not set off the mine but any man would.

This simple little device was about the cleverest thing I ever helped to design. It was a classic answer to the problem. It could be turned out in vast quantity quickly, easily and cheaply — about five shillings a time against the £2 each or more for the other contemplated designs — and above all it was completely safe to install. One just drilled a lot of holes in the ground with the augur, dropped in the mines and scattered earth over them, pulled out by attached strings wooden pegs which were put into the central tubes to keep the dirt out, drop in the igniter units and then put the striker units in place. It was the easiest job in the world to do and nothing could possibly go wrong. In fact, nothing ever did. For packaging we had cardboard tubes taking five mines and a round wooden block carrying the necessary five igniter units and five striker units. Also in the package was included one of our instruction leaflets.

Well within a month of giving myself this job, I was able to submit samples of the mine complete with highly satisfactory test reports and production estimates to the Ordnance Board. But it took another three months to get the device accepted, and it only happened then because of the pressure we were able to bring to bear and the fact that the official design department had still not even got off the mark. As anticipated, the use of cardboard was regarded with horror. Yet nobody could find anything against it. It was suggested that mines made this way would prove useless if they got wet so we threw dozens of them into one of our water tanks complete with striker and igniter units. When we fished them out again a fortnight later they all functioned perfectly.

Of course we were told that the igniter unit was of impracticable design and that it would be impossible to manufacture it in quantity.

Our answer to that was that we would be happy to undertake this and later on we did. Leslie Gouldstone acquired half a dozen or so of Wilson's safety detonator fixing outfits and the six little girls operating them turned out these units at a fantastic rate without hurting themselves at all.

For a long while, not an issue of O.B. Procs. appeared in which there was not a powerful minute from D.M.D.I. urging acceptance of the 'M' mine and one or two from other people urging the opposite In the end, this was one where I had to enlist the help of the Prof., and the P.M. through him, before I could make any progress and they made me waste my time talking to a number of VIP's about it including Duncan Sandys who was now Parliamentary Secretary to the MOS and my old friend Lucas.

However, in the end the 'M' Mine was accepted and as I say M.D.1 produced literally millions, contenting ourselves with making the igniters and sub-contracting the rest of the work as we had done with the S.T. Grenade. And there was a side effect here. When the RAF approached us asking for our help in devising means for protecting their airfields by surrounding them with alarm signals of some sort this was the answer. Wilson rapidly learnt something about fireworks and we merely filled the cardboard cases with some rocket mixture instead of high explosive. Soon we simplified even this device by making the igniter unit itself a firework which when initiated would give a bright flash in a choice of several colours. The cardboard container was just left empty. It still offered the cheapest and simplest way of installing the device.

These alarm mines caught on like wildfire for protecting all kinds of installations such as camps as well as airfields. They cost only about 2/6d a time and it was so easy to put them down and leave them down. They did their job perfectly and, if any silly clot belonging to the place trod on one by mistake, no harm was done either to him or to the installation. Just drop in another igniter unit and striker and the damage was repaired. Of course I chose the title of 'M' Mine but I was not too pleased with that and considered I could have done better and thought up a descriptive one in the Limpet and Clam class given the opportunity. But unfortunately the O.B. started to refer to this device in their Proceedings as the 'Macrae Mine'. Apart from giving me publicity that I was not seeking, when this was noticed in the establishment it started to arouse feelings because the O.B. had just refused to permit one of our weapons to be named after Jefferis.

I hastily urged them to abbreviate the name to the 'M' Mine which could upset nobody and they obliged.

Another device I perpetrated through reading O.B. Procs was an anti-lift one for anti-tank mines. Apparently the Germans had something of the sort and we suffered from not having it, it being annoying if one took a lot of trouble to lay a minefield and the other fellow could just lift the mines and walk off with them. Again this need was voiced in various minutes in O.B. Procs. and again it seemed that nothing much was being done to fill it.

By this time we had such a nice selection of booby traps that it was merely a matter of seeing which one could best be modified to do this little job. The A.P. Switch lent itself to it, but of course firing a cartridge was no good and anyway it had to operate in reverse, firing not when a weight was applied to it but when one was removed from it. However, we could keep the spike which offered the very secure mounting needed for this sort of mechanism. Such booby traps must not be free to wobble about.

Actually, the Anti-Lift device was a combination of the AP Switch and the Pull Switch plus our special igniter. The head consisted of a round metal container $3''$ in diameter by $\frac{3}{4}''$ deep filled with C.E. or composition explosive to initiate the mine when it was fired. A central tube passed through this head and extended for $2\frac{1}{2}''$ into the spiked tube of an AP switch which was used for mounting. This central tube carried a spring-loaded striker identical with that used in the Pull Switch, the split tube attached to the striker head passing through a restricted orifice at the base of the tube and being secured by a $\frac{1}{8}''$ rod inserted into it.

This rod, which had a head rivetted to it, was first dropped into the tube and followed by a compression spring. Then the head tube, complete with striker held in the cocked position, was inserted and pushed home against the main compression spring. This operation resulted in the pin penetrating the split tube and securing the striker in the cocked position. Finally, a starting pin with a length of wire attached kept the head in place by passing through a split bearing formed in a flange which topped the spike tube and an ear attached to the head.

To install this device was very simple and quite safe. It was issued fully assembled. When the hole for the mine had been prepared the spike was pushed into the ground at about its centre until the head sat on the ground. Then the igniter unit was dropped into the tube —

upside down this time as the striker was below it. The mine laying could then proceed and when the job was finished the device could be armed by drawing out the starting or safety pin with the attached wire. There was no cause for concern over this, for again the pin was of the self-trapping variety having a necked down portion at its centre. The weight of the mine was adequate to maintain the head of the device in the seated position so that it could not possibly fire accidentally. But if the installation had been badly carried out and the weight was not on the anti-lift device the starting pin could not be removed through being trapped and that was all there was to it. The mine layer would have to try again, but he could not get hurt. As a further safety feature, as no hair trigger effect was needed here, the securing pin for the striker head was of such a length that the mine had to be lifted two inches before the unfortunate lifter left this world. It was a nasty device; but the other side had the same kind if thing so we had to reciprocate. It took only a month to complete this design and get into production with it and only three months to get it accepted for service use. It was christened Switch No. 12. The device was completely disarmable once it had been installed and the only answer to it was to detonate the mine from a safe distance. 450,000 were issued before the war ended.

Soon after we were established at Whitchurch we were run to earth by a Commander Goodeve who had started a special weapons depart ment for the Admiralty known as the Directorate of Miscellaneous Warfare. The Prof. had put him on to Millis and out he came. Like myself, Goodeve was an opportunist. He himself had only indifferent research and development facilities whereas we could offer him everything. So he asked if he could attach some of his people to us to work on his projects and we were happy to oblige. In due course along came some naval officers and ratings headed by a Lieutenant Brinsmead, RNVR, and we were in business together for the rest of the war. Personally, I was delighted to have them all because apart from fitting into the community very well indeed they were always ready to give a hand in any emergency — such as having to stage a demonstration for the P.M. at Risborough in a hurry!

Their most important work was an anti-submarine weapon called the Hedgehog which will be described later. Where small devices were concerned, Brinsmead produced a couple of winners. The first was called an acoustic decoy. Now that magnetic mines had become harmless through the degaussing of our ships, the Germans were using ones initiated by underwater sound vibrations, and if the engines of a ship are running such vibrations must be broadcast. What the Acoustic Decoy did was to broadcast them first in advance of the ship. When thrown overboard, this little gadget would descend to the bottom of the sea making a suitable whirring noise which would set off a mine if one were there. I do not know how successful this device was, but it was certainly used.

The countermining pistol was Brinsmead's great success, however, and he was rightly given a useful award for inventing it. It was not an aggressive device at all, but was concerned with the clearing of wrecks which of course was becoming an ever increasing problem with the salvage people. The drill was to send down divers to affix a considerable number of heavy explosive charges at strategic points. It was necessary to fire them all simultaneously which meant either linking them up with Cordtex instantaneous fuse or bringing up separate leads from each to an electrical firing point. Either was a difficult operation.

By now we knew to our cost the phenomenon of sympathetic detonation, when exploding one charge can accidentally set off others. Brinsmead decided to make use of this and made a little fuse which would fire a charge when a shock wave reached it. It was a matter of getting the movement of a diaphragm to initiate firing and as usual the problem was to make the device 100 per cent safe. After a lot of experimental work Brinsmead succeeded in this and the country was saved an enormous amount of money in conducting salvage operations.

14

The Prof. and Others

WHEN HE FIRST commissioned me to write this book my publisher, who I should disclose is the Gordon Norwood who was with me right from the War Office days and is therefore in a position to make sure I tell the truth, wanted it to be entitled 'Secret Weapons of the Second World War' and take the form of a descriptive illustrated catalogue of the products of M.D.1. That struck me as being rather dull so I induced him to let me write the story of M.D.1. instead and bring people into it as well as mechanisms. I now propose to leave weapons alone for this chapter and deal with the people instead.

Taking them in order of priority at the start, Winston Churchill must come first and although I could not claim to know him at all well, I might have noticed a few aspects of him that have been missed by his biographers. For, as a journalist before I joined the army, it often fell to my lot to interview celebrities and write articles about them.

To me, the most remarkable thing about Winston Churchill was the way in which without conscious effort he would dominate any scene in which he was playing a part, regardless of who else was present. His Midnight Follies meetings, first held when he was First Lord of the Admiralty, were always attended by very distinguished people indeed including at various times the Prime Minister and every member of the Cabinet. Yet so powerful was Churchill's personality compared with theirs that one hardly noticed they were there.

The amount of information he could store away in that great head of his was fantastic. In discussion, he could without effort remember the present location of almost every important ship in the Fleet and could do the same where Army divisions were concerned. Millis calculated that it would take about six Admirals or Generals combined to equal this performance and I think he underestimated.

One of the myths that sprang up about Winston Churchill was that he would make important decisions on his own without first seeking advice and that nobody could then stop him from putting these decisions into practice. This idea was quite wrong. When faced with any problem the first thing Churchill would do would be to summon a selection of people best able to give him information on the subject and another selection best able to advise him as to the decision to be taken. Very seldom would he go against their advice. He knew that he had all the power in the world and that it would pay him to be careful how he used it.

It is true that he wrote every word of those wonderful speeches of his — he had to because nobody else could imitate his style and make words sit up and beg as he did. But every fact in every speech had to be most carefully checked. I was on many occasions one of a dozen or so officers who would be summoned to Chequers at the week-end because he was preparing one of his speeches and proposed to make some reference to the departments we represented or their work. We just had to hang around perhaps for an hour or so until somebody would bring us a couple of typewritten sheets in the enormous type which was the only kind he would allow to be used for documents he was expected to read. These sheets would contain the statements we had to check and it was our job either to pass them as correct or put them right if they were wrong. Seldom did a correction have to be made but, if it were made, it would be accepted without question.

At our demonstrations at Princes Risborough we saw another side of Winston Churchill altogether. He would be like a small boy on holiday. The faithful Commander Thompson would be in attendance carrying a Sten gun and when there was any lull in the proceedings Winston would lower himself to the ground and bang away with this thing at the nearest target. He could be very troublesome on these occasions through his reluctance to take shelter when necessary — a trait which he also exhibited during air raids to the intense concern of his staff. I was in charge of these Risborough demonstrations and on one occasion after Winston had finished playing with his gun and dusted himself off I told him I proposed to go on to the next item in the programme. This was the firing of a charge of very considerable size underneath a tank and there was every probality of pieces of shrapnel whizzing around so I asked the

P.M. kindly to step inside the splinterproof shelter we had put there for his protection. But he perched himself on a little mound nearby and said: 'No. I'll watch from here. Go ahead with the firing.'

I argued with him and he got quite cross. 'Get on with it,' he said 'I'll take the responsibility.' I had to tell him that the responsibility was mine not his and that if he refused to enter the shelter I refused to give the order to explode the mine. Reluctantly he gave way but he cheered up at once when the bang was over because it had been an impressive one and lumps of metal had flown around.

On this particular occasion Winston had brought along his daughter Mary who was having a grand time chatting away to the kilted Highlanders who were carrying out the range duties for us. Of course she asked me the classic question 'What do they wear underneath?' I told her she had better go and look and I believe she did. Mary proved to be a very good friend to M.D.1. We had always been trying to lure the P.M. to Whitchurch after these demonstrations but never succeeded. This time he turned down my invitation once again, but Mary was there. 'Oh, come on, Daddy,' she said, 'I want to go and you know jolly well you can spare an hour.' He went off with her like a lamb, and they spent over an hour at The Firs. It made the day for everyone at the establishment and the little Welsh factory girls nearly burst themselves with cheering.

The P.M. did have a drink in the Mess on his arrival and another before leaving. But the other idea that got around that he needed to be topped up with brandy at frequent intervals to keep him going was entirely wrong. Not knowing whether or not it was true I played for safety and at these demonstrations I had a truck fitted up as a mobile bar, the driver being instructed to follow the P.M. around and have his wares handy if wanted. They were never wanted — not by the P.M. anyway. The story that he got through a vast number of cigars every day was not true either. He always carried one — it was a bit of an act like the funny hats of his earlier days. But it was out a lot of the time and there was no risk of his smoking himself to death.

Finally, to revert to this unwillingness of Winston Churchill to exercise his power unless driven to do so. We suffered from this at M.D.1. as described in the Chapter headed 'Trials and Tribulations'. Our fate hung in the balance for months. Winston had created us and wanted us. He had only to write a four-line minute stating that we were to come directly under him as Minister of Defence and that would have settled the matter. Nobody could possibly have opposed this move or have the pluck to try to do so. But he just would not do that and wanted the problem to be solved in a constitutional manner. He did turn on the heat a bit in the end, but the Prof. had to work hard on him to get him to do it. The same thing applied when the adoption of some of the M.D.1. devices was opposed. The P.M. would refuse to interfere until he could be assured that there was no hope of persuading the opposers to change their minds. Then, if he were convinced that the cause was a good one, he would put all of his considerable weight behind it and push it along regardless. The 'Sticky Bomb — Make one million — WSC' minute is a good example of this.

I find it difficult to stop writing about Winston Churchill once I have started. But I doubt if I have anything more to say about him that has not been said before, so I pass on from the greatest man I have ever known or will know, to the Prof. Very few people understood the Prof. and I doubt if he understood himself. It would be difficult to find anyone who succeeded in making himself more unpopular than he did. That he did not succeed in making more friends than he did during his lifetime is not so surprising because he never tried to make friends. When after his death he was subject to attack in the Press, which seems always to be the fate of great men, it was sad to find that so few people rallied to his defence. Fellow peers such as Lord Snow and Lord Boothby could hardly wait to burst into print with quite absurd statements to the effect that he was an evil man responsible for the bombing of Dresden, that he nearly lost us the war through refusing to recognise the danger offered to us by the German 'V' weapons, and that he dissipated the resources of the country by having his own private research establishment (which meant M.D.1. of course) where he insisted on experiments being carried out on his crackpot ideas none of which proved to be any use at all.

The now retired Managing Editor of The Daily Telegraph, Sir Colin Coote, who had known the Prof. was a bit sympathetic towards the Prof. when this campaign started and published an article from me in his defence. But I did not see any others although some may have been written. It was easy enough to shoot down these assertions. The Prof. could no more have ordered the bombing of Dresden than I could have done — or the P.M. for that matter. The story must haven arisen in this way. Early on in the war it was found that our bombing was ineffective because apart from failing to hit the targets we were going for the wrong ones. Some statistics were needed here and neither the Air Ministry nor the Royal Air Force were able to provide them. So the P.M. asked the Prof. to start an organisation to do the job which he promptly did, taking a house at Marlow as his headquarters for this work and roping in some famous statisticians.

As Winston Churchill says in his History of the War, Vol. 2 ('Their Finest Hour') this department came to be of great value to him by furnishing him with statistics on all kinds of subjects. Where bombing policy was concerened, what it could and did do was to tabulate the results of past bombing raids and deduce from them what kind of target it paid to go for. No doubt Dresden would have appeared in one of these lists but it is unlikely the Prof. would have put it there himself. He merely controlled the machine that formulated these suggestions. They would then be considered first by the War Cabinet and then by the Chiefs of Staff Committee before any firm decisions were taken. So to accuse the Prof. of being responsible for the bombing of Dresden was quite ridiculous.

As one who was dug out of bed on instructions from the Prof. in the early hours of the morning to go off and inspect the remains of almost the first V Bomb to land here, I can state that he was very much aware of this danger. In fact it had been discussed endlessly at Whitchurch and for a long time we had been receiving the most up to date reports on the subject. Prof. certainly never suggested that nothing need be done about the V weapon; on the contrary he was always urging us to try to think up some brilliant counter measure against it which we were unable to do. What he did maintain, though, was that the weapon as described in the intelligence reports was a non-starter. They claimed that it would have a warhead carrying 10 tons of high explosive. The Prof., who was of course a brilliant mathematician, worked out that this was impossible, that the maximum size of warhead for a flying bomb of the sort described would enable no more than one ton of high explosive to be carried, and that therefore the weapon would not have such devastating effect as had been suggested. He did *not* say it would have no effect at all. Millis, who was also a brilliant mathematician, was asked by the Prof. to calculate this one independently and he came up with the same answer. They were both dead right. The V1 carried one ton of high explosive.

I wish we could have done something by way of counter measures against the V weapons because this would have been conclusive proof that the Prof. was taking the matter seriously. As a matter of fact we were working on a guided interception missile but even with our facilities we could not produce one quickly. Where the other accusation is concerned, I think I have already said enough in this book to prove that the Prof's private research establishment was by no means useless. We were never called upon to work on any of his crackpot ideas because he did not have any. Very seldom would he put forward any proposals in connection with a new weapon and he would content himself with suggesting that we should try to meet some specific requirement which he knew to be vital. For instance, he wanted a bomb that would damage a battleship more severely than the existing ones we produced them.

Time and again in my diary there is a note to the effect that the Prof. suggested we should work on some project or other. But he never insisted on our doing so and often there is another note later on stating that we advised him that we would prefer to leave this one alone. He never argued over a matter of this sort. In the same way, although we did not have to get his permission to undertake some new project, we always advised him about it as a matter of courtesy and asked for this permission. It was never refused, although on occasion he might express the view that we were not on a good wicket.

The Prof. was always keenly interested in everything we were doing at Whitchurch and when he came on his weekly visit to us I always tried to arrange things so that he could watch a few experiments and talk to the design officers concerned about the progress they were making. Then we would retire to the front office where, after dealing with any paperwork I had saved up for him, he would settle down to a discussion with Millis on some project or other. Generally some of the others would be there — Norman Angier, Ralph Farrant and James Tuck — and inevitably sooner or later mathematics would come into it. Right from the start it had been evident that this would happen so in this front office I had provided a nice big blackboard and coloured chalks. They all loved it.

I remember particularly one evening when we had been over at the RAF station at Wing dropping material called 'Window' out of aeroplanes to see if it worked. 'Window' consisted of strips of silvered tape which when dropped by our bombers would fox the enemy radar and put his fighters off the trail. The trouble was that if we started to use this stuff the Germans would soon get on to it and follow suit, in which case Fighter Command here would be faced with the same difficulty and be unable to locate and shoot down the German bombers. So there was a great dispute going on between Bomber Command and Fighter Command about whether or not we should start using 'Window'. One of the Prof.'s attackers after his death raised this one too and said he was increasing the hazards for our bomber crews by persuading the P.M. not to permit the material to be used. But of course this was complete nonsense. The Prof. had no say at all in this decision — it was purely a matter for the Chiefs of Staff Committee and the RAF. His job and ours was to make 'Window' work so that it was there if wanted.

On this particular occasion, there was a roll of this material on Millis's desk. The Prof. asked how much it weighed. Nobody knew, but James Tuck said he could soon find out. He then retired to the blackboard and after what appeared to me to be an unnecessarily complicated piece of calculation announced that it would weigh $8\frac{1}{2}$ ounces. 'No, no, James,' said the Prof., 'you should try it this way,' whereupon he proceeded to carry out an even more elaborate calculation which produced a different answer — a fraction over 7 ounces. Not to be outdone, Millis then had a go and came up with yet another answer. During the mathematical argument that ensued, I took the reel into the next office, weighed it on a letter scale, and returned to announce that it was precisely $6\frac{1}{2}$ ounces. Nobody was in the slightest interested, and the mathematical argument went on for a further half-hour.

Prof. was not only a teetotaller and non-smoker but also a most sincere vegetarian. He would not even eat the yolk of an egg. This made it very difficult to entertain him. When he was coming to Whitchurch I would always offer to have any vegetarian dish prepared for him but he would always refuse and produce his own little packet of sandwiches. He had a very large frame, and how he managed to subsist on so little was a mystery. He made no attempt whatsoever to persuade others to follow his example and when I went to lunch with him at his rooms at Christchurch or his flat at Marsham Court he would always provide me with an excellent meal and plenty to drink.

This teetotalism put us in a bit of a spot when he first started coming to Whitchurch. After six o'clock in the evening, one had only to press the bell in the front office for drinks to appear as if by magic; it was a fine system. But with the Prof. there we did not like to take advantage of it and would sneak away in turn to the bar instead. The Prof. got on to this on about his second visit and said: 'Please don't let me stop you from having drinks if you want them.' From then onwards the bell was pressed. On one occasion to our utter astonishment the Prof. plunged his hand into his trouser pocket and said: 'Let me pay for this round.' But of course we didn't.

Why the Prof. made himself so unpopular was because he not only sincerely believed that there was no better brain in the world than his with the one exception of Winston Churchill but also because he made no attempt whatever to conceal this view. Everyone who disagreed with him was a fool. A row had been going on for some time between himself and Professor Tizard, whom he had supplanted as the chief scientific adviser to the government when Churchill became P.M. He ever afterwards referred to 'that ass Tizard' which was very stupid of him because Tizard certainly had as good a brain as he had. Tizard really took it very well, but other scientists did not.

The Prof. did not like people very much or rouse any affection in them. Few of those who worked with or for him would say anything much in his favour even if they said nothing against him. He was regarded as just a cold fish. Yet he could inspire loyalty in people, one example being the faithful Harvey who looked after him like a mother and served as his secretary, cook-housekeeper and chauffeur all at once. I suppose another example was me, although I cannot quite understand how this came about. When the Prof. first met me at the Admiralty over operation 'Royal Marine' it was evident that he regarded me as less than the dust beneath his chariot wheel. I was not a scientist or mathematician but a nonentity — just somebody who worked for that brilliant fellow Jefferis. It was not until we got to Whitchurch that the Prof. began to realise that I had some kind of a brain and was using it. His respect for me greatly increased when he found that I was not only running the establishment, which he had sense enough to see that Millis was not well fitted to do, but was doing my full share of design and development work. In time he grew to rely on me for keeping the good ship M.D.1. on an even keel even though I was not the Captain.

It would be an exaggeration to say that the Prof. got fond of me but he did find my company very tolerable and quite liked talking to me. Sometimes he would be almost affable and tell me about funny incidents in the House of Lords. He never appeared to have any interest in women but once when I told him I had met Lady Bath over the week-end and she had sent him her kind regards his face lit up and he said: 'Isn't she lovely?' When I asked him for advice about

173

a career for my elder son he said: 'My dear fellow, make him a university don like me. It's the softest job in the world.'

Almost bashfully one day the Prof. invited me to have lunch with with him at Marsham Court and then listen to a speech he was going to make that afternoon in the House of Lords. 'I doubt if you will be able to hear a word I say,' he told me, 'because nobody does.' He was quite right. After the war when Millis had left M.D.1. and I had taken over the Prof. did not come to Whitchurch so much but liked me to run over to Christchurch once a week to tell him what was going on. We would walk round the garden which went with his rooms and of which he was very proud. When M.D.1. was finally closed down and I decided to quit the army he made considerable efforts to get me a job although he was no longer in power and could now pull few strings. When I went after one myself he wrote me a most glowing reference, and so did Brigadier Hogg.

Nobody could stand more on his dignity than could the Prof., and he was very troublesome over this. He would refuse to attend a meeting which he did not chair unless the chairman was somebody he considered to be of something like equal rank. Once as the result of a complaint he had taken up about an M.D.1. weapon being turned down he insisted on a special meeting of the Ordnance Board being called to discuss the matter and announced that he would be present. But when the President of the O.B., Admiral Pridham, went sick and the Prof. was told that a deputy would have to take the chair the Prof. refused to attend.

The same kind of thing happened when the citizens of Whitchurch got a bit restless and sent in a petition to the government saying that they had put up with The Firs and the noises we made there throughout the war but saw no reason why they should have to go on doing that now so would they please close down the place. This was a bit unfair, because we had been a godsend to the village during the war, bringing much wanted business to the shopkeepers and pubs, finding employment for anyone who wanted it, and providing free entertainment at our social and cinema shows. And we were still going on doing that.

However, appeasement seemed to me to be the best plan and, as I was now the head of the establishment, I decided to run a whale of a party and invite to it everybody who mattered. In particular I wanted the Prof. to be there. He said he would consider the matter and would I let him have a list of guests? I did that and thought it quite an impressive one. It included names like that of Sir Charles Ellis, who like the Prof. was an FRS, Nubar Gulbenkian, who was quite a famous figure, and a host of other celebrities. But after peering through it the Prof. could find nothing to suit him and said that although he would come if this were a matter of very great importance to me he would prefer to stay away. Probably the party went better without him, and it did serve its purpose.

The Prof. grew very proud of M.D.1. in time and nothing pleased him more than to bring out some VIP to see the place. Generally it would be somebody with some technical problem to discuss such as Sir Robert Watson-Watt, the inventor of radar. In one of the attacks on the Prof. after his death he was accused of opposing Watson--Watt and hindering the development of radar. This too was utter nonsense. He always encouraged Watson-Watt and went on doing it now. I was instructed to give him every assistance should he want to carry out some experimental work at Whitchurch. The same applied to Sir Barnes Wallis when he came out to discuss his cannon ball bomb with us. Most people had discouraged him but the Prof. had not.

The Prof's enemies did not realise how intensely patriotic he was. His entire energies were devoted to winning the war. I am told that throughout it he refused to accept any salary even as a Cabinet Minister and would not make use of the official car to which he was fully entitled or anything of that sort. Harvey had to drive him about in an enormous but ancient Packard. When it passed out at Whitchurch one day, I persuaded him to let our transport section do a bit of work on it and had quite a job to convince him that there was no need to pay. Whilst the Packard was out of action he would let me drive him about in my own car but would not let me put an army car and driver at his disposal.

It was all too easy to wind up the Prof. into a state of great indignation. Millis had only to suggest to him that somebody was obstructing our work for him to breathe fire and thunder and set about getting whoever it was removed from his job. The difficulty here was that Millis could quite often be in the wrong and would fancy he was being badly treated although in fact the other fellow was not being unreasonable but merely wanted more information. I often had great difficulty in smoothing out these situations and preventing drastic action being taken. Indeed, the only thing I could do sometimes was to visit the Prof. on the quiet, assure him that the offending official was now being more co-operative and urge him to forget the whole business. Even when we were all behaving nicely, M.D.1. was unpopular enough in many quarters and we could not afford to be hated.

Although the Prof. was easily put out in this way he was very slow to take offence where any of us were concerned. I provided him with a very nice office at 'The Firs' equipping it with a 'scrambler' telephone and one of the large type typewriters we now had to use for all official minutes that might be seen by the P.M.

On his next two visits to Whitchurch, the Prof. inhabited his new office for perhaps five minutes and then joined us in the front office. During the next six months he never entered it at all. By this time we were desperately short of space in the house so I had this room converted into a bedroom for one of the secretaries. My mistake was in not mentioning this to the Prof. Some months later on arrival at 'The Firs' he announced that he proposed to do some work in his office and that put me nicely on the spot. I could only explain the situation as best I could. But the Prof. felt I had slighted him in some way and it took me a little time to get back into favour.

I never saw him get cross with Millis, although he would have done on one occasion if he had known the facts. One time when Millis was away on leave and I had to visit the Prof., after we had run through a few matters he suddenly turned quite fierce and said: 'Now what has happened over that sabotage weapon? This really is too bad.' I always boasted that I knew of everything that was going on at Whitchurch, but this one beat me. I probed about a little and discovered that over a fortnight back the Prof. had for once actually asked Millis to knock up a sample of some little device for the ready wrecking of radio sets. Millis should have told me about it as this was in my line, but in fact it had completely escaped his memory. What is more, when the Prof. had telephoned to ask how this job was going, Millis assured him that it would be finished in another day or so — and then forgot it for the second time. I did not find this out until afterwards, but I assured the Prof. that Millis would have put the work in hand and that some unforeseen snag must have arisen since his departure. A little quick work was done, and when the Prof. came out to Whitchurch a couple of days later I was able to hand over to him a prototype of this device which he accepted with grace. None of this mattered much because there is an entry in my diary a fortnight later saying: "Instructed by the Prof. not to proceed further with the

176

development of his sabotage weapon."

The Prof. literally adored Winston Churchill. There were one or two other people such as, oddly enough, Ernie Bevin whom he really liked. But there is no question that Millis came top of the form and that he developed a sincere affection for him. The fact that it was not very heartily reciprocated did not seem to worry the Prof. at all. One would think that when Millis tried so hard to duck away from under his patronage and go over to the opposition that would have been the end of a beautiful friendship so far as the Prof. was concerned. When the situation was at last happily resolved the Prof. simply must have realised that Millis had not returned to his fold under his own power and that we had to drag him there by his heels. Yet there was no sign of his bearing a grudge. On the contrary, he favoured Millis more than ever and took a great deal of trouble to induce the P.M. to have his name included in the Dissolution Honours list for the award of the KBE. This, incidentally, put the cat amongst the pigeons once again as there were many other Major Generals who considered they should have come first if KBEs were being handed out. But the Dissolution Honours list is not subject to the same scrutiny as the normal ones and nobody could stop this award going through.

People used to say that the Prof. was mean-minded, but surely this action proves the contrary. Few big men in such circumstances would have shown such loyalty and generosity to a friend. As I started off by saying, nobody understood him and he did not understand himself. I never became his favoured friend as did Millis, but his death came as a blow to me and I missed him very much.

I have in the course of my story shown so many facets of Millis' character that I should not need to say much more about him. But I want to put something right. Someone whom I asked to read the first few chapters of this book and give me their comments on it said: 'What an awful fellow that Jefferis must have been. I can't see how you managed to get along with him at all.' He was *not* awful and on the whole I got on with him extremely well. But I was so shaken by this assertion that I went through the chapters again with the idea of deleting any lines which might be construed as knocks at Millis. I found it impossible to do that and still give a true record of what happened at M.D.1. and why it happened. So let me attempt the the almost impossible task of trying to explain what made Millis tick.

For a start, he was an out-and-out genius — there could be no question about that. This frequently made him moody and irritable because, when he had a problem on his mind, he did not want to think about anything else and resented anyone trying to make him do so. In the intervals when he came up for air, though, he could be a charming and attractive companion, full of fun and good humour. Here is an example. At the start of the war Ruth and Millis and Mary and myself both lived in caravans which we parked at Elstree. Ruth got a bit tired of hers when an oil stove went wrong whilst she was out and she found everything covered with a thick film of black soot. So the two women hunted around and found a little house at Mill Hill which we rented and shared.

It was not a very nice little house and the ladies had a very poor time of it except on the rare occasions when Millis brightened up and we had a party. Normally we would not get away from the War Office until quite late in the evening and even then Millis might be reluctant for us to go home. We would stop at some pub on the way back, not so much for drinks, as to enable Millis to go on talking about whatever project was uppermost in his mind, which he knew would be impossible when we got home.

As I say, the ladies had a poor time. They seldom complained, but one morning as we were setting off they did say: 'You never even buy us any flowers. You might think of that some time.' And to my surprise Millis did. After a little brooding as we went along he said to me: 'You know Crom Varley once got in a spot like this. He had one set of tails and one dinner jacket that were so old they were falling to pieces. His wife kept on about it and threatened to stop going out with him unless he bought some new clothes. Crom held out as long as he could because he was very attached to the old ones. But he lost in the end, and one day there was delivered to his home a parcel containing six sets of tails and six sets of dinner suits. When almost in tears his wife pointed out that this was a wicked waste of money and that he would never need all these clothes Crom retorted that this was not the point at all. He had been badgered for the past two years to buy new clothes. If he bought only one set this would happen all over again in a few years' time. Therefore he had now taken steps to ensure that it never could happen again. He had solved the problem.'

'And', said Millis, 'we will now solve ours in the same manner. 'There's a flower shop at Hendon Central, isn't there?. You just pull up there.'

I was a bit slow on the uptake here and had not yet worked out the association of ideas. But I did as I was told, and we both walked into

178

the shop. 'We want,' said Millis pulling out a cheque book,' to buy the contents of the shop please, and will you have them delivered to this address?' The astonished lady was quite ready to oblige so that she could close the shop and take the day off. When we got home that night we had great difficulty in getting into the little house. There were flowers, flowers everywhere including a palm tree in the lavatory which made it impossible to sit down. But the treatment worked. Flowers were never mentioned again.

One of Millis's greatest faults was that he was completely and utterly honest where money was concerned, which was more than could be said for me. He had a frightful conscience over expenses and that sort of thing. When we visited contractors and were invited to lunch he was always reluctant to accept and wanted to pay for himself out of his own pocket. He reproved me on several occasions for allowing myself to be taken out to lunch or dinner, which I did with impunity. His argument was that this might put me under an obligation to the contractor concerned. I was a bit hurt at the suggestion that my sense of duty could so easily be suborned, and took the trouble to produce notes proving that, even when contractors entertained me, I continued to bully them to get their prices down and did not hesitate to reject their products if they were found not to be up to standard.

Really upright people like Millis are often unlucky. It was not long before an inspector at Whitchurch lodged a complaint at the Ministry of Supply not against me but against Millis. He accused him of misappropriating funds, wild extravagence at the expense of the government, graft, and Heaven knows what else. I have never been more furious in my life than when I was told about this. I stormed up to London to see Brigadier Hogg about it and anyone else I could find and I must say that, even those who did not like Millis much, knew that he was quite incapable of this sort of conduct and were almost as indignant as I was.

The complaint had been lodged officially and there was no way in which it could be cancelled. The inspector concerned was suspended from duty and lived on full pay doing nothing for several months. Then a Court of Enquiry was held at which of course not a scrap of evidence could be produced against Millis and that was the end of that. British justice is a peculiar thing. It is extraordinary that any little would-be trouble maker of this sort can lodge a complaint against an honourable man and get away with it. So far as I know, this fellow never suffered in any way for having done this dastardly thing. Of course after his paid holiday he never came back to Whitchurch although I would happily have taken him on again — and made sure that he met with an accident. He was posted somewhere else instead of being sent to jug.

Millis's mentality over our bag of gold was difficult to understand. When we were given it at the War Office he considered it fair enough to use it for any proper purpose and paid my expenses out of it before I was taken on the strength. It could be used for paying some of the IBC staff overtime to save me having to argue about that with the War Office finance people. When we first went to Whitchurch, the bag of gold was still working and proved invaluable in getting the the place going, enabling me to take on extra staff and pay them until such time as they could be brought on to the establishment officially. I could also pay bonuses to selected members of the staff if we all agreed that they were underpaid.

I explained earlier on that, when the War Office golden goose ceased work, I contrived to keep things going by getting money from our fortunate friends in the Cloak and Dagger business. I kept quiet about this for as long as I could, but had to own up to Millis in the end. His reaction was as expected — the fund must be closed down and only official payments could be made in future. Bonus payments must cease forthwith. Of course everything went completely haywire. I had all kinds of odd people working about the place on urgent jobs and had to lay them off because they could not be paid. Those few people who were receiving what we called bonus payments were naturally disgruntled when they did not receive them in their pay packet at the end of the week.

Let me make it quite clear that we were not being over generous with government money. The pay scales were very poor indeed and under the regulations we could not pay a man what he was worth but only what the tables said he should get. As an example here we had an excellent though unqualified accountant whose name I will not mention in case it might embarrass him. Because he was unqualified the MOS would agree to his being paid only £8 per week. I asked for an increase for him. I was told to furnish full particulars of his duties and the number of staff he had working for him — which in fact totalled six ladies. This little department paid the bills, paid the staff and kept the books. The answer came back in a month or so that this accountant was earning the top rate for his grade. If, however, his staff was increased to twelve or more, for which permission would be granted, then he would come into a different category and could be paid £10 per week.We called it a day and paid him the extra £2 out of the bag of gold — thereby saving the country the cost of taking on six unwanted ladies.

This bag of gold business went up and down like a yo-yo for a while. When Millis's conscience got the better of him, which it did all too easily, he would tell me to wash out the whole thing and cause me much bother. Norman Angier would then get to work on him and get him to reverse his decision — he was always able to do that more easily than I could. On one occasion, having repaid the substantial balance standing in the bag of gold account to some department or other and then having decided to start the thing going again, Millis wrote his own cheque for £90 which he refused to have repaid to him when we were in funds again. The Prof. solved this one for us in the end. Although he had plenty of money himself, he felt that it would be a good thing for his brother, Brigadier Lindemann, to contribute to the running of M.D.1. From then onwards, £200 per month was automatically paid into our bag of gold account by his bankers. Both the Lindemanns were patriots.

There was a sad ending to this bag of gold business. When Millis was about to leave M.D.1. after the war was over, he came back from town one day and informed me that to clear things up he had dropped in to the finance branch at the War Office and told them I had a lot of secret funds and that he had instructed me to render them a full account and give them a cheque for the balance. This put me in real trouble. The War Office was of course no longer concerned with this bag of gold and Millis should have gone to the MOS if to anyone. Much confusion resulted, during which I ran a severe risk of being court martialled for misappropriation of public funds. However, it all came right in the end and I was able to produce my carefully kept account books and a cheque for something over £1,000 — in neither of which was anybody interested.

Millis' good nature was another of his troubles and mine. He would suddenly take a liking to somebody and order me to find them a job at The Firs. I could never seem to make him understand that, even though we were now a large establishment and could do much as we liked in the long run, we had to toe the line to some extent where taking on additional staff was concerned. I had to submit a case to the Ministry for doing so and wait perhaps a month or more for the necessary approval. When the bag of gold was operating, this simplified the matter and I could pay the person concerned until he or she was made legitimate. When Millis had locked the till the problem was a more difficult one. Very reluctantly I would give way to him on occasion and engage an Assistant Administrative Officer or somebody like that as a draughtsman — happening to have a draughtsman's post vacant. But I hated to have to do it because I could so easily be found out, and frequently was. When that happened I tended to lose the confidence of the MOS officials whose goodwill I had so carefully cultivated.

These difficulties were brought about entirely through Millis' good nature. He was like a weathercock. On the way to town in the duty car one day he decided that none of us was doing enough for the war effort. He solemnly told me that he was now working a minimum of 16 hours a day and that he thought I and everybody else in the establishment should do the same. I maintained that this outlook was stupid. All of us were doing more than our fair whack, and if I drove myself or anybody else any harder, all that would happen would be that they would have to go sick and their output would be lowered. I told Millis that unless he let up a bit himself this was what would happen to him and I was quite right. Later on he was compelled to take so much sick leave that he would have done much better to work only an eight-hour day.

I lost this battle. But a month later on my return from a visit to Scotland I was astonished to find that Millis had posted a notice in the factory over his own signature stating that it would be closed down for a week and all staff could have a holiday on full pay. Somebody, probably Norman Angier, had suggested to him that the factory hands were overworked which was true and this was his immediate reaction. The extraordinary thing was that Leslie Gouldstone, who was in charge of the factory but away at the time, had not been consulted either. Utter chaos resulted. As the factory was only just running to programme we could not possibly afford to close down for a whole week and, if we did, the MOS would not agree to making this an extra week's paid holiday. Yet once the hands had been officially informed that they were to have a week's holiday this could not be withdrawn from them. Leslie had to settle down to work out a holiday rota and find some way of fiddling the books. We both joined together in cursing Millis. But as I say, he did not make this move with malice aforethought. It was just his good nature getting the better of him and the failure of his brain to function where administration matters were concerned.

This really explains all Millis' troublesomeness. Like most brilliant scientists, mathematicians and so forth he readily convinced himself that with a brain such as his he could solve problems of administration quite easily without having to put any real thought into it. This I am sure accounted for his wish to take M.D.1. over to Beaverbrook. He could have thought the matter out before deciding to make this move and consulted some of us about it but he just didn't. Probably he conceived the idea in between planning a guided missile and concocting a new theory of prime numbers and then never gave it further serious thought.

One other remarkable thing about Millis was his ability suddenly to throw overboard all his responsibilities for the war effort for a while and concentrate on something that was of no real consequence. When we were in the heat of the fray at Whitchurch he got involved in producing a new theory of prime numbers and it became very difficult to get him to think about anything else. The trouble was that the Prof. thoroughly approved of this and contrived to bring out G. A. Taylor and other famous mathematicians for discussions on this matter. I found it very difficult indeed to get on with the war. From time to time Millis would get involved in these mathematical problems and, in the middle of devising some new weapon, would write a treatise on the formulae governing the calculation of compression spring movements under varying loadings or something of that sort.

His final effort in this direction was a mathematical concept related to jet propulsion which involved not only sheets and sheets of figures but also making up a peculiar machine on a high priority basis which we christened Katherine. Katherine did nothing useful except emit piercing shrieks at intervals and provide Millis with information which enabled him to predict mathematically and entirely correctly that it was possible to build a jet propelled engine. In the meantime Whittle was building the engine so on this occasion M.D.1. was able to make no useful contribution to the good work.

Of course I grew fond of Millis — nobody could help it in spite of his little idiosyncrasies. It was very sad indeed when he died after a long illness through which Ruth had looked after him with complete devotion. He is the third great man whose death I have to mention in this book.

Next on my list of celebrities comes Lord Melchett. We saw a lot of him, particularly after ICI undertook the manufacture of the PIAT for us — a weapon which is described in a later chapter. He was one of the few people the Prof. respected and they got on extremely well together. Another bond between them was that they both loved Millis. Melchett would pay frequent visits to Whitchurch, sometimes bringing with him his son who had just joined the Navy as an able-bodied seaman. At other times, Millis and I would visit Melchett at his magnificent estate at Sharnbrook in Bedfordshire. What impressed me most about his mansion was that the lavatories in addition to being close carpeted were equipped with pedestals having plush covered seats instead of the usual plastic or wooden ones.

The ICI headquarters in Buckingham Palace Road was rather like an annexe to the Palace itself except that it was conducted with more formality. A number of gentlemen in what appeared to be full evening dress took the place of the usual uniformed messengers and the top executives were accommodated in drawing room suites rather than offices. The first time I had to visit Lord Melchett there to make some arrangements with him, in the middle of our discussion a question arose which he decided must be referred to Lord Burnham. He pressed a button and very promptly one of the gentlemen in evening dress appeared.

'The Deputy Chairman,' said Lord Melchett, 'craves a meeting with the Chairman and would like to bring with him the Deputy Director of M.D.1. — Colonel Macrae.' The gentleman bowed and departed, to return five minutes later to report that the Chairman would be happy to receive us now. He then led us down the corridor to another drawing room suite, flung open a door, and announced us as if we were attending a reception. I began to realise why this organisation was known to top civil servants as the Ministry of ICI.

Lt-Colonel Blacker has been frequently mentioned in previous chapters and as I stated achieved fame through being one of the first men to fly over Mount Everest. Why this was so I never understood because I should have thought almost anyone could do it given a suitable aircraft. But there was no question that Blacker was a character in his own right quite apart from this particular feat. An Irishman, he was of course born with the gift of the gab, but he was in addition extremely well read.

Blacker would settle down in a chair after dinner and start off talking to me with some such remark as: 'Have you ever considered, dear boy, how remarkable is the history of the development of what is now known as the common bayonet but started life in the Turkish army in 1643 as a form of scimitar?' He would then run on for an hour or more quoting specific dates and names of battles in which the gradually improved scimitar was being used, without even faltering. And this was only one of his subjects. He could talk on almost any other. I never really knew whether he was telling a true story or making it up as he went along. There was no way of finding out because it would have been a life work to check up on all the facts he purported to give.

I always felt Blacker ought to have been an actor, and in fact to a great extent he was one. He was one of the most courteous and charming of men, kind and considerate to everyone. He would argue with anyone quite cheerfully and politely but would never in any circumstances get heated and lose his temper. I think perhaps it was this 'unruffability' that irritated Millis so much. These two were both brilliant in their differing ways and I tried very hard to turn them into a team. But they proved to be incompatible. Blacker, too, died a few years back and I lost yet another friend.

One of the celebrities posted to us during the war was Major Sir Malcolm Campbell. He had been running some kind of motor corps which had now been absorbed by another unit and was therefore at a loose end. We were experimenting with tank ploughs at that time — ploughshare contrivances for fitting to the front end of a tank which would plough up and detonate any anti-tank mines the enemy had been unkind enough to install on the route. It was not an easy problem to solve. I also got Campbell involved with Nobby Clarke's rocket-operated bridge which is described in Chapter XV.

What surprised me about Malcolm Campbell was his quiet and retiring manner. As the holder of the world's land speed and water speed records I had expected him to be rather a dashing type. He was the complete opposite. Once when we had to attend a demonstration at Chobham in Surrey he offered to drive me down there in his little Ford Prefect of which he seemed very proud, perhaps because he had been appointed a director of the Ford Company. I tried to take a good hold on my nerves and visualised having to go round corners on two wheels and that kind of thing. I doubt if we exceeded 30 mph during the entire journey and we certainly never passed another vehicle. When we had to travel over a field, Malcolm Campbell was really in a state of agony in case he broke a spring and we hardly moved at all. He was an extremely nice man, though, and so was his son Donald whom I came to know after the war.

To list all the celebrities who visited us at Whitchurch and comment on them would be an impossible task. But without exaggeration I think I can say that at one time or another we were privilegd to meet the top brass in all three Services plus a fair number of politicians. In the course of my story I have mentioned quite a number of the officers we had posted to us at Whitchurch and, as I said in my introduction, to list them all would be impracticable. But I should like to name Major Stribling who came to us as a Captain to replace Captain Faber when he went off to India to demonstrate M.D.1. products. 'Strib,' who was found for me by Brigadier Hogg, served the department well and truly until he died of a kidney complaint. Captain Rosling, who came along later, grappled with the problems of tank ploughs with some success and was adored by my cat whilst Major Fields who naturally enough became known to everybody as 'Gracie' Fields ran the ranges and stayed with M.D.1. to the bitter end. To my sorrow, I learnt recently that he, too, had died.

15

Some Rather Larger Weapons

AMONGST THE MISCELLANEOUS ironmongery belonging to Lt-Colonel Blacker which we had excavated from the ruins of the Portland Place workshop was what he called a spring gun. Being very spigot minded, on the grounds that a bigger and better round could be fired off a spigot than through a barrel, Blacker had worked on this device as a complementary one to his Blacker Bombard. The Bombard fired a bomb weighing 20 lbs and this necessitated having it firmly mounted. Blacker wanted a mobile spigot job which would fire about a 2 lb round and which could be used like a rifle and fired from the shoulder.

If the spigot was a fixed one and the bomb had to be thrown 200 yards or so anyone plucky enough to fire the contraption would find himself performing backward somersaults because of the recoil. To avoid this discouraging outcome, Blacker devised a moveable spigot, mounted in a tube, which could slide back into it against the influence of a powerful compression spring. To start the proceedings, a strong man could cock the device by the means provided and retract the spigot until it was held by the trigger mechanism. The bomb was then placed in a cradle in front of the spigot. On pulling the trigger the spigot would be released to enter the tail tube of the bomb and its striker end would fire a propellant cartridge. Off would go the round and its back kick would obligingly push the spigot back against the spring until it was recocked. During this process, a great deal of the recoil would be absorbed by the spring so that the firer had a good chance of remaining upright.

Millis, having nothing much to do one morning for a change, was poking about the workshops when he discovered Blacker's prototype of this contrivance under a bench. It did not look very impressive —

just a long and rusty old spring with a few components attached to it. However, he ruined the front office carpet by taking this thing to pieces and then brooded over it. The next day he rang Stewart Blacker and said: 'Stewart, I'm pinching one of your ideas — that old spring shoulder gun thing which is kicking about the workshop. Do you mind?' I could not hear the other end of the conversation but apparently Blacker did not mind.

About a couple of days later, having completely disorganised the workshops through insisting that this weapon must be rebuilt in a hurry, Millis trotted down to the ranges to try it out. His idea was to fire 2″ mortar rounds from it so we had fitted up a dozen or so dummy ones with the necessary tail tubes and fins which we hoped would keep them stable in flight. Millis insisted on firing this menace himself which was just as well because nobody else volunteered for the job and we onlookers were very pleased to find him the right way up when he had done it. But he admitted that the kick was pretty unpleasant.

After studying spring design and devising an entirely new formula for calculating the requirements for compression springs used in shoulder guns, Millis made another prototype which worked very well indeed. But nobody wanted it. The argument against its adoption, which seemed to be quite reasonable, was why have a special shoulder gun for firing a 2″ mortar round when it could be fired perfectly well from the standard 2″ mortar. This argument bowled me over completely, but it left Millis indignant but undefeated. He did a bit more thinking. As luck would have it some time back he had become interested in shaped or hollow charges operating under what was known as the Neumann effect. The idea was that, if a charge of high explosive were placed behind a metal cone with the concave part of the cone facing forwards and the device was stood off from the target for a prescribed distance, on detonation the explosive would be focussed so that, instead of midly affecting a wide area, it would give great penetration over a small one — in other words, bore a small hole through thick armour plate.

Work on this theory had been going on for some time at M.D.1. and elsewhere but there was a great number of variables to sort out. The best metal to use for the cone had to be ascertained, the angle of the cone was critical, so was its thickness — likewise the stand off distance from the target. Ably assisted by Norman Angier and James Tuck, Millis had worked out a lot of these answers on the black-

188

board in the front office. But the remainder could only be found empirically, so the boys were busy working through a trials programme on the ranges. This leisurely programme was rudely interrupted when Millis demanded a $2\frac{3}{4}$ lb hollow charge round in no time at all, but his order was executed.

Trials with prototype rounds showed that Millis was really on to something now. Remarkable penetration of armour plating was at once achieved. The final version as issued to the services would penetrate the heaviest armour used on German tanks. True the hole would be only a small one but the blast effect was lethal. After the new weapon had been tested at Whitchurch, its birth was reported to the Ordnance Board and quite soon a demonstration for it was staged at Bisley at which the top brass of the Army was to be present. The target was a heavy armour plate and as full precautions must be taken when trying out a new weapon, especially when it has to be fired at rather short range to make sure that the target is not missed, the firer was placed in presumed safety behind an armour plate screen in which was cut a comparatively narrow slot through which the front end of the projector could protrude.

The Small Arms School at Bisley appointed one of their Warrant Officers to fire this weapon. When he pulled the trigger there was a satisfying bang as the round hit the target and, as was afterwards found, punched a nice hole in it. But the firer fell back seriously injured. It was soon found that a slug of metal had come back through the slot in his screen and gone through him.

When he had been taken care of, Millis without the slightest hesitation took his place and fired several rounds with excellent results. These M.C.s in general and Millis in particular could do things like that. Then we retired to Whitchurch to find out what had gone wrong. The experts soon did that. It seemed that when the hollow charge round detonated the intense heat formed the apex of the cone into a metal slug which was shot back through the tail tube at very high velocity like a bullet from a gun. It was just a matter of luck which way the tube was aiming and in this case it was sighted right back at the firer — a chance about level with that of winning the football pools. Once this trouble was found, it was very quickly cured by redesigning this rear end of the bomb and for good measure using a special cartridge case which could not come back in the same way.

To perfect what we wanted to call the Jefferis Shoulder Gun but which the Ordnance people insisted must be called the Projector Infantry Anti-Tank, or PIAT for short, did not take long. The design of the projector had to be cleaned up and made suitable for rapid production. Here ICI came into the picture and Lord Melchett arranged for the resources of ICI's factory at Billingham to be devoted to this work. They handled the entire output, obtaining components from sub-contractors as required. They also made and filled the rounds, which consisted of the hollow charge anti-tank one, an anti-personnel or fragmentation one, and an inert one for practice firing which was the one I myself liked best. At first we had some trouble in getting stable flight from these rounds but a drum tail with fins was found to be the answer.

A special nose fuse was needed to detonate this round. There was a competition on between the orthodox design department and M.D.1. to produce an acceptable design. Of course our Mr Smith won easily and produced satisfactory prototypes of what was to become known as the fuse 425 before the opposition had even got started on the job. At once The Firs factory went into production with this device and soon we were turning it out in thousands. Smith and Wilson then devised a most ingenious and more refined form of it which was accepted as fuse 426. Very sensibly M.D.1. was appointed the sole supplier of this fuse and we churned out thousands of them until the end of the war.

Undoubtedly the PIAT was by far the most effective anti-tank weapon produced for the infantryman in the last war, not excepting the American Bazooka which came along later. It was as popular with our side as it was unpopular with the enemy! A report from John Redfern who was with the Eighth Army, dated June 1, 1944 says: 'From now onwards, the men of a famous North Country regiment will not be parted from their PIATs. The officers say they go to bed with them.'

Here is another report from Matthew Halton from Normandy dated June 19, 1944. ' . . . German tanks rushed back and forth across our slit trench, spraying the Canadians with fire and steel. In reply, the Canadians stalked those huge tanks with PIAT mortars. You know the PIAT mortar? If you fire it from fifteen to twenty feet, you are likely to be caught in the blast. The Canadians were crawling to within five or ten feet, and from that distance the mortar bombs went through the German armour. The Jerries inside got the blast. Twenty nine Panther and Tiger tanks were burnt out.' As a matter of fact, provided they hit the target, the so called mortar bombs would have gone through the German armour just the same if they had been fired from 200 yards away. But why be fussy about that?

I forget how many V.Cs the PIAT earned for soldiers throughout the war but it was about five or six. It should have been more. It was quite a heavy weapon to cart about and was supposed to be operated by a two-man team — one to carry and fire the projector and the other to carry the rounds and do the loading. But some PIAT enthusiasts insisted on working as one-man bands and lugging the whole outfit about by themselves. How they managed it I just do not know. Recently to oblige the BBC, who were working on a programme describing tanks and anti-tank weapons, I cheerfully agreed to fire a PIAT for them if they could find one. Having fired the first one made and many of the production ones, I felt I knew all about the job.

They did find one — a museum piece. There is no doubt about it, 25 years does make a difference. When demonstrating the PIAT, I used to be able to carry it to the site and fire off several rounds from a standing position without discomfort. This time the weapon seemed to weigh a ton instead of 60 lbs. By the time I got it to the appointed site on the ranges I was exhausted. The producer then expected me to hurl myself complete with PIAT into the long grass and fire at a target 200 yards away. When I rehearsed this act he complained that I made it look as if the weapon were heavy, which it definitely was. He punished me by making me throw myself down in the approved manner until he was satisfied.

By this time, the effect of the drinks kindly furnished to me by the officers in the Mess had worn off and I was feeling discouraged. First, I had been made to sign a form stating that if, in firing this PIAT, I were injured or killed the Ministry of Defence would not be responsible. Next, the gentleman who had acquired this PIAT from the museum told me he had tried it out earlier on, which I thought was rather brave of him, and had been concerned because something had whistled back past his ear — probably, he suggested, part of the cartridge case. His advice to me was to refuse to fire this weapon until I could be provided with a tin hat, although for some unknown reason these commodities appeared to be in short supply on these particular ranges and he had so far been unable to locate one.

When no tin hat was forthcoming, gritting my false teeth and remembering the epic story of Millis at Bisley who was firing live rounds when I was firing only inert ones, I shut my eyes and pulled the trigger. Needless to say, I missed the target and the only impressive thing that happened was that I was propelled rapidly backwards but not fast enough to avoid the PIAT which hit me on the forehead with its rear sight. This was fortunate, because a spot of blood appeared and the producer was so concerned about it that he abandoned his idea of asking me to fire a few more rounds. However, I was more than ever convinced that everyone who fired a PIAT should have been awarded the V.C.

Let me continue with the story of these hollow charges. We made a whole range of them and called them Beehives because they looked like them. The smallest weighed only 6 lbs but would drill a nice hole through 2 inches of armour plate or a yard of concerte. Larger sizes would penetrate any concrete pillbox and that was what they were wanted for. The demand for these useful stores became terrific as D Day drew nearer. M.D.1. was overwhelmed with orders for them and although we pulled out all the stops, and had our favourite contractors working overtime, we found we were losing ground. Urged by the MOS, I put on my best uniform and visited the key factories concerned, there to give the factory girls a carefully rehearsed pep talk about how important it was to speed up production of these wares. They seemed to like me and cheered me like anything. I returned to Whitchurch satisfied, only to be advised a fortnight later that as a result of my efforts production had been increased by 20 % but no more.

This was not nearly good enough. In desperation, I asked that General Montgomery should arrange to visit these same factories and see if he could do better. He did. Immediately after his visits, production started to soar and by D Day we near enough met the orders. This hurt my ego a bit, particularly as I am said to look rather like the General and was often mistaken for him at places like the Cafe Royal if I went there in battledress until it was found that I was not wearing a beret with two badges.

Once Millis had the hollow charge bit between his teeth he raced off with it. The PIAT round and the Beehive series was followed by hollow charges for both artillery and bombs. Where guns were concerned, hitherto the only way to pierce armour had been to fire a missile at it which would go through by sheer velocity and ignorance. Millis at once realised that with hollow charge rounds velocity mattered not at all — the high explosive would supply that when it got there. The round had only to be lobbed on to the target and the hollow charge would do the rest. So he looked round for suitable guns to fire his hollow charge rounds.

There were none, but quite undeterred by this Millis said he would make some. The design of guns is an old established art allied to witchcraft, and nobody is supposed to undertake this occupation unless he can prove that his forbears have been engaged in it for many generations. On learning that Millis proposed to design some guns the Ordnance Board in toto nearly had a thrombosis. However, Millis having acquired and read all the literature that could be found on the subject expressed the opinion that these old gun designers were a lot of poor hoots with no real knowledge of mathematics. After writing a treatise on how guns should be designed he then very quickly produced at Whitchurch two which were immediately accepted for service use. The first was a 4.5" Naval gun for use by MTBs against trawlers. This fired a 15 lb plastic round which poulticed itself on to the target, Millis having momentarily abandoned hollow charges and reverted to his first Sapper love for a poulticed charge. The second gun was the 7.5" AVRE which mounted on a tank fired a larger plastic round, still at low velocity — about 800 ft/sec. This proved to be just the job for knocking down buildings.

Having produced these satisfactory guns firing their poulticing rounds Millis felt he had been faithful to the Sapper philosophy and was now entitled to have another go at hollow charges. In rapid succession, he produced the Capital Ship or C.S. Bomb, the Anti-Submarine or A.S. Bomb, an anti-tank round for low velocity howitzers and a hollow charge head for rockets. All these weapons were officially adopted and were highly successful.

In this chapter, the weapons seem to have grown up in size too quickly for me. I shall therefore carry on with the big boys and return to the little ones later. Perhaps the most spectacular was a mine we called the Bobber but which was given the official title of the J. W. Bomb, which was not so bad as it meant Johnnie Walker. It consisted of a sizeable naval mine designed to be dropped into a harbour gently by means of a parachute. When the parachute had detached itself and gone away, the mine sank to the bottom of the harbour and after a short rest started to search it. It would ascend to the surface at an angle and if it failed to hit anything go down to the bottom and try again. Millis and his mathematicians maintained that they had worked out the plan so that in the course of time this J.W. mine would explore every part of the harbour and if there were any ships there it must soon find one and blow it up. After many setbacks, Norman Angier made the thing work and it went into service.

Skating over tank ploughs of one sort and another, which were supposed to dig out anti-tank mines laid by the enemy without hurting themselves, we come to Journey's End. Unfortunately this one never got off the ground, but it is an excellent example of how Millis could think ahead of anyone else. He devised a long distance rocket which slowly rotated so that it could be steered towards its target by the radio firing of a subsidiary rocket at right angles to the axis. Millis worked out all the complicated trajectory correction sums on the blackboard in the front office, made up a one sixth scale model of the device and was just about to go ahead with a full scale one when the war ended. Of course this is all easy stuff for the aerospace boys nowadays, but Millis was well ahead of them.

The Hedgehog was an out-and-out winner. It grew up from the Blacker Bombard or Spigot Mortar. As has been stated earlier on, Commander Goodeve, who had created a new Admiralty department called 'Miscellaneous Weapons' for producing special weapons, on hearing about the spigot mortar was struck with the idea of attacking submarines by firing off a pattern of bombs from spigots — which could be done much more easily than dropping a pattern of depth charges. When through the good offices of the Prof. he came out to Whitchurch to discuss his idea with Millis, he was welcomed with open arms. Millis obligingly did the arithmetic for him to show at what angles the spigots must be set to give the right pattern, had a rough model of the device made, and produced some 60 lb bombs for firing from it. By this time Commander Goodeve had invaded Whitchurch with our full consent and we found that we had attached to us a large section of the Navy which carried on with the development of this equipment and lobbed these 60 lb bombs about our ranges until they were full of potholes. However, they did a good job and the P.M. was delighted when he came to Whitchurch to see the Hedgehog demonstrated. He kept on demanding a repeat performance until we ran out of rounds. The Hedgehog went into service rather late in the day but was credited with 37 confirmed submarine killings — which is not bad.

To show that we were versatile, I must mention the 20 lb J Bomb which was a superior incendiary device developed by James Tuck. He used a solid napthaline filling instead of the orthodox petrol one and devised an initiator that was much more ferocious than thermite.

194

For good measure his bomb included a 'Window Breaker' which went bang after a predetermined delay to remove all nearby glass and let some air into the place. We soon learnt from experience that it is very disappointing just to drop an incendiary bomb into a building and let it go at that. It can easily go out. The thing to do is to ensure that plenty of air can enter the building to encourage combustion.

I have intentionally reserved the last place in this list of bigger weapons for Nobby Clarke and his 'Great Eastern' — which by the way is not the famous ship. The earlier history of Nobby has been recounted. He designed the Limpet with me. And when I mentioned to Winston Churchill that he had worked on a trench forming machine similar to that being developed by a Mr Hopkins of the Naval Design Department, Mr Churchill promptly had him attached to that department. In due course, Nobby managed to escape from this job which he disliked intensely and to get himself taken on by what was now known as Station E.S.6 of the Special Operations Executive, which was the place at Aston House from which he had been ejected in earlier days for spurning security measures. They got a bit frightened of him there so General Gubbins, who was now in charge of SOE, posted him to Station 17 in Hertford where he was made the O.C. and entrusted with the job of training saboteurs.

This was just Nobby's cup of tea and enabled him to become a bigger menace than ever. He had no guards on the gates of his magnificent estate. One just drove in and then found the vehicle being battered by rounds fired from spigot mortars set off by trip wires. Nobby would emerge smiling and point out that if they had been live rounds the occupants of the vehicle would no longer be in this world. But that was little consolation to the driver who had to explain how the bodywork of his vehicle had been badly bashed.

Nobby made a hobby of raiding the local RAF and transformer stations with his trainees, leaving dummy charges all over the place, and then ringing up the fellow in charge to point out that his security measures were lousy. This made him unpopular, and although Colin Gubbins liked him he felt that he might be of more use elsewhere and approached me about it. As Nobby had served me and MIR (c) well in the early days I felt that something ought to be done here and got Millis to agree to my taking him on. In fact I contrived to get him promoted to Major. Nobby was a bit restless, but soon managed to get himself sent to Italy to demonstrate the PIAT and write a rude son net on the River Po. There he fell foul of the D of As' representative

195

who was a Brigadier and came home with his tail between his legs. Thoroughly disgruntled, he retired hurt to his Bedford home without bothering to tell anybody that he was back and I had quite a job to get him out of a Court Martial on grounds of desertion.

After finding a little excitement by going out in Sunderland flying boats from St Eval to see what happened when they dropped our anti-submarine bombs, Nobby returned to The Firs where I tried hard to find him suitable work without much success. When he thought up an idea for a rocket-operated tank bridge it was a great relief to me. It seemed most unlikely the thing would work but developing it would get Nobby out of my hair for a while. So I got Millis to approve the project.

It was quite an impressive one, calling for many men and much equipment. But by now we were quite influential, and I had no difficulty at all in getting a couple of Churchill tanks complete with drivers right away. Nobby got to work, hardly pausing for sleep, and quickly produced some sketches which some genius at G. A. Harvey Ltd of Greenwich managed to translate into masses of girderwork. Large lorries brought this heavy gear to Whitchurch and after we had armed the workshop staff with much bigger spanners they made something of it.

Came the day when Nobby was prepared to demonstrate his creation to one and all. It was a kind of Bailey Bridge carried on the back of a Churchill tank in a folded up position. The idea was that on reaching a canal or narrow river that must be crossed the tank driver halted on the brink of the bank and pressed Button A. This resulted in rockets being fired to throw over the folded part of the contrivance to form a bridge over which tanks could run.

As the pioneer, Nobby of course insisted on being the presser of Button A and nobody else wanted the job anyway. Unfortunately he had not consulted Millis about the mathematics for this venture and had just installed a large number of 3″ rockets to make sure the bridge was thrown over. It was, and it very nearly took the Churchill with it. The driver of the tank was not in good shape but Nobby remained unshaken and signalled to the drivers of another Churchill tank and a Sherman tank who were standing by to climb over his bridge. This the brave fellows did and the viability of Nobby's project was proven.

The rockets were tamed, and quite quickly Nobby's 'Great Eastern' became one of our show-pieces.

We used to poop it off and then send tanks of all shapes and sizes over it. The big brass loved this, and I had a lot of fun devising means for recovering the bridge reasonably quickly ready for the next demonstration. The experience I gained helped me a lot when after the war I went into the Territorial Army as a Commander, Royal Electrical & Mechanical Engineers, in which capacity I had to specialise in these recovery jobs.

In due course, the first ten Great Easterns were completed and Nobby accompanied them to France after D Day. They were used and did good work; but unfortunately they were a bit late in the day. If they could have been made available in hundreds it would have made a lot of difference.

16

The Jumpers and Others

OUR FIRST EFFORT in the way of jumpers was the 'K' or Kangaroo Mine described earlier on, the business part of which popped up to plaster itself on the belly of a tank and then explode. By now, I had adopted Millis' trick of developing any novel principle in every possible direction. He had done it with poultice and hollow charges so I would do it with jumpers. I studied the market for them.

Once again, O.B. Procs. gave me the opening I wanted. It seemed that the standard 8lb fragmentation bomb being dropped in clusters from aircraft was very ineffective against entrenched troops. It did not detonate until it hit the ground, whereupon the shrapnel pieces sailed harmlessly overhead. What was wanted was a bomb which would detonate 20 feet or so before it reached the ground but to design that was just about impossible. A time fuse was no answer, as the height at which the cluster would open was governed by an atmospheric switch which could not be set to close limits. So the bomb might go off a couple of hundred feet above ground and do no damage at all or sit on it for some seconds before detonating — which was just as bad. To consider using some kind of proximity fuse was quite out of the question on the grounds of both cost and complication.

This was a natural for the jumper idea. Instead of trying to detonate the bomb before it reached the ground the thing to do was to let it land and then bounce it back in the air to a height of 20 feet and detonate it. The 'K' Bomb did take a few months to develop and get into production because we had to evolve an entirely new kind of fuse for it. It also proved very necessary for the bomb to land at reduced velocity and the right way up. The body was formed of two metal hemispheres welded together so we fitted it with a spring loaded fabric tail which popped up like an old fashioned opera hat without a top when the bomb was released from the cluster. This did the job nicely.

The standard cluster carried 49 of these bombs. They were as safe as houses whilst they remained packed into it. On release, apart from the tail springing out a little propellor or air vane in the nose would start to revolve because of the draught and would in a little while withdraw a striker to permit a shutter carrying a 1.7 grain detonator to move over into the armed position. On impact, the striker would be driven into this detonator, which would then fire a black powder propellant charge through a 0.2 second delay. The delay was to ensure that the bomb had settled down before it was shot back into the air.

A secondary delay of 0.4 seconds was ignited at the same time as the propellant charge. This would burn through when the bomb had reached a height of between 15 feet and 20 feet and fire a flash detonator or azide sleeve to detonate the high explosive filling of the bomb through the medium of a stemmed disc or C.E. pellet.

The assessors soon decided that the 'K' Bomb was at least five times more effective than the existing F8 bomb and it was at once accepted as a service issue. A first order for one million was placed with M.D.1. But by now the people who used these devices were becoming more ambitious. In August 1944 we were asked if we could fit a delay to these bombs so that when dropped they would lie dormant for a predetermined period and then come to life and do their jumping act.

This was a pretty tall order, so I put three of our design teams on to the job and also had a go at it myself. I must say I was pretty pleased with myself when Millis, who had been appointed judge, picked my design as the winner. It was quite a neat job. The same air vane as before was used, and had to perform 12 revolutions before the stem would withdraw far enough to free a detent interposed between a striker and a 1.7 grain detonator so that the device became armed — a very safe arrangement. On impact the detent would run forward, but instead of firing taking place this would merely result in a spring load being applied to one of our famous lead elements as used in the 'L' Delay. The bomb would then stay put for any period that had been chosen from five minutes to 28 days whilst the lead had its neck stretched until it broke. The drill would then be the same as before, the bomb jumping up to a height of 20 feet and detonating.

Of course we could not carry out trials by dropping these bombs from aircraft all day long because aircraft were in great demand for other purposes. But Wilson got over this one by fixing up one of our 29 mm spigot mortars on the ranges so that it would fire a bomb carried in a cup to a height of around 600 feet, the bomb would fall out of the cup when it reached the top of its flight and then come down just as if it had been dropped from an aircraft. This was a brilliant idea of his and saved us weeks of time. And from it we learned something else. As we did not want to hang about for hours until these bombs popped up again we set out to find how short we could make the delay period — and finished up with 45 seconds! We found it as hard as anyone else to believe that a delay operating on this stretch of lead principle could be so astonishingly accurate. But it was.

After the usual hitches had been overcome, this delayed action 'K' Bomb passed all its field trials with flying colours and was officially adopted in place of its direct action predecessor. For it served both purposes. If direct action firing were required all one had to do was to omit the lead element. The approving authorities liked this fuse much better than its predecessor, which they had accepted only under pressure because it had not properly complied with their rules about the shuttering of detonators. This latest version did comply.

We went into full production with the 'K' Delay Bomb, making the fuses at Whitchurch. But it was not long before the war finished and production had to stop. What amazed me, however, and still amazes me is that it was never restarted. Here was a weapon which was absolutely ideal for use in the small wars that followed — Korea and so forth. There is nothing to rival it. Using it not only enables the enemy to be attacked with an anti-personnel bomb five times more effective than any other. It also enables any selected area be sterilised against occupation by the enemy for anything up to a month. If the action is a police one, the other side have merely to be informed that if its members enter certain territory they risk getting killed. There were 49 bombs to every cluster and they could be given a variety of timings. If anyone were brave enough to try to locate these hundreds of bombs which would be going off at unknown times he would be on a bad wicket. For a start, they would be most difficult to locate because for them we used a tail which collapsed when the bomb landed. More often than not the bomb would bury itself in the ground complete with tail, so that it would take a lot of spotting. If it were spotted, even if it did not go off itself there was an excellent chance that a brother a few yards distant might do so. The only answer would be to go away until the maximum delay period had expired. But only the side which had dropped the bombs would know what this was.

I pulled out all the stops I could to get production of the 'K' Bomb continued after the war. I also tried to get the Air Ministry to adopt this 'L' delay fuse minus the propellant charge for other bombs, for it was miles ahead of anything they had. But the Prof. was out of power and others such as General Ismay were unable to help much. They did get the Chief of Air Staff to consider the matter and write me a charming letter saying how good the 'K' Bomb was and what a clever fellow I had been to design it but that did not help. He explained that now the war was over they had run out of money and could not contemplate making any new weapons for a while. I then got permission from the War Office to offer the design to the Americans and Canadians. But although both of them liked it they gave me the same kind of answer.

In due course, all the beautiful tools and fixtures we had set up at Whitchurch for making this really remarkable bomb and fuse were like the rest of our apparatus taken away and thrown on the rubbish heap. However, I have retained a full set of drawings. Does anyone want to buy a nice bomb?

The next jumper was a 3″ mortar round. It was meant to behave in the same manner as the "K" Bomb and use a very similar fuse, so that after landing it popped up in the air to detonate and hurt the poor fellow in the trenches below. Again we were asked for both direct action and delay action types. I kept fairly clear of this one myself and left Nobby Clarke and John Marston to sort it out. It took them some time to do that because they started a kind of private competition, each producing his own design and prototypes and going off to different ranges to carry out firing tests in great secrecy. They won in the end, and between them produced an acceptable round of the kind required. But this never went into service as the war finished at just about the same time they did. Again, I should have thought this weapon could with advantage have been adopted for service use and issued to the fellows who on occasion find themselves given the job of firing 3″ mortar rounds against entrenched troops, an operation which can be most unrewarding. This, however, was not to be.

The Puff Ball was one of Millis' poultice charge affairs for the aerial attack of tanks. One day, the Prof. brought out to Whitchurch a Group Captain Pendril who had been flying fighters in the Middle East in sorties against enemy tanks and had not had much success in these operations. To try to drop single bombs on tanks was a waste of time; nor was it any good trying to shoot them up with machine guns. What Pendril wanted to do was to be able to fly over a tank or a railway train dropping a string of small bombs, one of which would be almost certain to hit the target and finish the job.

Millis got on to this one like mad, and produced a little 9 lb soft nosed bomb complete with suitable dropping gear to enable it to be layed in the required string pattern. It reminded me of my First World War contraption for dropping Mills grenades in much the same fashion. Pendril made a rather better dropping gear which he showed to us installed in his Hurricane at the RAF Station at Wing, so we adopted that instead. Unlike the other design departments, we had no need to be touchy if somebody came along with a design which was better than ours.

We were using metal containers for these bombs and as they were to be dropped in a string, right at the start we tried them out for sympathetic detonation. They were quite all right when spaced over 10 feet apart; but we were not quite happy about this and decided to change over to plastic containers which we found would let this distance be decreased to two feet. After several successful trials with the metal cased bombs, we were suddenly asked to provide another batch in a hurry for a trial at Orford. We decided to use these new plastic cased bombs instead to be on the safe side and by working all night had them ready in time. But Pendril was not very keen on using them as they were untried and pointed out that anyhow he could not do so without permission from the Director of Armaments Development, Air Ministry. So off he went with some of the original metal cased bombs.

He was killed. Making his first run over the target tank he came in too low. The string of bombs straddled it, and one detonated against it. This started off a chain reaction of sympathetic detonation until the last bomb went off. It had only just left the Hurricane, which immediately burst into flames. Poor Pendril landed, but it was quite impossible to get him out. It was a very unpleasant affair and caused me to start a movement for providing pilots of fighter planes with means whereby they could inject themselves with some instantaneous poison in cases like this so that they could avoid having to fry to death. I believe this move was successful. The saddest aspect of this tragedy was that even though Pendril was flying too low he would have been all right if he had been dropping the plastic bombs. He was a fine fellow, and we all felt his loss severely.

Another device which enabled us to make ourselves unpopular with the official Armaments Design Department was an attachment to the service shrapnel mine. This mine was a jumper too; but it was an expensive and pretty poor contraption and did not give value for money. It was operated by a trip wire, and the idea was that if the enemy were unkind enough not to trip over it some subsidiary means of initiation should be provided. O.B. Procs. again indicated that having brooded over this problem for a year ADD had got nowhere at all. As these shrapnel mines cost £2 a time the obvious answer was to use eight 'M' Mines at 5/- a time instead. But this was not acceptable, so we decided to tackle the job, and in a fortnight produced an answer that was approved. We used a number of converted AP Switches which could be set in the ground around the Shrapnel Mine. If any one were trodden on, it would through a flexible cable set off the shrapnel mine. This one too was reluctantly accepted for service use.

Of course we had our failures. We were asked to find some way of quickly breaking through a standard barbed wire field. This was quite a problem. To cut a way through a few coils of this horrible stuff is not too difficult, but the job gets harder as one goes on. Millis had a brilliant idea. After studying Roman history and learning about arquebuses, catapults and so forth he decided that what was needed was a whacking great and heavy flywheel. Mounted on a suitable stand, this potential missile would then be wound up to high revolutions by a petrol engine operating through a variable gear. When it was going flat out, its axle would be removed so that it would trot off and barge through any obstacle such as wire.

This was almost a good idea, but not quite. The trouble was that the flywheel would start off all right and then tend to get its course deflected. In fact it seemed to have a tendency to perform a 'U' turn and come back to the firing point. Even Millis found this rather frightening and agreed that the project should be abandoned.

His next idea for solving this problem was to have a 6 foot length of heavy angle iron vertically disposed and backed by a directed or hollow charge, at designing which he was now rather clever. In theory, when fired this chunk of iron would travel in an upright posture and just sweep through any amount of wire. In practice, it proved to have a tendency to travel in anything but a vertical plane. It might either bury itself in the ground close ahead or go sailing up into the air. If it happened by chance to take the proper path it would never get quite through the wire and would leave the last few coils intact.

Millis got a bit despondent about this and handed the job over to me to enable him to tackle something more important. I plugged along for a while, getting slightly better results all the time, but never quite making it. Then one morning I decided to use a much bigger and better charge and a longer piece of angle iron. Probably I was careless this time and had not made sure that the device was securely supported. Presumably it was not, because instead of proceeding along the proper path this massive chunk of angle iron sailed up into the air. Running alongside our ranges was the main road, and running along this main road were about as many telephone wires as anyone could cram on to poles. They served not only M.D.1. and local requirements but also provided the main communications lines to RAF, Wing which was a fully operational station.

My piece of angle iron swept through this pack of telephone lines and cleaned the whole lot away. For several hours I was the most unpopular fellow in Buckinghamshire if not the country, but fortunately nobody could get me on the telephone to tell me so. I must say the Post Office people came to my rescue very smartly indeed and helped by my signallers did a wonderful repair job. In fact we were back to normal in a couple of hours. However, I was too disheartened to carry on with this project and Millis agreed that it could be scrubbed from our list and classed as an M.D.1. failure. We had only a few anyway.

All kinds of odd things went on at Whitchurch once Commander Goodeve and his DMWD crowd had invaded us and it was sometimes difficult for me to keep myself up to date about them. One day I found a Jeep parked in the yard outside the experimental workshop with half the navy doing things to it. On enquiry, I learnt that this was to be an invasion vehicle. The idea was that it should motor along and when a canal or narrow river were reached it should continue without faltering. When the bank was reached the driver would press a button which would result in rockets being fired so that the outfit sailed up into the air and its momentum enabled it to breach the gap and land on the other side.

I forget who was in charge of this operation. It might have been

Nevil Shute who under the name of Lt. Norway was involved in these DMWD projects. Or it could have been Ian Fleming who at that time had not got round to inventing No 007 James Bond. Anyhow, this venture was not my responsibility, so after assuring myself that Nobby Clarke had nothing to do with it and after suggesting it might be a good idea to have a parachute I left it alone.

A few days later when I was sitting in my office I was advised that there had been quite a nasty accident with this flying Jeep. As a first move, it had been decided to shoot the vehicle straight up into the air from a stationary attitude instead of trying this when it was proceeding at speed — which was perhaps just as well. Unfortunately the Naval types concerned had not consulted Millis or any of our mathematical experts about what rockets to use and had just planked for a number of large ones. As a result, on the trial the Jeep with its brave but unfortunate occupant shot up to a height of some 20 feet and then did not even have the decency to land on its wheels but came down sideways. Things might have been worse, as we were able to get this hero off to hospital without delay and they patched him up all right. Commander Goodeve then responded to my plea that he should please transfer this experiment to somewhere else as we had enough casualties of our own and did not need contributions from the Navy.

Do not get the idea that I have described every weapon or device worked on by M.D.1. for this is not so. I have contented myself with dealing with most of the 30 odd ones which we developed and which were actually accepted for service use. In many other cases, such as those of the Mobile Mine and the One Man Submarine, we carried out the initial development work and when the project was proved to be a viable one handed it over to some other department.

17

Life at The Firs

THERE IS A LOT to be said for living in a closed community. There is no wear and tear on the mind and body travelling to work every day, and there is no need to live by the clock. One can just get on with the job and not worry. Of the more than 250 inhabitants of the station, most worked for at least a 10 hour day and many made it 12 hours. This applied to the officers and senior executives who would start off at 9 am and very often would not finish until 9 pm or later. It was not so tough as it sounds. We were living in the utmost comfort with everything laid on. The exhausted worker could knock off for a drink any time he liked because we had no fixed hours.

It was an odd life in a way, though. So far as M.D.1. was concerned, throughout most of the war such things as week-ends simply did not exist. We would discover it was a Sunday only when we tried to ring up some other department. When entertainment was wanted we had no need to go in search of it. We had our own cinema with a full sized 35mm projector and I became an accomplished stand-by operator for it. We had dances and socials galore and there was competition between the departments to see which could lay on the best one. I rather think Gordon Norwood won the title with the popular series of affairs he put on down at his carpenter's shop under the title of 'Woodchoppers Balls.' But the Drawing Office under Leslie Harris came a close second. Like most Drawing Offices they had a flair for devising entertainments of one sort or another. They were particularly good at producing in their spare time, if any, all kinds of ingenious sideshows for the local church fête, which was generally held in our grounds anyway. But the finest job of work they did, for which I shall be for ever grateful to them was to launch 'The Firs Magazine' at a time when morale was pretty low, and keep it going to the bitter end. It did a lot of good.

In view of the fact that we had soldiers and sailors and airmen and little Welsh girls, apart from our other female staff, what was really surprising was that in spite of the fact that they all lived in the same encampment we had remarkably few sex problems. Of course they were all worked to death, but that alone could not account for it. Much credit must go to Fairy Wond who controlled the hostel we had built for these girls. She seemed to have the gift of being able to keep her little brood in good order without appearing to be a disciplinarian.

She and the army Captain who was later attached to us as Welfare Officer could between them cope perfectly well with everyday incidents and would never bother me about them. But as the establishment's Administrative Officer, on the few occasions when they got stumped they would come along to me and I was supposed to be able to exercise the judgement of Solomon.

They were having difficulty with a young lady working in the factory — not a Welsh girl. It seemed that late at night she was constantly being found in one of the sentry boxes complete with sentry. What was surprising was that although quite a big girl she favoured a little sentry, who was now serving a month's detention. Wishing to get all the angles on this case before hearing it I whistled up the Sergeant Major and demanded a report. He assured me that the attraction to the little sentry was understandable because he was not built in the normal proportions and that in his opinion she had attacked the little fellow and he was not really to blame.

Armed with this information, I got the welfare experts to bring the lady along to my office to see what could be done about it. In a highly paternal manner, I pointed out to her that she was being most unkind and unfair to her soldier friends by behaving like this. They could be severely punished for such an offence whereas no action could be taken against her. Therefore I must appeal to her better nature and if she would promise me that she would leave the men alone in future that would be the end of the matter.

She burst into tears and assured me that this was no answer to the problem. She had already given Miss Wond several such promises and had broken them immediately. She just could not help it. Always she had been very attracted to men, and when they were in uniform she found them irresistible. At this she gave me an enchanting smile and looked me over until I quivered a bit. If she might give me some

207

advice, the only possible way out of this difficulty would be for me to send her to work somewhere else, preferably where there were no men in uniform. I had to do just that, but I was quite sorry to see her go. She was certainly honest.

The next worker I had to get transferred for somewhat similar reasons was a Scottish welder. Sitting in my front office late one summer's evening polishing off some paperwork, I was startled when the door suddenly flew open and a naval officer — who shall remain nameless — came flying in. The window giving access to the courtyard outside was wide open and without pause he flew out through this.

Just as I was pondering over this strange occurrence another figure burst in, this one being attired in a boiler suit, and carrying a very heavy spanner. He performed the same act. This could be classed as an 'unusual happening' and I felt sure that these fellows could not be rehearsing for one of our plays without telling me about it. So I summoned the guard and declared a state of emergency.

Fortunately two of them grabbed the welder before he caught up with the naval officer, so there was no bloodshed. I learnt next day that he had fallen violently in love with one of our attractive office ladies, which was quite understandable. She was on rather good terms with the naval officer and had been taking a walk with him around the estate. Eventually they arrived outside the experimental workshop where this welder was on night shift. The sight of them together was too much for him and he went berserk, chasing his rival into the house and then out again. Off he went back to Scotland the next day.

Now I come to think of it, people like myself who were able to go away for days on end attending trials and meetings and that sort of thing had a much better time than those who were more or less tied to the establishment. In their place, I doubt if I should have remained as contented and tractable as most of them did. They must have regarded me as a Good Time Charlie. Some of these trials were magnificently staged. For instance, when ICI wanted to demonstrate the PIAT to top brass, which seemed to be about once a fortnight, they would temporarily take over the luxury hotel nearest to the ranges for those attending and everything would be on the house.

The Air Ministry went one better when organising some bomb dropping trials in Wales, which both Millis and I were invited to attend. The invitation merely asked us to be at Paddington Station at 11 pm on a certain day. We arrived there a little late, so I abandoned our car in the roadway outside Platform 1 and we dashed in. Our idea was that we had been booked on some regular train where if we were lucky we would be given a third class sleeping compartment and perhaps a cup of tea in the morning. But this was not so at all. A reception committee ushered us into a royal train definitely more magnificent than the one in which we had accompanied Winston Churchill to Dover. A Mr Grand, who apparently owned the Great Western Railway, welcomed us, invited us to be his guests, and pointed out that the bar was open and would remain like that. Would we please order anything we liked? We did.

In the small hours of the morning we retired to our luxury first class sleeping berths and in the larger ones we woke up to find ourselves in a siding at Fishguard. After a substantial breakfast, we were transferred to a funny little two coach train which puffed us along a single line track to our destination. It too was provided with a well stocked and permanently open bar and refreshment facilities.

We lived in this little train during the daytime whilst the trials were in progress and at night were taken back to our more luxurious quarters. Nothing could possibly have been more pleasant. Evidently Mr Grand knew how to lay on an operation of this sort in a big way. It transpired that we had made a non stop run to Fishguard in the first place through Mr Grand having had the forethought to kidnap the Traffic Superintendent Mr Matthews who had ordered all trains to be cleared out of our way on pain of death and ridden down on the footplate himself to make sure that they were. Immediately on arrival, a couple of telephone lines had been installed so that we could get in touch with our respective departments at any time we liked.

All good things come to an end, and in due course we got back to our train one evening to find that the programme had been completed. Mr Matthews then spoke into both telephones at once and gave orders that the line to London must at once be cleared. We would be starting off after dinner. Mr Matthews invited me to accompany him on the footplate and as this idea appealed to me immensely I nearly accepted. But on enquiry I found that I should have to spend the whole night there because the train was not stopping anywhere and there was no way of getting back to the coaches from the locomotive. So I weakened and went off to my comfortable bed later on. I have regretted that ever afterwards because it would have been an experience that there will be no opportunity to repeat. For that matter, neither can the trip be repeated. Since nationalisation, such luxury and such service cannot be provided. Neither can the facility for leaving a car at Paddington Station for several days free of charge and fines.

To return to The Firs, time marched on and in due course we arrived at May 8 1945 or V.E. Day. I did not enjoy myself at all. Everybody went mad. It was obvious that there must be a little trouble here and there and that it would be unfair to appoint a duty officer to deal with it and deprive him of the fun and games. So I ordered all the Military Police, poor fellows, to remain on duty, turned my office into a kind of report centre and awaited the worst.

Millis, having stoked up nicely in the bar, collected a Sherman tank from the ranges and contrived to get it into our front drive where he whizzed it round until he had scattered most of the gravel. Fortunately he got tired before knocking down any walls and decided to go home — without the tank. But it was soon spotted by Brian Passmore, who had been in the bar with my wife Mary, celebrating. They thought it would be a good idea if they went off for a ride in this machine although Brian had no idea how to drive it. Apparently on the run they came over all religious and decided to go to church to give thanks. For half an hour later it was reported to me that they had arrived at a church in the next village but were having trouble in getting the tank to go inside. I despatched a rescue party and waited for the next incident.

It soon came along. Norman Angier felt it was an occasion for fireworks. He therefore acquired a large batch of quite big rockets and proceeded to poop them off, selecting as his firing site a point at the summit of a concrete road which led down to the ranges and the CMP's camp. Unlike the Guy Fawkes day rockets, these were not provided with sticks for poking into the ground to keep the bodies upright; but Norman had fixed up some sort of stand for doing this. All went well for a while and the show was most spectacular. Then Norman got careless. A rocket he had just initiated was not properly secured. It fell over, and instead of going up vertically proceeded at speed in the near horizontal plane. A weary CMP was walking along this road on his way back to the camp. The rocket struck him right on target. Luckily he was not seriously hurt and we soon whipped him off to hospital. The trouble was to make him believe that the attack was not intentional. He had been the victim of a 1000 to 1 chance.

210

There were no other major incidents, so at 4 am I called off the emergency procedure and went to bed. I made my wife pay for the repair of the church steps, which was perhaps rather mean of me.

The end of the European war took the head of steam out of things for a while. All armaments contracts had of course to be reviewed and priorities readjusted to meet the requirements of the Far East. However, our devices were all in great demand by the Americans so we were able to keep going although we felt like people who had been pushing a bus up an incline for a long while and now saw it disappearing over the top.

It was now that my nefarious plot for making Millis a General matured. We were advised that we had been made a Grade A Directorate. Millis' promotion to Major General was published on June 16, 1945 and mine to full Colonel on June 21. Everything was looking pretty rosy for us and the Prof. was constantly telling us that the future of M.D.1. was assured. He had asked both Millis and myself to write papers on how best to run armaments development and research in peacetime and we had not hesitated to put forward our views. Naturally we had both made M.D.1 a key establishment in the plan. The Prof. told us that the P.M. had found time to study our papers, fully approved our plans, and proposed to put them into practice almost right away. We seemed to be all set for life.

18

After the Ball is Over

ALL OUR BEAUTIFUL DREAMS about the future of M.D.1 vanished into thin air on July 26, 1945 when the Great British Public was ungrateful enough and stupid enough to vote Winston Churchill out of power. It was obvious that our number would be up directly the Japanese war ended if not before. Our enemies could descend on us now that we had no protection.

V.J. Day came sooner than expected — on August 15. It did not give me the same trouble as V.E. Day for everyone took it quietly. On the following day, everything went as flat as a pancake. Without exception, everyone at The Firs had been working flat out to help with the war effort. Now the spirit had suddenly gone out of us and there was no incentive to go on. However, I was determined to keep things going somehow or other. The development projects were all right because as yet nobody could stop us from carrying on with them. But the factory was almost out of work through orders for our devices being cancelled.

Idle hands soon destroy morale, so I scouted round and found work for us by going to some of our contractors and turning the tables on them. I pointed out to them that they would now have to get into production again with their civilian lines and that was where M.D.1. could help. We now had capacity at our factory for making bits and pieces. Geoffrey Hawkes was most responsive and at once placed enough orders with me to keep our automatics busy for some while. He also gave me a development contract for devising means for tuning harmonicas or mouth organs by electronic means. This was obviously one for Smith and Wilson so I gladly accepted it. Other contractors reciprocated in like manner. A visit to the Atomics people at Harwell resulted in my getting a very large order from them which they wanted executed in a hurry; so we were soon quite busy again.

The prediction I had made in 1940 that given the chance the orthodox Armaments Design Department would take us over and then dispose of us came true all too quickly. On September 26, 1945, only two months after Winston Churchill and the Prof. had lost their power, the Chief Engineer and Superintendent of Armaments Design, Ministry of Supply, came over from Fort Halstead to visit us to say that he was taking over the place at once. Millis went to see Lord Melchett to learn if he was still interested in the idea of acquiring M.D.1. for ICI. But he was not. I tried the Atomic Energy Research Establishment, but they were so busy expanding at Harwell that they did not want to acquire an outstation. The War Office, maybe as a diplomatic move, then offered Millis the post of Engineer-in-Chief to the Pakistan army which he promptly accepted. I was a bit hurt when he did not suggest I should go with him as his second-in-command, but I could not have accepted such an offer anyway. Having done much towards the creation of M.D.1., I felt it was up to me to stay put and try to keep the establishment in being so that those who wanted to could retain their jobs.

It took the Ministry of Supply only a month to finalise the arrangements for us to be taken over by ADD. This compared favourably with the several months they had taken to approve our establishment in the first place. We were to lose our title of M.D.1. and become Group 9 of the Armaments Design Department. As Millis had left, I was put in charge of Group 9, appointed Assistant Chief Engineer and Superintendent of Armaments Design, and allowed to retain my rank of Colonel. All this was implemented on November 1 1945.

Millis went off to Pakistan on November 16 having returned from leave to throw a fearful farewell party at The Firs which went on for most of the night. I then started to get down to my new job. It was a most depressing business. We had of course run the show during the war without the need for much red tape; but now I found myself surrounded with demands for estimates, monthly reports on the progress being made with the twenty or more development projects we had on hand, and so forth. I had to estimate how long it would take in man hours to complete each project and what the expenditure would be on materials. It was quite impossible to do that so I just put down any old figures, which I am sure is what the Heads of the other Groups did. Then I found myself on the mat for accepting work for the factory from outside contractors. A stiff note told me that this practice must stop immediately and that anyway the MOS had no machinery for receiving payments for work of this sort.

I did win on this one because I happened to know that one Ordnance factory to keep its staff employed had taken on a big contract for making bath taps at prices which showed them a heavy loss whilst on our work we were at least making a profit. But I was still unpopular with my new boss because as was only to be expected Group 9 did not fit in at all with any of the other ADD Groups. We were built to run quickly and it was impossible for us to get down to their slow speeds. When I was asked how long it would take us to develop an improved PIAT I said three months which I thought was well over the odds because under the previous management I should have had to do it in half the time. Back came the answer that it was quite impossible to complete such a development in this time and that I must change the estimate to two years. This ruling was soon followed up by an instruction that all short term projects were to be abandoned and that the only items that could remain on my list were ones which would take five years or more to complete. This notice went to all Heads of Groups and I could never discover the reason for the ruling. I think it must have been issued to make things awkward for me as I was the only Group Head who had no five year or longer projects on his list. Six months was the most I could give to any one of them.

I knew that this argument was likely to prove academic and that soon the second half of my prediction would come true and the establishment would be abolished. For it was certain that this was the intention. Sure enough on February 28, 1946, exactly four months after ADD had taken us over, CEAD advised me that Group 9 was to be axed. Of course I fought like a wild cat to save it, and even the Prof. fought like a not very tame one. But he was almost powerless now and had to pay for the unpopularity he had gained for himself. The high officials he had been able to override when he was Winston Churchill's right hand man now had opportunities to get their own back and did not hesitate to seize them. If by any chance one of them gave sympathetic consideration to his proposal that M.D.1. should be revived others would soon spring up to knock the idea on the head.

Whilst the Prof. was campaigning, I managed to keep the shop open in one way or another until the beginning of May, 1946, which was quite a feat and one that increased my unpopularity with CEAD. My best gambit was to induce the Atomics boys, who now had all the priority in the world, to tell the MOS that we were carrying out most important contracts for them and must be allowed to complete them. The Prof. then managed to pull a string which really looked like working something. He got Lord Portal, the Atomic Weapons chief, interested in the idea of taking over The Firs as an experimental station to specialise in the design of fuses for atomic weapons.

Of course we were the ideal set-up for that sort of work, and in fact there was no other establishment with the staff and equipment to undertake it. So this one simply must be a winner and we should after all live happily ever after. But this was not to be. There was a long delay, during which the opposition evidently worked on Lord Portal to good effect. It was agreed that he should send one of his experts to inspect The Firs and decide on whether or not we could tackle this work. The one chosen was CEAD's opposite number on the research side at Fort Halstead. He reported back that we were quite unsuitable and that was that. This held up the atomic fuse development business for a long time until a new station could be started for doing the job

We dragged along until the end of October whilst all this chicanery was going on. I was then offered a choice between two rather attractive jobs, either of which would have permitted me to stay in the army without any drop in rank. But I am an obstinate fellow and I still felt I could keep The Firs going somehow or other. Besides, The Firs Magazine was publishing declarations from me assuring everyone that everything was coming right and I could not very well walk off whilst this was going on. I tried everything I knew. I even came to terms with my mortal enemies at the Ministry of Works and persuaded their engineering side that they should take over the place. They immediately applied to the MOS for it and were promptly turned down. Then Geoffrey Hawkes was so pleased with our mouth organ work for him that he planned to take over the establishment for the manufacture of these contrivances and other musical instruments. Again the MOS turned down the proposal very smartly indeed. The Prof. did manage to get it referred to Sir Stafford Cripps at the Board of Trade and Geoffrey and I went to see him. That did no good at all.

It was now more than ever evident that the plan was to wipe

M.D.1. off the earth as completely as possible. The plant must go, the equipment must go and the staff must go. As a first move, most, of the staff were fired by the MOS, although I managed to get some of them such as Smith and Wilson transferred to other Ministry establishments. Then the place was put in charge of the Director of the Rocket Research establishment at nearby Westcott, who promptly ordered that I must not be allowed on the premises. This left the way clear for the Ministry of Works to tear down all the factory equipment, load it together with most of the machinery into trucks, and take it to Westcott where it was thrown on the rubbish dump.

Shell now put in a bid for the premises, which they said they proposed to use as a gas turbine research centre. Obviously this was a put up job because, if they had wanted The Firs for that, they would have taken it over when it was in full working order. However, their bid was accepted and in theory they took over right away. In practice they did nothing more about it and merely appointed as caretaker — one of my Warrant Officers who had a cottage on the estate. Some six months later Shell sold The Firs to some large steel corporation which wanted a country residence for use by its directors and nothing more. The MOS had certainly done a good job of work. Not a trace now remained of M.D.1.

As the fact will not be on record elsewhere, let me stress that M.D.1. was the finest and best equipped weapons development establishment in this country and probably in the world. The Americans envied us and freely admitted that they could not rival us here. We had the materials, the men, the equipment and the know how. As an asset to the country, the M.D.1. establishment could be valued in millions of pounds. Yet it was totally destroyed through jealousy!

Just before ADD took over, the Prof. had instructed me to create a museum showing all the weapons that had been developed by M.D.1. during the war. Winston Churchill had requested this and it was certainly a good idea. We went at it with a will, making sectioned models of all the devices together with written descriptions of them and photographs showing the results of trials. It was a lot of work, but it seemed worth it. Soon after ADD took over it was ruled that this museum must be transferred to their headquarters at Fort Halstead. I knew what would happen to it there and hastened to tell the Prof. He got really busy, and came to see me a few days later in a very satisfied state of mind. He had been able to arrange

216

for Winston Churchill to request that all this material should be transferred to the Imperial War Museum where a special section was to be devoted to it.

I knew this would not work, but it was no good saying so. Visit the Imperial War Museum to-day and you may find one Sticky Bomb tucked away in the corner of a showcase with nothing to say what it is and an early PIAT hung up on a wall. There is no other exhibit from M.D.1. and no mention is made of the name. In fact it is difficult to find such a mention in any official documents, for no effort has been spared to deny our existence.

Fortunately the enemies of M.D.1. cannot prevent the publication of this book, otherwise I am sure they would do so. It gives the true story of how — inspired by Winston Churchill — we created an establishment which contributed more to the war effort than any other weapons design department. If this were not so and we had been a failure, nobody would have bothered to try to erase us from history.

Appendix 1

Attack on Enemy Shipping with Limpets.

The incidents described below in which enemy shipping was damaged or sunk through being attacked with Limpet Mines have been selected from a large number of official Admiralty reports on the subject.

1. On December 7, 1942 a raid against shipping at Bordeaux was carried out under the code name 'Operation Frankton'. The Limpeteers were Royal Marines in five canoes, taken to the Gironde Estuary by S.M. TUNA. The following enemy vessels were damaged in this raid:-

   S.S. ALABAMA (5641 tons), S.S. TANNENFELS (7840 tons), S.S. PORT-LAND (7132 tons) and S.S. DRESDEN (5567 tons)

2. On January 3, 1943 four Chariots carrying Limpets carried out an attack on Italian shipping in Palermo Harbour. Cruiser ULPIO TRAIANO was sunk and S.S. VIMINALE was damaged. Limpets laid on CICLONE, GRECALE, and S.S. GIMMA were removed by the enemy before they detonated.

3. On April 28, 1943 a number of German steamers was sunk in Oslo Harbour and at Koppernvik in the Haugesund with Limpets. One officer and three ratings in canoes blew up and sank a German mine-locating craft off Koppernvik.

4. On September 25, 1943, a raid against shipping in Singapore Harbour was carried out by British and Australian Navy personnel under the command of Major Ivor Lyon of the Gordon Highlanders. With their canoes, they were carried to the area in an ex-Japanese sailing vessel KRAIT. The following Japanese merchant ships were sunk in this raid:-

   KIZAN MARU (5072 tons), KARUSAN MARU (2197 tons), YAMAGATA MARU (3807 tons), TASYO MARU (6000 tons), SHINKOKU MARU (10,000 tons), and NASUSAN MARU (4399 tons).

5. On June 18, 1944, a raid against German shipping in Portolago (Leros) was carried out by Allied sabotage forces commanded by Lt. J.F. Richards, R.M. under the code name 'Operation Sunbeam'. With the exception of a small water tanker, the ships concerned were all alongside the jetty. In all, five ships were attacked with the following results:-

219

Patrol Vessel G.D. 91 (Trawler) blew up and sank, Salvage Tug TITAN sunk, small Water Tanker beached to avoid sinking, Torpedoboat TA 14. Two mines blew large holes in her port side forward but the crew succeeded in keeping her afloat. Torpedoboat T.A. 17. Five mines caused extensive damage to the after part of the ship.

6. On June 22, 1944, a raid against shipping at Spezia, on the North West coast of Italy, was carried out by four English and six Italian naval personnel using Limpets. As a result, the BOLZANO (10,000 tons) capsized.

7. On July 31, 1945, a raid was carried out against Japanese cruisers in Johore Strait by Midget Submarines carrying limpets. A Japanese craft, the TAKOA, (9850 tons) was seriously damaged by limpets placed by Midget Submarine XE 3.

Appendix II

The following extracts from the Supplement to the *London Gazette* are reproduced by permission of the Controller H. M. Stationery Office

War Office, 13th July 1944.

The KING has been graciously pleased to approve awards of the VICTORIA CROSS to the undermentioned:

No. 3663590 Fusilier Francis Arthur Jefferson, The Lancashire Fusiliers. (Ulverston, Lancs)

On 16th May 1944, during an attack on the Gustav Line, an anti-tank obstacle held up some of our tanks, leaving the leading Company of Fusilier Jefferson's Battalion to dig in on the hill without tanks or anti-tank guns. The enemy counter attacked with infantry and two Mark IV tanks, which opened fire at short range causing a number of casualties and eliminating one P.I.A.T. group entirely.

As the tanks advanced towards the partially dug trenches, Fusilier Jefferson entirely on his own initiative, seized a P.I.A.T. and running forward alone under heavy fire, took up a position behind a hedge; as he could not see properly, he came into the open, and standing up under a hail of bullets, fired at the leading tank, which was now only twenty yards away. It burst into flames and all the crew were killed.

Fusilier Jefferson then reloaded the P.I.A.T. and proceeded towards the second tank, which withdrew before he could get within range. By this time our own tanks had arrived and the enemy counter attack was smashed with heavy casualties.

Fusilier Jefferson's gallant act not merely saved the lives of his Company and caused many casualties to the Germans, but also broke up the enemy counter attack and had a decisive effect on the subsequent operation. His supreme gallantry and disregard of personal risk contributed very largely to the success of the action.

Department of National Defence, Ottawa, 13th July 1944

THE CANADIAN ARMY

The KING has been graciously pleased to approve the award of the VICTORIA CROSS to:

Major John Keefer Mahony, The Westminster Regiment (Motor)

221

On 24th May, 1944, 'A' Company of the Westminster Regiment (Motor) under the command of Major Mahony was ordered to establish the initial bridgehead across the river Melfa . . .

Shortly after the bridgehead had been established, the enemy counter attacked with infantry supported by tanks and self-propelled guns. The counter attack was beaten off by the Company with its P.I.A.Ts 2" mortars and grenades, due to the skill with which Major Mahony had organised his defences. With absolute fearlessness and disregard for his own safety, Major Mahony personally directed the fire of his P.I.A.Ts throughout this action, encouraging and exhorting his men. By this time, the Company strength had been reduced to 60 men, and all but one of the Platoon Officers had been wounded. Scarcely an hour later, enemy tanks formed up about 500 yards in front of the bridgehead and in company with about a Company of infantry launched a second counter attack. Major Mahony, determined to hold the position at all costs, went from section to section with words of encouragement, personally directing fire of Mortars and other weapons . . .

War Office 17th August 1944.

The KING has been graciously pleased to approve the award of the VICTORIA CROSS to:

Warrant Officer (Company Sergt. Major) Stanley Elton Hollis The Green Howards (Middlesborough).

W. O. Hollis prevented the enemy from holding up the advance on to the Normandy Beaches at critical stages on D-day . . .

Later the same day, in the village of Crepon, the company encountered a field gun and crew armed with spandaus at 100 yards range.

Hollis pushed right forward to engage the gun with a P.I.A.T. from a house at 50 yards range. He was observed by a sniper, who fired and grazed his right cheek, and at the same moment the gun swung round and fired at point-blank range into the house.

To avoid fallen masonry, Hollis moved his party to an alternative position. Two of the enemy gun crew had by this time been killed, and the gun was destroyed shortly afterwards.

War Office, 7th September 1944.

The KING has been graciously pleased to approve of the award of the VICTORIA CROSS to:

Rifleman Ganju Lama, 7th Gurkha Rifles, Indian Army.

On the morning of 12th June the enemy put down an intense artillery barrage on our positions north of the village of Ningthoukhong causing heavy casualties. This was immediately followed by a strong enemy attack supported by five medium tanks. After fierce hand to hand fighting the perimeter was driven in in one place and enemy infantry supported by three medium tanks broke through pinning our troops to the ground with intense fire.

B.Company 7th Gurkha Rifles, was ordered to restore the situation. Shortly

222

after passing the starting line it came under heavy medium machine gun and tank machine gun fire at point blank range. Rifleman Ganju Lama, the No. 1 of the P.I.A.T. gun, on his own initiative, crawled forward and engaged the tanks single handed. In spite of a broken left wrist and two other wounds, one in his right hand and one in his leg caused by cross fire concentrated upon him, Rifleman Ganju Lama brought his gun into action within 30 yards of the enemy tanks and knocked out first one and then another, the third tank being destroyed by an anti-tank gun.

In spite of his wounds he moved forward and engaged with grenades the tank crews who now attempted to escape. Not until he had killed or wounded them all, thus enabling his company to push forward, did he allow himself to be taken back to the regimental aid post.

It was solely due to his prompt action and brave conduct that a critical situation was averted, all positions were regained, and very heavy casualties were inflicted on the enemy.

Index

224

225

228